Frommer's®

French PhraseFinder & Dictionary

1st Edition

D0840273

WILEY

Wiley Publishing, Inc.

Published by:

Wiley Publishing, Inc.

111 River St.
Hoboken, NJ 07030-5774

ISBN-13: 978-0-471-77329-0
ISBN-10: 0-471-77329-8

French Editor: Marc Nadeau
Series Editor: Maureen Clarke
Photo Editor: Richard H. Fox
Cover design by Fritz Metsch

With special thanks to Jennifer Reilly.

Interior Design, Content Development, Translation, Copyediting, Proofreading,
Production, and Layout by:
Publication Services, Inc., 1802 South Duncan Road, Champaign, IL 61822
Linguists: Frederique Vincent-Goodall, John Garvey, Aimee Ehrs

For information on our other products and services or to obtain technical support,
please contact our Customer Care Department within the U.S. at 800/762-2974, outside the U.S. at 317/572-3993 or fax 317/572-4002.
Wiley also publishes its books in a variety of electronic formats. Some content that
appears in print may not be available in electronic formats.

Manufactured in the United States of America

5 4

Contents

An Invitation to the Reader

In researching this book, we discovered many wonderful sayings and terms useful to travelers in France. We're sure you'll find others. Please tell us about them, so we can share the information with your fellow travelers in upcoming editions. If you were disappointed with an aspect of this book, we'd like to know that, too. Please write to:

Frommer's French PhraseFinder & Dictionary, 1st Edition
Wiley Publishing, Inc.
111 River St. • Hoboken, NJ 07030-5774

An Additional Note

The packager, editors, and publisher cannot be held responsible for the experiences of readers while traveling. Your safety is important to us, however, so we encourage you to stay alert and be aware of your surroundings. Keep a close eye on cameras, purses, and wallets, all favorite targets of thieves and pickpockets.

Frommers.com

Now that you have the language for a great trip, visit our website at **www.frommers.com** for travel information on more than 3,000 destinations. With features updated regularly, we give you instant access to the most current trip-planning information available. At Frommers.com, you'll also find the best prices on airfares, accommodations, and car rentals—and you can even book travel online through our travel booking partners. At Frommers.com, you'll also find:

- Online updates to our most popular guidebooks
- Vacation sweepstakes and contest giveaways
- Newsletter highlighting the hottest travel trends
- Online travel message boards with featured travel discussions

INTRODUCTION: HOW TO USE THIS BOOK

As a Romance language, French is closely related to Latin, Spanish, Italian, Portuguese, and Romanian. The most widely taught second language after English, French is spoken by more than 75 million people in countries throughout the world including France, Belgium, parts of Switzerland, Algeria, Tunisia, and Morocco, many nations of West Africa, Tahiti, several Caribbean islands, and Canada. French was also the official language of the English courts for centuries—from the Middle Ages until 1731—and its effect on English is extensive and indelible; roughly 45 percent of modern English vocabulary is of French origin.

Our intention is not to teach you French; we figure you'll find an audio program for that. Our aim is to provide a portable travel tool that's easy to use. The problem we noticed with most phrasebooks is that you practically have to memorize the contents before you know where to look for a term you might need on the spot. This phrasebook is designed for fingertip referencing, so you can whip it out and find the words you need fast.

Like most phrasebooks, part of this book organizes terms by chapters, like the chapters in a Frommer's guide—getting a room, getting a good meal, and so on. And within those sections, we tried to organize phrases intuitively, according to how frequently most readers are likely to use them. But let's say you're in a cab and you've received the wrong change, and you forget which chapter covers money. With Frommer's PhraseFinder, you can quickly look up "change" in the dictionary, and learn how to say "Sorry, but this isn't the right change." Then you can follow the cross reference for numbers, and quickly learn how to specify how much you're missing.

What will make this book most practical? What will make it easiest to use? These are the questions we asked ourselves constantly as we assembled these travel terms.

Our immediate goal was to create a phrasebook as indispensable as your passport. Our far-ranging goal, of course, is to enrich your experience of travel. And with that, we offer the following wish: *Bon voyage!*

CHAPTER ONE

SURVIVAL FRENCH

If you tire of toting around this phrasebook, tear out this section. With the right hand gestures, you'll get a lot of mileage from the terms in the next 43 pages.

BASIC GREETINGS

For a full list of greetings and introductions, see p119.

Hello.	**Bonjour!**
	boh~-zhoohr
How are you?	**Comment allez-vous?**
	koh-maw~-tah-lay-voo
I'm fine, thanks.	**Bien, merci.**
	bee-yeh~ mayhr-see
And you?	**Et vous?**
	ay voo
My name is ____.	**Je m'appelle ____.**
	zhuh mah-pehl
And yours?	**Et vous?**
	ay voo
It's a pleasure to meet you.	**Ravi(e) de faire votre connaissance.**
	rah-vee duh fayhr voh-truh koh-nay-sans
Please.	**S'il vous plaît.**
	seel voo play
Thank you.	**Merci.**
	mayhr-see
Yes.	**Oui.**
	wee
No.	**Non.**
	noh~

OK.	**D'accord.**
	dah-kohr
No problem.	**Pas de problème.**
	pah duh proh-blehm
I'm sorry, I don't understand.	**Je suis désolé(e), je ne comprends pas.**
	zhuh swee day-zoh-lay zhuh nuh koh~-praw~ pah
Would you speak slower, please?	**Pouvez-vous parler plus lentement, s'il vous plaît?**
	poo-vay-voo pahr-lay plue law~t-maw~ seel voo play
Would you speak louder, please?	**Pouvez-vous parler plus fort, s'il vous plaît?**
	poo-vay-voo pahr-lay plue fohr seel voo play
Do you speak English?	**Parlez-vous anglais?**
	pahr-lay-voo-zaw~-glay
Do you speak any other languages?	**Parlez-vous d'autres langues?**
	pahr-lay-voo doh-truh law~g
I speak ____ better than French.	**Je parle ____ mieux que le français.**
	zhuh pahrl ____ mee-yeuh kuh luh fraw~-say
Would you spell that, please?	**Pouvez-vous épeler cela?**
	poo-vay-voo-zay-play suh-lah
Would you please repeat that?	**Pouvez-vous répéter cela, s'il vous plaît?**
	poo-vay-voo ray-pay-tay suh-lah, seel voo play
Would you point that out in this dictionary?	**Pouvez-vous me le montrer dans ce dictionnaire?**
	poo-vay-voo muh luh moh~-tray daw~ suh deek-see-oh~-ayhr

THE KEY QUESTIONS

With the right hand gestures, you can get a lot of mileage from the following list of single-word questions and answers.

Who?	**Qui?**
	kee
What?	**Quoi?**
	kwah
When?	**Quand?**
	kaw~
Where?	**Où?**
	oo
Why?	**Pourquoi?**
	poohr-kwah
How?	**Comment?**
	koh-maw~
Which?	**Quel / Quelle?**
	kehl
How many / much?	**Combien?**
	koh~-bee-yeh~

THE ANSWERS: WHO

For full coverage of pronouns, see p22.

him	**lui**
	lwee
her	**elle**
	ehl
them	**eux / elles**
	euh / ehl
I	**moi**
	mwah
you (singular)	**toi / vous**
	twah / voo
you (plural)	**vous**
	voo
us	**nous**
	noo

THE ANSWERS: WHEN

now	**maintenant**
	maw~t-naw~
later	**plus tard**
	plue tahr
in a minute	**dans une minute**
	daw~-zoon mee-noot
today	**aujourd'hui**
	oh-zhoohr-dwee
tomorrow	**demain**
	duh-meh~
yesterday	**hier**
	yayhr
in a week	**dans une semaine**
	daw~-zoon smehn
next week	**la semaine prochaine**
	lah smehn proh-shen
last week	**la semaine dernière**
	lah smen dayhr-nyayhr
next month	**le mois prochain**
	luh mwah proh-sheh~
At ____	**À ____**
	ah
ten o'clock this morning.	**dix heures ce matin.**
	dee-zoehr suh mah-teh~
two o'clock this afternoon.	**deux heures cet après-midi.**
	doeh-zoehr seh-tah-pray-mee-dee
seven o'clock this evening.	**sept heures ce soir.**
	seh-toehr suh swahr

For a full list of numbers, see p7.

THE ANSWERS: WHERE

here	**ici**
	ee-see
there	**là**
	lah
near	**près**
	pray
closer	**plus près**
	plue pray
closest	**le plus près**
	luh plue pray
far	**loin**
	lweh~
farther	**plus loin**
	plue lweh~
farthest	**le plus loin**
	luh plue lweh~
across from	**de l'autre côté de**
	duh lo-truh koh-tay duh
next to	**à côté de**
	ah koh-tay duh
behind	**derrière**
	day-ree-yayhr
straight ahead	**tout droit**
	too dwah
left	**à gauche**
	ah gohsh
right	**à droite**
	ah dwaht
up	**en haut**
	aw~-noh
down	**en bas**
	aw~ bah
lower	**plus bas**
	plue bah

higher	**plus haut**
	plue-zoh
forward	**en avant**
	aw~-nah-vaw~
back	**en arrière**
	aw~-nah-ree-yayhr
around	**autour**
	oh-toohr
across the street	**l'autre côté de la rue**
	loh-truh koh-tay duh lah roo
down the street	**bas de la rue**
	bah duh lah roo
on the corner	**au coin de la rue**
	oh kweh~ duh lah roo
kitty-corner	**à l'opposé**
	ah loh-poh-zay
_____ blocks from here	**à _____ rues d'ici**
	ah _____ roo dee-see

For a full list of numbers, see the following page.

THE ANSWERS: WHICH

this one	**celui-ci / celle-ci**
	suh-lwee see / sehl see
that one	**celui-là / celle-là**
	suh-lwee lah / sehl lah
this (here)	**ceci**
	suh-see
that (there)	**cela**
	suh-lah
these ones (here)	**ceux-ci / celles-ci**
	soeh-see / sehl see
those ones (there)	**ceux-là / celles-là**
	soeh-lah / sehl lah

NUMBERS & COUNTING

one	**un**	eighteen	**dix-huit**
	uh~		*dee-zhweet*
two	**deux**	nineteen	**dix-neuf**
	deuh		*deez-noehf*
three	**trois**	twenty	**vingt**
	twah		*veh~t*
four	**quatre**	twenty-one	**vingt-et-un**
	kah-truh		*veh~-tay-uh~*
five	**cinq**	twenty-two	**vingt-deux**
	saw~k		*veh~t-deuh*
six	**six**	thirty	**trente**
	sees		*traw~t*
seven	**sept**	forty	**quarante**
	seht		*kah-raw~t*
eight	**huit**	fifty	**cinquante**
	hweet		*seh~kaw~t*
nine	**neuf**	sixty	**soixante**
	noehf		*swah-saw~t*
ten	**dix**	seventy	**soixante-dix**
	dees		*swah-saw~t-dees*
eleven	**onze**	seventy-one	**soixante-et-onze**
	oh~z		*swah-saw~-tay-*
twelve	**douze**		*oh~z*
	dooz	seventy-two	**soixante-douze**
thirteen	**treize**		*swah-sa~t-dooz*
	trehz	eighty	**quatre-vingt**
fourteen	**quatorze**		*kah-truh-vaw~*
	kah-tohrz	eighty-one	**quatre-vingt-un**
fifteen	**quinze**		*kah-truh-vaw~-*
	keh~z		*tuh~*
sixteen	**seize**	ninety	**quatre-vingt-dix**
	sehz		*kah-truh-vaw~-*
seventeen	**dix-sept**		*dees*
	dee-seht		

ninety-one	**quatre-vingt-onze**	two hundred and one	**deux cent un**
	kah-ruh-vaw~-toh~z		*doeh saw~-tuh~*
		one thousand	**mille**
one hundred	**cent**		*meel*
	saw~	two thousand	**deux mille**
two hundred	**deux cents**		*doeh meel*
	doeh saw~		

FRACTIONS & DECIMALS

one-eighth	**un huitième**
	uh~ hwee-tee-ehm
one-quarter	**un quart**
	uh~ kahr
one-third	**un tiers**
	uh~ tee-yayhr
one-half	**un demi / une demie**
	uh~ duh-mee / oon duh-mee
two-thirds	**deux tiers**
	doeh tee-yayhr
three-quarters	**trois quarts**
	twah kahr
double	**double**
	doo-bluh
triple	**triple**
	tree-pluh
one-tenth	**un dixième**
	uh~ dee-zyehm
one-hundredth	**un centième**
	uh~ saw~-tyehm
one-thousandth	**un millième**
	uh~ meel-yehm

MATH

addition	**l'addition**
	lah-dee-see-yoh~
2 + 1	**deux plus un**
	doeh plue-zuh~

subtraction	**la soustraction** *lah soo-strahk-see-yoh~*
2 – 1	**deux moins un** *doeh mweh~ uh~*
multiplication	**la multiplication** *lah muel-tee-plee-kah-see-yoh~*
2 × 3	**deux fois trois** *doeh fwah twah*
division	**la division** *lah dee-vee-zee-yoh~*
6 ÷ 3	**six divisé par trois** *sees dee-vee-say pahr twah*

ORDINAL NUMBERS

first	**premier / première** *preh-mee-ay / preh-mee-yayhr*
second	**deuxième** *doeh-zee-yehm*
third	**troisième** *twah-zee-yehm*
fourth	**quatrième** *kah-tree-yehm*
fifth	**cinquième** *saw~kee-yehm*
sixth	**sixième** *see-zee-yehm*
seventh	**septième** *seh-tee-yehm*
eighth	**huitème** *hwee-tee-yehm*
ninth	**neuvième** *noeh-vee-yehm*
tenth	**dixième** *dee-zee-yehm*
last	**dernier / dernière** *dayhr-nyay / dayhr-nee-yayhr*

MEASUREMENTS

Measurements will usually be metric, though you may need a few American measurement terms.

inch	**pouce**
	poos
foot	**pied**
	pee-yay
mile	**mile**
	meel
millimeter	**millimètre**
	mee-lee-meh-truh
centimeter	**centimètre**
	saw~-tee-meh-truh
meter	**mètre**
	meh-truh
kilometer	**kilomètre**
	kee-loh-meh-truh
hectare	**hectare**
	ehk-tahr
squared	**carrés**
	kah-ray
short	**court / courte**
	koohr / koohrt
long	**long / longue**
	loh~ / loh~g

VOLUME

milliliter	**millilitre**
	mee-lee-lee-truh
liter	**litre**
	lee-truh
kilo	**kilo**
	kee-loh

ounce	**once**
	oh~s
cup	**tasse**
	tahs
pint	**pinte**
	peh~t
quart	**quart**
	kahr
gallon	**gallon**
	gah-luhn

QUANTITY

some	**quelques**
	kehl-kuh
none	**aucun / aucune**
	oh-kuh~ / oh-kuen
all	**tous / toutes**
	too / toot
many / much	**beaucoup**
	boh-koo
a little bit (can be used for quantity or for time)	**un peu**
	uh~ pueh
dozen	**une douzaine**
	oon doo-zeh~n

SIZE

small	**petit / petite**
	puh-tee / puh-teet
the smallest (literally "the most small")	**le plus petit / la plus petite**
	luh plue ptee / lah plue peh-teet
medium	**moyen / moyenne**
	mwah-yaw~ / mwah-yaw~n
a little medium	**un moyen de taille petit**
	uhn mwah-yaw~ duh tie ptee

big	**grand / grande**
	graw~ / graw~d
fat	**gros / grosse**
	groh / grohs
really fat	**très gros / très grosse**
	tray groh / tray grohs
the biggest	**le plus grand / la plus grande**
	luh plue graw~ / lah plue graw~d
wide	**large**
	lahrzh
narrow	**étroit / étroite**
	ay-twah / ay-twaht
too	**trop**
	troh
not enough	**pas assez**
	pah-zah-say

TIME

Remember that civilians in Europe and French-speaking Canada make use of the 24-hour clock. After 12 noon, hours continue upward, so that 1:00 PM is the 13th hour, 2:00 PM is the 14th hour, and so on. The French also write time differently: Instead of separating hours from minutes with a colon, they use a lowercase "h." For example: 11:30 AM is 11h30; 11:30 PM is 23h30.
For full coverage of numbers, see p7.

HOURS OF THE DAY

What time is it?	**Quelle heure est-il?**
	keh-loehr ey-teel
At what time?	**À quelle heure?**
	ah keh-loehr
For how long?	**Pendant combien de temps?**
	paw~-daw~ koh~-bee-yeh~
	duh taw~

It's one o'clock.   **Il est une heure.**
eel ayt-oon oehr

It's two o'clock.   **Il est deux heures.**
eel ay doeh-zoehr

It's two thirty.   **Il est deux heures trente.**
eel ay doeh-zoehr traw~t

It's two fifteen.   **Il est deux heures et quart.**
eel ay doeh-zoehr ay kahr

It's a quarter to three.   **Il est trois heures moins quart.**
eel ay twah-zoehr mwah kahr

It's noon.   **C'est midi.**
say mee-dee

It's midnight.   **C'est minuit.**
say mee-nwee

It's early.   **Il est tôt.**
eel ay toh

It's late.   **Il est tard.**
eel ay tahr

in the morning   **au matin**
oh mah-taw~

in the afternoon   **dans l'après-midi**
daw~ lah-pray mee-dee

at night   **dans le soir**
daw~ luh swahr

at dawn   **à l'aube**
ah lohb

DAYS OF THE WEEK

Monday   **lundi**
luh~-dee

Tuesday   **mardi**
mahr-dee

Wednesday   **mercredi**
mehr-kruh-dee

Thursday	**jeudi**
	zhoeh-dee
Friday	**vendredi**
	vaw~druh-dee
Saturday	**samedi**
	sahm-dee
Sunday	**dimanche**
	dee-maw~sh
today	**aujourd'hui**
	oh-zhohr-dwee
tomorrow	**demain**
	duh-maw~
yesterday	**hier**
	ee-yayhr
the day before yesterday	**avant-hier**
	ah-vaw~-tee-yayhr
one week	**une semaine**
	oon seh-meh~n
next week	**la semaine prochaine**
	lah smeh~n pro-sheh~n
last week	**la semaine dernière**
	lah smeh~n dayhr-nayhr

MONTHS OF THE YEAR

January	**janvier**
	zhaw~-vee-yay
February	**février**
	fay-vree-yay
March	**mars**
	mahrs
April	**avril**
	ah-vreel

May	**mai**
	may
June	**juin**
	zhweh~
July	**juillet**
	zhoo-ee-ay
August	**août**
	oot
September	**septembre**
	seh-taw-bruh
October	**octobre**
	ohk-toh-bruh
November	**novembre**
	noh-vaw-bruh
December	**décembre**
	day-saw-bruh
next month	**le mois prochain**
	luh mwah proh-shaw~
last month	**le mois dernier**
	luh mwah dayhr~nyay

SEASONS OF THE YEAR

spring	**le printemps**
	luh preh~-taw~
summer	**l'eté**
	lay-tay
autumn	**l'automne**
	loh-tuhn
winter	**l'hiver**
	lee-vayhr

Faux Amis

If you try winging it with "Frenglish," beware of false cognates, known as faux amis, "false friends"—French words that sound like English ones, but with different meanings. Here are some of the most commonly confused terms.

gros(se)	fat
dégoutant(e)	gross
bras	arm
soutien-gorge	bra
main	hand
principal(e)	main
raisin	grape
raisin sec	raisin
pain	bread
douleur	pain
boulette	small ball (like a meatball)
balle	bullet
vacances	holiday
chambres libres	vacancies
injurer	to insult
blesser	to injure
résumé	synopsis
curriculum vitae	résumé
manger	to eat
mangeoire	manger
robe	dress
peignoir	robe
assister	to attend an event
aider	to help
attendre	to wait
librairie	bookstore
bibliothèque	library

FRENCH GRAMMAR BASICS

ALPHABET & PRONUNCIATION

French uses the same alphabet as English, with the addition of the ligature **œ**, used in words like **sœur** (sister) and **œil** (eye). French pronunciation can seem quite difficult. There are several **"nasal vowels"** that are sometimes used when **m** or **n** follows a vowel. Only the nasal is pronounced, not the **m** or **n**, unless another vowel comes along afterward.

The **nasal** will be represented with a **~**. Try this example by tightening your throat as if to whine, snort, or hum:

a good white wine   **un bon vin blanc**
                       uh~ boh~ veh~ blaw~

Another tricky bit is the guttural French **r**. It's sounded in the back of the throat, somewhere near a German "ach." Because the French **r** is all but impossible without practice or prior experience, we'll help you hint at it by adding *hr* to pronunciations.

Letter	Name	Pronunciation
a	*ah*	**ah** as in *father*
		au: oh as in *so*
		ai, aie: ay as in *paid*
		ail: ie as in *tie*
		an: aw~ as in *long*
b	*bay*	**b** as in *bay*
c	*say*	**ca, co, cu:** hard **k** sound as in *car*
		ce, ci: s sound before **i, e**, as in *cent*
d	*day*	**d** as in *day*
		d at end of word is usually silent
e	*uh*	**uh** as in *women,* unstressed, but with lips more pursed
		e at end of word is usually silent
		ein: eh~ as in *men*
		en, em: aw~ as in *long*
		ent: at end of word is usually silent
		er: at end of word, **ay** as in *face*

Letter	Name	Pronunciation
		es at end of word is usually silent
		et, ez: at end of word, **ay** as in *face*
		eu, eue: oeh like German **oe, oeh**
e stressed	*eh*	**eh** as in *vet*
e stressed (é)	*ay*	**ay** as in *say*
f	*ehf*	**f** as in *father*
g	*zhay*	**ga, go, gu:** hard **g** sound as in *gold*
		ge, gi: zh as **g** in *massage* or **s** in *vision*
h	*ahsh*	silent
i	*ee*	**ee** as in *machine*
		il: at end of word, **ee** as in *see*
		in, im: eh~ as in *men*
j	*zhee*	**zh** as **g** in *massage* or **s** in *vision*
k	*kah*	hard **k** sound as in *kitten*
l	*ehl*	**l** as in *million*
m	*ehm*	**m** as in *money*
n	*ehn*	**n** as in *nothing*
		n, nd, nt: at end of word, **~** nasalizes preceding vowel
		ne: at end of word, as in *phone*
o	*oh*	**o:** inside word, at end of word, or before silent final letter, **oh** as in *so*
		o: before nonsilent final letter, **uh** as in *come*
		oe, œ: uh like German but lower
		oi: wah as in *bourgeois*
		on: oh~ as in *phone*
		ou: oo as in *routine*
p	*pay*	**p** as in *pay*
q	*koeh*	**qu:** hard **k** sound as in *liquor*
r	*ehr*	**r, hr: r** as in *argument*, usually far back in throat

Letter	Name	Pronunciation
s	*ehs*	**s** as in *sister*
		s: between vowels, including final silent e, **z** as in *misery*
		s at end of word is usually silent
t	*tay*	**t** as in *tea*
		t at end of word is usually silent
		tre, ttre: at end of word, as in *bet*
u	*ueh*	**ue, ueh** as in *due*, but shorter
		un, um: uh~ as in *under*
v	*vay*	**v** as in *volt*
w	*doo-bluh-vay*	**v** as in *volt*
x	*eeks*	**x:** before unstressed vowel, **ks** as in *fixed*
		x: before stressed vowel, **gz** as in *examine*
		x at end of word is usually silent
y	*ee-grehk*	**ee** as in *mighty*
		y: before vowel, **y** as in *yank*
z	*zehd*	**z** as in *zip*
		z at end of word is usually silent

GENDER & ADJECTIVE AGREEMENT

All nouns in French are assigned a masculine or feminine gender, most often accompanied by a masculine or feminine definite article (**le** or **la**). Definite articles (the), indefinite articles (a), and related adjectives must also be masculine or feminine and singular or plural, depending on the noun they're modifying (see the examples in the following boxes).

Unlike English adjectives, French adjectives generally follow the noun, and they must agree in number and gender with the nouns they modify. Some common adjectives do come before the noun, however. These generally have to do with beauty, age, number, goodness, and size.

Quirks of Gender

A group of people always takes the masculine form unless the group is completely composed of females.

John and his sisters are blonds.

Jean et ses sœurs sont blonds.
zhah~-nay say soehr soh~ bloh~

The Definite Article ("The")

	Singular	Plural
Masculine	*le* petit magasin cher (the small, expensive store)	*les* petits magasins chers (the small, expensive stores)
Feminine	*la* petite chambre chère (the small, expensive room)	*les* petites chambres **chères** (the small, expensive rooms)

When a singular definite article appears directly in front of a noun that begins with a vowel, it is contracted with an apostrophe:

	Singular	Plural
Masculine	**l'amour** (love)	**les amours** (loves)
Feminine	**l'église** (the church)	*les* églises (the churches)

The Indefinite and Partitive Articles ("A", "An," and "Any" / "Some")

	Singular	Plural
Masculine	**un grand magasin intéressant** (a big, interesting store)	**des grandes magasins intéressants** (some / any big, interesting stores)
Feminine	**une grande chambre intéressante** (a big, interesting room)	**des grandes chambres intéressantes** (some / any big, interesting rooms)

How Much Do You Really Want? (The "Partitive")

French often uses what's called "the partitive" to express some of a larger whole; the words "some" or "any" are never implied, as in English. In other words, if you went to the store for "milk" (rather than for "some" milk), it would suggest all the milk in the world to a French speaker. In French, the words "some" or "any" must always be explicit, as in the examples below.

de + la = de la glace   some ice
duh lah glas

de + le = du lait   some milk (or some
 doo lay   ice cream)

de + l' + vowel (f) = **de l'essence**   some gasoline
duh leh-saw~s

de + l' + vowel (m) = **de l'eau**   some water
duh loh

de + les (f) = **des aubergines**   some eggplant(s)
day-zoh-bayhr-zheen

de + les (m) = **des haricots verts**   some green beans
day-zay-ree-koh vayhr

THIS / THESE / THAT / THOSE

When modifying nouns, "this," "that," "these," and "those" must agree with the noun in gender and number.

	This / That	These / Those
Masculine	**ce château** (this / that castle) **cet immeuble** (this / that building)	**ces châteaux** (these / those castles) **ces immeubles** (these / those buildings)
Feminine	**cette maison** (this / that house) **cette usine** (this / that factory)	**ces maisons** (these / those houses) **ces usines** (these / those factories)

French does not usually make a distinction between "this and "that" or between "these" and "those." If necessary, the endings **-ci** (here, nearby) and **-là** (over there) can be added for emphasis:

I'd like this ring here, not that necklace there.	**Je voudrais cette bague-ci, pas ce collier-là.**
	zhuh voo-dray seht bahg-see pah suh kohl-yay-lah
You take these taxis right here, not those coaches over there.	**On prend ces taxis-ci, pas ces cars-là**
	oh~ praw~ say tahk-see-see pah say kahr-lah

When **ce** is used with **être** (to be) to mean "this is," it makes a contraction. The plural form of "these are" also uses **ce**, not **ces**:

That's his widow.	**C'est sa veuve.**
	say sah voehv
These are our husbands.	**Ce sont nos maris.**
	say soh~ noh mah-ree

PERSONAL PRONOUNS

English	French	Pronunciation
I	Je	zhuh
You (singular, familiar)	Tu	tueh
He / She / It	Il / Elle	eel / ehl
We	Nous	noo
You (plural / singular formal)	Vous	voo
They (*m / f*)	Ils / Elles	eel / ehl

Hey, You!

French has two words for "you": *tu*, spoken among friends and familiars when addressing only one person, and *vous*, used among strangers or as a sign of respect for elders and authority figures, and to address more than one person—even if you're speaking to a group of your family members or close friends. When speaking with a stranger, expect to use *vous* unless you are invited to use *tu*.

When a verb begins with a vowel, if the subject appears directly in front of it, **je** (I) forms a contraction. The plural subjects change in pronunciation, though:

English	French	Pronunciation
I like.	J'aime.	zhehm
You (singular, familiar) **like.**	Tu aimes.	tueh ehm
He / She / It likes.	Il / Elle aime.	ee-lehm / eh-lehm
We like.	Nous aimons.	noo-zeh-moh~
You (plural / singular, formal) **like.**	Vous aimez.	voo-zeh-may
They (*m* / *f*) **like.**	Ils / Elles aiment.	ee-lehm / eh-lehm

REGULAR VERB CONJUGATIONS

French verb infinitives end in **ER** (**parler**, to speak), **IR** (**choisir**, to choose), and **RE** (**vendre**, to sell). Most verbs (known as "regular verbs") are conjugated according to the rules for those endings. These are the present-tense conjugations for regular verbs.

Present Tense

ER Verbs	PARLER "To Speak"	
I speak.	Je parle.	zhuh pahrl
You (singular, familiar) **speak.**	Tu parle*s*.	tueh pahrl
He / She / It speaks.	Il / Elle parle.	eel / ehl pahrl
We speak.	Nous parl*ons*.	noo pahr-loh~
You (plural / singular, formal) **speak.**	Vous parl*ez*.	voo pahr-lay
They speak.	Ils / Elles parl*ent*.	eel / ehl pahrl

IR Verbs	CHOISIR "To Choose"	
I choose.	Je chois*is*.	zhuh shwah-zee
You (singular, familiar) **choose.**	Tu chois*is*.	tueh shwah-zee
He / She / It chooses.	Il / Elle chois*it*.	eel / ehl shwah-zee
We choose.	Nous chois*issons*.	noo shwah-zee-soh~
You (plural / singular, formal) **choose.**	Vous chois*issez*.	voo shwah-zee-say
They choose.	Ils / Elles chois*issent*.	eel / ehl shwah-zees

RE Verbs	VENDRE "To Sell"	
I sell.	Je vend**s**.	zhuh vaw~
You (singular, familiar) sell.	Tu vend**s**.	tueh vaw~
He / She / It sells.	Il / Elle vend. (no ending)	eel / ehl vaw~
We sell.	Nous vend**ons**.	noo vaw~-doh~
You (plural / singular, formal) sell.	Vous vend**ez**.	voo vaw~-day
They sell.	Ils / Elles vend**ent**.	eel / ehl vaw~d

Past Tense

One way of expressing past tense in French is the **passé composé**. The passé composé is formed like the construction "I have walked," in English—with a helping verb (the present tense of **avoir**, to have; or in rare cases, **être**, to be), plus the past participle of the action verb. For the verb "to walk," for example, it's equivalent to "I walked," "I did walk," or "I have walked" in English.

The past participle has a standard form for each type of regular verbs. The following boxes demonstrate how to conjugate **avoir** and then combine it with the past participle of regular ER, IR, and RE verbs to form the past tense.

Passé Composé / Past with Avoir

Present Tense	AVOIR "To Have"	
I have.	J'*ai*.	zhay
You (singular, familiar) have.	Tu *as*.	tueh ah
He / She / It has.	Il / Elle *a*.	eel / ehl ah
We have.	Nous av*ons*.	noo-zah-voh~
You (plural / singular, formal) have.	Vous av*ez*.	voo-zah-vay
They have.	Ils / Elles *ont*.	eel-zoh~ / ehl-zoh~

ER Verbs	AVOIR + PARLER "To Speak"	
I spoke.	J'*ai* parlé.	zhay pahr-lay
You (singular familiar) **spoke.**	Tu *as* parlé.	tueh ah pahr-lay
He / She / It spoke.	Il / Elle *a* parlé.	eel / ehl ah pahr-lay
We spoke.	Nous av*ons* parlé.	noo-zah-voh~ pahr-lay
You (plural / singular, formal) **spoke.**	Vous av*ez* parlé.	voo-zah-vay pahr-lay
They spoke.	Ils / Elles *ont* parlé.	eel-zoh~ / ehl-zoh~ pahr-lay
Past Participle:	parlé.	pahr-lay

IR Verbs	AVOIR + CHOISIR "To Choose"	
I chose.	J'*ai* chois*i*.	zhay shwah-zee
You (singular, familiar) **chose.**	Tu *as* chois*i*.	tueh ah shwah-zee
He / She / It chose.	Il / Elle *a* chois*i*.	eel / ehl ah shwah-zee
We chose.	Nous av*ons* chois*i*.	noo-zah-voh~ shwah-zee
You (plural / singular, formal) **chose.**	Vous av*ez* chois*i*.	voo-zah-vay shwah-zee
They chose.	Ils / Elles *ont* chois*i*.	eel-zoh~ / ehl-zoh~ shwah-zee
Past participle:	chois*i*	shwah-zee

RE Verbs	AVOIR + VENDRE "To Sell"	
I sold.	J'*ai* vend*u*.	zhay vaw~-doo
You (singular, familiar) **sold.**	Tu *as* vend*u*.	tueh ah vaw~-doo
He / She / It sold.	Il / Elle *a* vend*u*.	eel / ehl ah vaw~-doo
We sold.	Nous av*ons* vend*u*.	noo-zah-voh~ vaw~-doo
You (plural / singular, formal) **sold.**	Vous av*ez* vend*u*.	voo-zah-vay vaw~-doo
They sold.	Ils / Elles *ont* vend*u*.	eel-zoh~ / ehl-zoh~ vaw~-doo
Past participle:	vend*u*	vaw~-doo

Passé Composé / Past with Être

A few exceptional verbs—mostly involving verbs of motion—use **être** (to be) instead of **avoir** to form the **passé compose**. Like adjectives, past participles with **être** must agree with the subject in number and gender. Note that the pronunciation of the past participle never changes.

Present Tense	ÊTRE "To Be"	
I am.	Je *suis*.	zhuh swee
You (singular, familiar) are.	Tu *es*.	tueh ay
He / She / It is.	Il / Elle *est*.	eel / ehl ay
We are.	Nous *sommes*.	noo-suhm
You (plural / singular, formal) are.	Vous *êtes*.	voo-zeht
They are.	Ils / Elles *sont*.	eel soh~ / ehl soh~

IR Verbs	ÊTRE + PARTIR "To Leave"	
I left.	Je *suis* parti*(e)*.	zhuh swee pahr-tee
You (singular, familiar) **left.**	Tu *es* parti*(e)*.	tueh ay pahr-tee
He / She / It left.	Il *est* parti. / Elle *est* partie.	eel / ehl ay pahr-tee
We left.	Nous *sommes* parti*(e)*s.	noo-suhm pahr-tee
You (plural / singular, formal) **left.**	Vous *êtes* parti*(e)*s.	voo-zeht pahr-tee
They left.	Ils *sont* partis. / Elles *sont* parties.	eel soh~ / ehl soh~ pahr-tee

The following verbs use **être** as the helping verb for the **passé composé**:

aller (to go)	Je suis allé*(e)*. (I went.)	zhuh swee-zah-lay
arriver (to arrive)	Je suis arrivé*(e)*. (I arrived.)	zhuh swee-zah-ree-vay
descendre (to go down)	Je suis descendu*(e)*. (I went down.)	zhuh swee day-saw~-doo
devenir (to become)	Je suis devenu*(e)*. (I became.)	zhuh swee dehv-nueh
entrer (to come in)	Je suis entré*(e)*. (I came in.)	zhuh swee-zaw~-tray
monter (to go up)	Je suis monté*(e)*. (I went up.)	zhuh swee moh~-tay
mourir (to die)	Je suis mort*(e)*. (I died.)	zhuh swee mohr / mohrt
naître (to be born)	Je suis né*(e)*. (I was born.)	zhuh swee nay

partir (to leave)	Je suis parti(e). (I left.)	zhuh swee pahr-tee
rentrer (to come / go home)	Je suis rentré(e). (I went home.)	zhuh swee raw~-tray
rester (to stay)	Je suis resté(e). (I stayed.)	zhuh swee res-tay
retourner (to go back)	Je suis retourné(e). (I went back.)	zhuh swee ray-toohr-nay
revenir (to come back)	Je suis revenu(e). (I came back.)	zhuh swee reh-vnueh
sortir (to go out)	Je suis sorti(e). (I went out.)	zhuh swee sohr-tee
tomber (to fall)	Je suis tombé(e). (I fell.)	zhuh swee toh~-bay
venir (to come)	Je suis venu(e). (I came.)	zhuh swee vnueh

Having It All

Avoir means "to have," but it's also used to describe conditions, such as hunger or thirst, body pain, and age:

I'm hungry.	**J'ai faim.**	*zhay feh~*
I have a headache.	**J'ai mal à la tête.**	*zhay mah-lah lah teht*
I am ten years old.	**J'ai dix ans.**	*zhay dee-zah~*

Avoir is also used in the two common fixed expressions, *avoir besoin de*, "to need," and *il y a*, "there is," "there are":

| I need a pillow. | **J'ai besoin d'un oreiller.** *zhay beh-zwah~ duh~-noh-ray-ay* |
| There are two seats available. | **Il y a deux places libres.** *eel-yah doeh plas lee-bruh* |

The Future

For novice French speakers, the easiest way to express the future is to use the present tense of the irregular verb **aller** (to go) as a helping verb plus the infinitive. We use the same structure in English when we say things like "I'm going to eat."

Present Tense	ALLER "To Go"	
I go.	Je *vais*.	zhuh vay
You (singular, familiar) **go.**	Tu *vas*.	tueh vah
He / She / It goes.	Il / Elle *va*.	eel / ehl vah
We go.	Nous all*ons*.	noo-zah-loh~
You (plural / singular, formal) **go.**	Vous all*ez*.	voo-zah-lay
They go.	Ils / Elles *vont*.	eel / ehl voh~

ER Verbs	ALLER + PARLER "To Talk"	
I'm going to talk.	Je *vais* parler.	zhuh vay pahr-lay
You're (singular, familiar) **going to talk.**	Tu *vas* parler.	tueh vah pahr-lay
He / She / It is going to talk.	Il / Elle *va* parler.	eel / ehl vah pahr-lay
We're going to talk.	Nous *allons* parler.	noo-zah-loh~ pahr-lay
You're (plural / singular, formal) **going to talk.**	Vous *allez* parler.	voo-zah-lay pahr-lay
They're going to talk.	Ils / Elles *vont* parler.	eel / ehl voh~ pahr-lay

IRREGULAR VERBS

French has numerous irregular verbs that stray from the standard **ER**, **IR**, and **RE** conjugations. Rather than bog you down with too much grammar, we're providing the present tense conjugations for some of the most commonly used irregular verbs.

BOIRE "To Drink"

I drink.	Je b*ois*.	zhuh bwah
You (singular, familiar) **drink.**	Tu b*ois*.	tueh bwah
He / She / It drinks.	Il / Elle b*oit*.	eel / ehl bwah
We drink.	Nous b*uvons*.	noo bueh-voh~
You (plural / singular, formal) **drink.**	Vous b*uvez*.	voo bueh-vay
They drink.	Ils / Elles b*oivent*.	eel / ehl bwahv
Past participle:	b*u*	bueh

CONNAÎTRE "To Know" (a person / place)

I know Marc.	Je connais Marc.	zhuh koh-nay mahrk
You (singular, familiar) **know Nice.**	Tu connais Nice.	tueh koh-nay nees
He / She / It knows my parents.	Il / Elle connaît mes parents.	eel / ehl koh-nay
We know your (girl)friends.	Nous connaissons vos amies.	noo koh-nay-soh~ voh-zah-mee
You (plural / singular, formal) **know this hostel.**	Vous connaissez cet auberge.	voo koh-nay-say seh-toh-bayrzh
They know our children.	Ils / Elles connaissent nos enfants.	eel / ehl koh-nehs noh-zaw~-faw~
Past participle:	connu	koh-nueh

DIRE "To Say", "To Tell"

I say.	Je dis.	zhuh dee
You (singular, familiar) say.	Tu dis.	tueh dee
He / She / It says.	Il / Elle dit.	eel / ehl dee
We say.	Nous disons.	noo dee-zoh~
You (plural / singular, formal) say.	Vous dites.	voo deet
They sat.	Ils / Elles disent.	eel / ehl deez
Past participle:	dit	dee

ÉCRIRE "To Write"

I write.	J'écris.	zheh-kree
You (singular, familiar) write.	Tu écris.	tueh eh-kree
He / She / It writes.	Il / Elle écrit.	eel / ehl eh-kree
We write.	Nous écrivons.	noo-zeh-kree-voh~
You (plural / singular, formal) write.	Vous écrivez.	voo-zeh-kree-vay
They write.	Ils / Elles écrivent.	eel-zeh-kreev / ehl-zeh-kreev
Past participle:	écrit	eh-kree

"Faire" Weather

The verb *faire* (to do, to make) is also used impersonally to describe the weather:

It's hot / cold out.
Il fait chaud / froid.
eel fay shoh / fwah

The weather's nice / bad today.
Il fait beau / mauvais aujourd'hui.
eel fay boh / moh-vay oh-zhoohr dwee

FAIRE "To Do," "To Make"

I do.	Je fais.	zhuh fay
You (singular, familiar) do.	Tu fais.	tueh fay
He / She / It does.	Il / Elle fait.	eel / ehl fay
We do.	Nous faisons.	noo feh-zoh~
You (plural / singular, formal) do.	Vous faites.	voo feht
They do.	Ils / Elles font.	eel / ehl foh~
Past participle:	fait	fay

OUVRIR "To Open"

I open.	J'ouvre.	zhoovhr
You (singular, familiar) open.	Tu ouvres.	tueh oovhr
He / She / It opens.	Il / Elle ouvre.	eel / ehl oovhr
We open.	Nous ouvrons.	noo-zoo-vroh~
You (plural / singular, formal) open.	Vous ouvrez.	voo-zoo-vray
They open.	Ils / Elles ouvrent.	eel-zoovhr / ehl-zoovhr
Past participle:	ouvert	oo-vayhr

PARTIR "To Leave"

I leave.	Je pars.	zhuh pahr
You (singular, familiar) leave.	Tu pars.	tueh pahr
He / She / It leaves.	Il / Elle part.	eel / ehl pahr
We leave.	Nous partons.	noo pahr-toh~
You (plural / singular, formal) leave.	Vous partez.	voo pahr-tay
They leave.	Ils / Elles partent.	eel / ehl pahrt
Past participle:	parti (with être; agrees with subject)	pahr-tee

POUVOIR "Can," "To Be Able"

I can.	Je peux.	zhuh poeh
You (singular, familiar) can.	Tu peux.	tueh poeh
He / She / It can.	Il / Elle peut.	eel / ehl poeh
We can.	Nous pouvons.	noo poo-voh~
You (plural / singular, formal) can.	Vous pouvez.	voo poo-vay
They can.	Ils / Elles peuvent.	eel / ehl poehv
Past participle:	pu	pue

PRENDRE "To Take"

I take.	Je prend**s**.	zhuh praw~
You (singular, familiar) **take.**	Tu prend**s**.	tueh praw~
He / She / It takes.	Il / Elle prend.	eel / ehl praw~
We take.	Nous pre**n**ons.	noo pruh-noh~
You (plural / singular, formal) **take.**	Vous pre**n**ez.	voo pruh-nay
They take.	Ils / Elles pren**n**ent.	eel / ehl prehn
Past participle:	pr**is**	pree

SAVOIR "To Know" (a fact)

I know how to drive.	Je s**ais** conduire.	zhuh say koh~-dweer
You (singular, familiar) **know the route.**	Tu s**ais** la route.	tueh say lah root
He / She / It knows where.	Il / Elle s**ait** où.	eel / ehl say oo
We know the answer.	Nous sav**ons** la réponse.	noo sah-voh~ lah ray-poh~s
You (plural / singular, formal) **know his / her problem.**	Vous sav**ez** son problème.	voo sah-vay soh~ praw-blehm
They know the truth.	Ils / Elles sav**ent** la vérité.	eel / ehl sahv lah vay-ree-tay
Past participle:	s**u**	sue

SORTIR "To Go Out," "To Exit"

I go out.	Je sors.	zhuh sohr
You (singular, familiar) go out.	Tu sors.	tueh sohr
He / She / It goes out.	Il / Elle sort.	eel / ehl sohr
We go out.	Nous sortons.	noo sohr-toh~
You (plural / singular, formal) go out.	Vous sortez.	voo sohr-tay
They go out.	Ils / Elles sortent.	eel / ehl sohrt
Past participle:	sorti (with être; agrees with subject)	sohr-tee

VENIR "To Come"

I come.	Je viens.	zhuh vee-yeh~
You (singular, familiar) come.	Tu viens.	tueh vee-yeh~
He / She / It comes.	Il / Elle vient.	eel / ehl vee-yeh~
We come.	Nous venons.	noo vnoh~
You (plural / singular, formal) come.	Vous venez.	voo vnay
They come.	Ils / Elles viennent.	eel / ehl vee-yehn
Past participle:	venu (with être; agrees with subject)	vnueh

VOIR "To See"

I see.	Je vois.	zhuh vwah
You (singular, familiar) see.	Tu vois.	tueh vwah
He / She / It sees.	Il / Elle voit.	eel / ehl vwah
We see.	Nous voyons.	noo vwah-yoh~
You (plural / singular, formal) see.	Vous voyez.	voo vwah-yay
They see.	Ils / Elles voient.	eel / ehl vwah
Past participle:	vu	vue

You can say "I want" to make a request, but it's much more polite, just like in English, to say "I would like"—**je voudrais**. Therefore, we will provide this conditional tense rather than the present tense for this verb.

VOULOIR "To Want"

I would like to eat.	Je voudrais manger.	zhuh voo-dray mah~-zhay
You (singular, familiar) would like a beer.	Tu voudrais une bière.	tueh voo-dray oon bee-ayhr
He / She / It would like a knife.	Il / Elle voudrait un couteau.	eel / ehl voo-dray uh~ koo-toh
We would like some ketchup.	Nous voulions du ketchup.	noo voo-lee-oh~ doo keht-shup
You (plural / singular, formal) would like some books.	Vous vouliez des livres.	voo voo-lee-ay day lee-vruh
They would like to stay.	Ils / Elles voudraient rester.	eel / ehl voo-dray ruh-stay

REFLEXIVE VERBS

French uses more reflexive verbs than English. A verb is reflexive when its subject and object both refer to the same person or thing:

Marie looks at herself in the mirror.	**Marie se regard dans le miroir.** *mah-ree suh ruh-gahr daw~ luh meer-wahr*

The following common verbs are often used reflexively: **s'habiller** (to get dressed, literally to dress oneself), **s'appeler** (to be named, literally to call oneself), **se baigner** (to bathe oneself), and **se lever** (to wake up, literally to raise oneself).

To indicate that a verb is reflexive, French attaches a reflexive pronoun to the verb according to the subject:

SE LEVER "To Get Up"

I get up.	Je *me* lève.	zhuh muh lehv
You (singular, familiar) **get up.**	Tu *te* lèves.	tueh tuh lehv
He / She / It gets up.	Il / Elle *se* lève.	eel / ehl suh lehv
We get up.	Nous *nous* levons.	noo noo leh-voh~
You (plural / singular, formal) **get up.**	Vous *vous* levez.	voo voo leh-vay
They get up.	Ils / Elles *se* lève*nt*.	eel / ehl suh lehv

When a reflexive pronoun ending with a vowel comes before a verb that starts with a vowel, all but the **nous** and **vous** forms make contractions. Note the contractions and pronunciation changes for the following verb.

Reflexive verbs use **être** in the **passé composé** (remember to make the verbs agree). The reflexive pronoun goes directly before the helping verb.

She woke up.	**Elle s'est levée.**	*ehl say luh-vay*
They (a group of females) woke up.	**Elles se sont levées.**	*ehl suh soh~ luh-vay*

An impersonal usage of a reflexive verb appears in two common, useful phrases:

What's happening?	**Qu'est-ce qui se passe?**
	kehs kee suh pahs
What happened?	**Qu'est-ce qui s'est passé?**
	kehs kee say pah-say

S'AMUSER "To Have a Good Time"

I am having a good time.	Je *m*'amuse.	zhuh mah-muehz
You (singular, familiar) are having a good time.	Tu *t*'amuses.	tueh tah-muehz
He / She / It is having a good time.	Il / Elle *s*'amuse.	eel / ehl sah-muehz
We are having a good time.	Nous *nous* amusons.	noo noo-zah-mueh-zoh~
You (plural / singular, formal) are having a good time.	Vous *vous* amusez.	voo voo-zah-meuh-zay
They are having a good time.	Ils / Elles *s*'amusent.	eel / ehl sah-muehz

Who's Calling, Please?

Many reflexive verbs can also be used in a nonreflexive sense. The reflexive pronoun makes all the difference between *j'appelle Jean* (I'm calling John) and *je m'appelle Jean* (my name is John, literally I call myself John).

NEGATIVES

To render a statement negative, bracket the verb with **ne . . . pas**, as in the examples below. **Ne** contracts to **n'** in front of a vowel. (In spoken French, the **ne** is often omitted, so you'll need to listen for the **pas**.)

ALLER "To Go"

I am not going.	Je *ne* vais *pas*.	zhuh nuh vay pah
You (singular, familiar) are not going.	Tu *ne* vas *pas*.	tueh nuh vah pah
He / She / It is not going.	Il / Elle *ne* vas *pas*.	eel / ehl nuh vah pah
We are not going.	Nous *n'*allons *pas*.	noo nah-loh~ pah
You (plural / singular, formal) are not going.	Vous *n'*allez *pas*.	voo nah-lay pah
They are not going.	Ils / Elles *ne* vont *pas*.	eel / ehl nuh voh~ pah

Other Negatives

Here are some other negative expressions that follow a similar pattern.

NEVER: ne . . . jamais

I never like dancing.	Je *n'*aime *jamais* danser.	zhuh neyhm zhah-mey dah~-say

NO LONGER: ne . . . plus

I no longer like this.	Je *n'*aime *plus* ça.	zhuh neyhm plue sah

NO ONE: ne . . . personne

I like no one.	Je *n'*aime *personne*.	zhuh neyhm payhr-suhn

NOTHING / ANYTHING: ne . . . rien

I don't like anything.	Je n'aime *rien*.	zhuh neyhm ree-yaw~

ONLY: ne . . . que

I only like you.	Je n'aime *que* toi.	zhuh neyhm kuh twah

QUESTIONS

There are several ways to ask a question in French: The very simplest is just to use the tone of your voice. Just like in English, a sentence that drops in pitch at the end is a statement, but a sentence that rises in pitch is instantly a question.

You have (some) soap.	**Vous avez du savon.**
	voo-zah-vay due sah-voh~
Do you have (any) soap?	**Vous avez du savon?**
	voo-zah-vay due sah-voh~

Another easy and useful way to ask a question is to stick the fixed phrase **Est-ce que** onto the beginning of the sentence. There's no literal translation for **Est-ce que** that makes much sense; word-for-word it means "Is it that . . .?"

Do you have (any) soap?	**Est-ce que vous avez du savon?**
	ehs kuh voo-zah-vay doo sah-voh~

For other kinds of questions, see p3.

POSSESSIVES

French has no **'s** shorthand to show ownership. If you want to talk about "the girl's name," you have to say **le nom de la fille** (the name of the girl). The preposition de changes depending on which definite article follows it.

de + la = de la	la bouchon *de la* bouteille (the bottle's cork)	lah boo-shoh~ duh lah boo-tayh
de + le = du	les portes *du* restaurant (the restaurant's doors)	lay pohrt doo ruh-stoh-raw~
de + l' = de l'	la main *de l'*actrice (the actress's hand) le fil *de l'*ordinateur (the computer's cord)	lah meh~ duh lahk-trees luh fee duh lohr-dee-nah-toehr
de + les = des	la chanson *des* sœurs (the sisters' song) les valises *des* passagers (the passengers' suitcases)	lah shaw~-soh~ day soehrs lay vah-lees day pah-sah-zhay

Possessive Adjectives

Masculine Noun

My dog is black.	**Mon chien est noir.** *moh~ shee-yeh~-nay nwahr*
Your dog is pretty.	**Ton chien est beau.** *toh~ shee-yeh~-nay boh*
His / Her / Its dog is small.	**Son chien est petit.** *soh~ shee-yeh~-nay ptee*
Our dog is lost.	**Notre chien est perdu.** *nohtr shee-yeh~-nay pehr-due*
Your dog is dirty.	**Votre chien est sale.** *vohtr shee-yeh~-nay sahl*
Their dog is new.	**Leur chien est nouveau.** *loehr shee-yeh~-nay noo-voh*

Feminine Noun

My car is black.	**Ma voiture est noire.** *mah vwah-tuehr ay nwahr*
Your car is pretty.	**Ta voiture est belle.** *tah vwah-tuehr ay behl*
His / Her / Its car is small.	**Sa voiture est petite.** *sah vwah-tuehr at puh-teet*

Our car is lost.	**Notre voiture est perdue.**
	nohtr vwah-tuehr ay pehr-due
Your car is dirty.	**Votre voiture est sale.**
	vohtr vwah-tuehr ay sahl
Their car is new.	**Leur voiture est nouvelle.**
	loehr vwah-tuehr ay noo-vehl

Plural Noun (Masculine or Feminine)

My luggage is black.	**Mes bagages sont noir.**
	may bah-gahzh soh~ nwahr
Your luggage is pretty.	**Tes bagages sont beaux.**
	tay bah-gahzh soh~ boh
His / Her / Its luggage is small.	**Ses bagages sont petits.**
	say bah-gahzh soh~ ptee
Our luggage is lost.	**Nos bagages sont perdus.**
	noh bah-gahzh soh~ pehr-due
Your luggage is dirty.	**Vos bagages sont sales.**
	voh bah-gahzh soh~ sahl
Their luggage is new.	**Leurs bagages sont nouveaux.**
	loehr bah-gahzh soh~ noo-voh

DIRECTIONS

Although they have many other uses, the prepositions **à** and **de** have a variety of translations—such as "to," "from," "at," "for," or "of"—when people talk about places. See the rules for using **de**, **du**, **de l'**, and **des** on p42. **À** changes very similarly to **de**.

à + la = à la	**Tu reste à la gare.** (You're staying at the train station.)	*tueh rehst ah lah gahr*
à + l' = à l'	**Elle est à l'hôtel.** (She's at the hotel.)	*ehl ay-tah loh-tehl*
à + le = au	**Nous partons au théâtre.** (We're leaving for the theatre.)	*noo pahr-toh~ oh tay-ahtr*
à + les = aux	**Ils vont aller aux musées.** (They're going to go to the museums.)	*eel voh~-tah-lay oh mueh-zay*

CHAPTER TWO

GETTING THERE & GETTING AROUND

This section deals with every form of automated transportation. Whether you've just reached your destination by plane or you're renting a car to tour the countryside, you'll find the phrase you need in the next 30 pages.

AT THE AIRPORT

I am looking for ____	**Je cherche ____**
	zhuh shayhrsh
a porter.	**un porteur.**
	uh~ pohr-toehr
the check-in counter.	**l'enregistrement.**
	law~-ruh-zhee-struh-maw~
the ticket counter.	**les guichets.**
	lay gee-shay
arrivals.	**les arrivées.**
	lay-zah-ree-vay
departures.	**les départs.**
	lay day-pahrt
gate number ____.	**la porte numéro ____.**
	lah pohrt nue-may-roh

For a full list of numbers, see p7.

the waiting area.	**la salle d'attente.**
	lah sahl dah-taw~t
the men's restroom.	**les WC pour hommes.**
	lay vay-say poo-ruhm
the women's restroom.	**les WC pour femmes.**
	lay vay-say pour fahm
the police station.	**le bureau de police.**
	luh bue-roh duh poh-lees
a security guard.	**un agent de la sécurité.**
	uh~-nah-zhaw~ duh lah say-kue-ree-tay

the smoking area.	**la salle fumeur.** *lah sahl fue-moehr*
the information booth.	**le guichet d'information.** *luh gee-shay daw~-fohr-mah-see-yoh~*
a public telephone.	**un téléphone public.** *uh~ tay-lay-fohn pue-bleek*
an ATM.	**une billeterie automatique.** *oon bee-yeh-tree oh-toh-mah-teek*
baggage claim.	**la zone de récupération des bagages.** *lah zohn duh ray-kue-pay-rah-see-yoh~ day bah-gahzh*
a luggage cart.	**un caddie.** *uh~ kah-dee*
a currency exchange.	**un bureau de change.** *uh~ bue-roh duh shaw~zh*
a café.	**un café.** *uh~ kah-fay*
a restaurant.	**un restaurant.** *uh~ reh-stoh-raw~*
a bar.	**un bar.** *uh~ bahr*
a bookstore or newsstand.	**une librairie ou un kiosque à journaux.** *oon lee-brey-ree oo uh~ kee-yohsk ah zhoohr-noh*
a duty-free shop.	**une boutique hors taxe.** *oon boo-teek ohr tahks*
Is there Internet access here?	**Est-il possible d'accéder à l'Internet d'ici?** *ey-teel poh-see-bluh dahk-say-day ah leh~-tayhr-neht dee-see*

May I have someone paged, please?	**Pourriez-vous appeler quelqu'un par haut-parleur, s'il vous plaît?** *poo-ree-yay-voo ah-play kehl-kuh~ pahr oh pahr-loehr seel voo play*
Do you accept credit cards?	**Acceptez-vous les cartes de crédit?** *ahk-sehp-tay-voo lay kahrt duh kray-dee*

CHECKING IN

I would like a one-way ticket to ____.	**Je voudrais un aller simple pour ____.** *zhuh voo-dray uh~-nah-lay seh~- pluh poohr*
I would like a round-trip ticket to ____.	**Je voudrais un aller-retour pour ____.** *zhuh voo-dray uh~-nah-lay ruh- toohr poohr*
How much are the tickets?	**Combien coûtent les billets?** *koh~-bee-yeh~ koot lay bee-yay*
Do you have anything less expensive?	**Avez-vous quelque chose de moins cher?** *ah-vay-voo kehl-kuh shohz duh mwaw~ shayhr*
What time does flight ____ leave?	**À quelle heure le vol ____ part-il?** *ah keh-loehr luh vohl ____ pahr- teel*
What time does flight ____ arrive?	**À quelle heure le vol ____ arrive-t-il?** *ah keh-loehr luh vohl ____ ah- reev-teel*
How long is the flight?	**Combien de temps le vol dure-t-il?** *koh~-bee-yeh~ duh taw~ luh vohl duehr-teel*
Do I have a connecting flight?	**Y a-t-il une correspondance?** *yah-tee-loon koh-ray-spoh~-daw~s*

Common Airport Signs

Arrivées	Arrivals
Départs	Departures
Terminal	Terminal
Porte	Gate
Guichets	Ticketing
Douane	Customs
Récupération des bagages	Baggage Claim
Pousser	Push
Tirer	Pull
Interdit de fumer	No Smoking
Entrée	Entrance
Sortie	Exit
Hommes	Men's
Femmes	Women's
Navettes	Shuttle Buses
Taxis	Taxis

GETTING THERE

Do I need to change planes?	**Dois-je changer d'avion?** *dwah-zhuh shaw~-zhay dah-vee-yoh~*
My flight leaves at __:__ (time).	**Mon vol part à ____ heures ____.** *moh~ vohl pahr ah ____ oehr*
What time will the flight arrive?	**A quelle heure le vol va-t-il arriver?** *ah keh-loehr luh vohl vah teel ah-ree-vay*
Is the flight on time?	**Le vol est-il à l'heure?** *luh vohl ey-teel ah-loehr*
Is the flight delayed?	**Le vol est-il en retard?** *luh vohl ey-teel aw~ ruh-tahr*

For full coverage of numbers, see p7.
For full coverage of time, see p12.

From which terminal is flight _____ leaving?

De quel terminal le vol _____ part-il?
duh kehl tayhr-mee-nahl luh vohl _____ pahr-teel

From which gate is flight _____ leaving?

De quelle porte le vol _____ part-il?
duh kehl pohrt luh vohl _____ pahr-teel

How much time do I need for check-in?

De combien de temps ai-je besoin pour l'enregistrement?
duh koh~-bee-yeh~ duh taw~ ay-zhuh buh-zweh~ poohr law~-reh-zhee-struh-maw~

Is there an express check-in line?

Y a-t-il une file d'enregistrement express?
yah-teel oon feel daw~-reh-zhee-struh-maw~ ehk-spray

Do you have electronic check-in?

Y a-t-il un point d'enregistrement électronique?
yah-teel uh~ pwah daw~-rehzh-ee-strumaw~ ay-lehk-troh~-ik

Seat Preferences

I would like ____ ticket(s) in ____	**Je voudrais ____ billet(s) de ____** *zhuh voo-dray ____ bee-yay duh*
first class.	**première classe.** *preh-mee-yayhr klahs*
business class.	**classe affaire.** *klahs ah-fayhr*
economy class.	**classe économique.** *klahs ay-koh~-noh-meek*
I would like ____	**Je voudrais ____** *zhuh voo-dray*
Please don't give me ____	**S'il vous plaît, ne me donnez pas de place ____** *seel voo play nuh muh doh-nay pah duh plahs*
a window seat.	**une place côté hublot.** *oon plahs koh-tay oo-bloh*
an aisle seat.	**une place côté couloir.** *oon plahs koh-tay kool-wahr*
an emergency exit row seat.	**une place côté issue de secours.** *oon plahs koh-tay ee-sue duh suh-koohr*
a bulkhead seat.	**une place au premier rang.** *oon plahs pruh-mee-yay raw~*
a seat by the restroom.	**une place près des toilettes.** *oon plahs pray day twah-leht*
a seat near the front.	**une place à l'avant de l'avion.** *oon plahs ah lah-vaw~ duh lah-vee-yoh~*
a seat near the middle.	**une place au milieu de l'avion.** *oon plahs oh meel-yoeh duh lah-vee-yoh~*
a seat near the back.	**une place à l'arrière de l'avion.** *oon plahs ah lah-ree-yayhr duh lah-vee-yoh~*

GETTING THERE

Is there a meal on the flight?	**Un repas sera-t-il servi durant le vol?**
	uh~ ruh-pah suh-rah-teel sayhr-vee due-raw~ luh vohl
I'd like to order ____	**Je voudrais commander ____**
	zhuh voo-dray koh-maw~-day
a vegetarian meal.	**un repas végétarien.**
	uh~ ruh-pah vay-zhay-tah-ree-yeh~
a kosher meal.	**un repas kasher.**
	uh~ ruh-pah kah-shayhr
a diabetic meal.	**un repas spécial diabétique.**
	uh~ ruh-pah spay-see-yahl dee-ah-bay-teek
I am traveling to ____.	**Je vais à ____.**
	zhuh vay ah
I am coming from ____.	**Je viens de ____.**
	zhuh vee-yeh~ duh
I arrived from ____.	**Je suis arrive(e) de ____.**
	zhuh sweez-ah-ree-vay duh

For full coverage of countries, see English / French dictionary.

May I ____ my reservation?	**Puis-je ____ ma réservation?**
	Pwee-zhuh ____ mah ray-suhr-vah-see-yoh~
change	**changer**
	shaw~-zhay
cancel	**annuler**
	aw~-nue-lay
confirm	**confirmer**
	koh~-feer-may
I have ____ bags / suitcases to check.	**J'ai ____ sacs / valises à enregistrer.**
	zhay ____ sahk / vah-leez ah aw~-reh-zhee-stray

For a full list of numbers, see p7.

Passengers with Special Needs

Is that handicapped accessible?	**Ce vol est-il accessible aux personnes à mobilité réduite?**
	suh vohl ey-teel ahk-suhs-see-bluh oh payhr-suh-nah moh-bee-lee-tay ray-dweet
May I have a wheelchair / walker, please?	**Puis-je avoir une chaise roulante / un déambulateur, s'il vous plaît?**
	Pwee-je ah-vwahr oon shehz roo-law~t / uh~ day-aw~-bue-lah-toehr seel voo play
I need some assistance boarding.	**J'ai besoin d'assistance à l'embarquement.**
	zhay buh-zweh~ dah-sees-taw~s ah law~-bahrk-maw~
I need to bring my service dog.	**J'ai besoin d'emmener avec moi mon chien aidant.**
	zhay buh-zweh~ daw~-m-nay ah-vek mwah moh~ shee-yeh~-nay-daw~
Do you have services for the deaf?	**Offrez-vous des services spéciaux aux malentendants?**
	oh-fray-voo day sayhr-vees spay-see-yoh oh mah-law~-taw~-daw~
Do you have services for the blind?	**Offrez-vous des services spéciaux aux malvoyants?**
	oh-fray-voo day sayhr-vees spay-see-yoh oh mahl-vwah-yaw~

Trouble at Check-In

How long is the delay?	**Le retard est de combien de temps?**
	luh ruh-tahr ay duh koh~-bee-yeh~ duh taw~
My flight was late.	**Mon vol avait du retard.**
	moh~ voh-lah-vay due ruh-tahr
I missed my flight.	**J'ai manqué mon vol.**
	zhay maw~-kay moh~ vohl

GETTING THERE

When is the next flight?	**À quelle heure part le prochain vol?**
	ah keh-loehr pahr luh pro-shaw~
	vohl
May I have a meal	**Puis-je avoir un chèque-repas?**
voucher?	*pwee-zhuh ah-vwahr uh~ shek-*
	ruh-pah
May I have a room	**Puis-je avoir un bon de chambre?**
voucher?	*pwee-zhuh ah-vwahr uh~ boh~*
	duh shaw~-bruh

AT CUSTOMS / SECURITY CHECKPOINTS

I'm traveling with a group.	**Je voyage avec un groupe.**
	zhuh vwah-yahzh ah-vek uh~
	groop
I'm on my own.	**Je voyage seul(e).**
	zhuh vwah-yahzh soehl
I'm traveling on business.	**Je voyage pour affaires.**
	zhuh vwah-yahzh pooh-rah-fayhr
I'm on vacation.	**Je suis en vacances.**
	zhuh swee-zaw~ vah-kaw~s
I have nothing to declare.	**Je n'ai rien à déclarer.**
	zhuh nay ree-yeh~-nah day-
	klah-ray
I would like to	**Je voudrais déclarer ____.**
declare ____.	*zhuh voo-dray day-klah-ray*
I have some liquor.	**J'ai de l'alcool.**
	zhay duh lahl-kool
I have some cigars.	**J'ai des cigares.**
	zhay day see-gahr
They are gifts.	**Il s'agit de cadeaux.**
	eel sah-zee duh kah-doh
They are for personal use.	**Ils sont pour mon usage personnel.**
	eel soh~ poohr moh~-nue-sahzh
	payhr-suh-nehl

Listen Up: Security Lingo

Veuillez enlever vos chaussures / bijoux.	Please remove your shoes / jewelry.
Veuillez enlever votre blouson / pull.	Please remove your jacket / sweater.
Veuillez placer vos bagages sur le tapis roulant.	Please place your bags on the conveyor belt.
Veuillez vous mettre de côté.	Please step to the side.
Nous désirons vous fouiller.	We have to do a hand search.

That is my medicine.

Ce médicament est à moi.
suh may-dee-ka-maw~ ey-tah mwah

I have my prescription.

J'ai l'ordonnance qui va avec.
zhay lohr-doh~-naw~s kee vah ah-vek

My children are traveling on the same passport.

Mes enfants figurent sur le même passeport.
may-zaw~-faw~ fee-guehr suehr luh mehm pahs-pohr

May I have a male / female officer conduct the search?

Puis-je être fouillé(e) par un officier du sexe masculin / féminin?
pwee-zhuh eh-truh foo-wee-yay pahr uh~-noh-fee-see-yay due sehks mah-skue-law~ / fay-mee-naw~

Trouble at Security

Help me. I've lost ____	**Veuillez m'aider. J'ai perdu ____**
	voeh-yay may-day; zhay payhr-due
my passport.	**mon passeport.**
	moh~ pahs-pohr
my boarding pass.	**mon bordereau d'embarque-ment.**
	moh~ bohr-droh daw~-bahrk-maw~
my identification.	**ma pièce d'identité.**
	mah pee-yehs dee-daw~-tee-tay
my wallet.	**mon portefeuille.**
	moh~ pohr-tuh-foeh-yuh
my purse.	**mon sac à main.**
	moh~ sah-kah meh~
Someone stole my purse / wallet!	**On a volé mon sac à main / mon portefeuille.**
	oh~-nah voh-lay moh~ sah-kah meh~ / moh~ pohr-tuh-foeh-yuh

IN-FLIGHT

It's unlikely you'll need much French on the plane, but these phrases will help if a bilingual flight attendant is unavailable or if you need to talk to a French-speaking neighbor.

I think that's my seat.	**Je pense que c'est ma place.**
	zhuh paw~s kuh say mah plahs
May I have ____	**Puis-je avoir ____**
	pwee-zhuh ah-vwahr
mineral water?	**de l'eau minérale?**
	duh loh-mee-ney-rahl
water (plain)?	**de l'eau non-gazeuse?**
	duh loh due noh~-gah-zoehz
sparkling water?	**de l'eau petillante / de l'eau mousseuse?**
	duh loh peh-tee-yaw~t / duh loh moo-soehz

orange juice?	**un jus d'orange?**
	uh~ zhue doh-raw~zh
a soda pop?	**un coca?**
	uh~ koh-kah
a diet soda?	**un coca allegé / un coca light?**
	uh~ koh-kah ah-lay-zhay / uh~ koh-kah liet
a beer?	**une bière?**
	oon bee-yahr
some wine?	**du vin?**
	due veh~

For a full list of drinks, see p96.

a pillow?	**un oreiller?**
	uh~-noh-ray-yay
a blanket?	**une couverture?**
	oon koo-vayhr-tuehr
headphones?	**un casque?**
	uh~ kahsk
a magazine or newspaper?	**un magazine ou un journal?**
	uh~ mah-gah-zeen oo uh~ zhoohr-nahl
When will the meal be served?	**Quand le repas sera-t-il servi?**
	kaw~ luh ruh-pah suh-rah-teel sayhr-vee
How long until we land?	**Dans combien de temps allons-nous atterrir?**
	daw~ koh~-bee-yeh~ duh taw~ ah-loh~-noo ah-teh-reehr
May I move to another seat?	**Puis-je changer de place?**
	pwee-zhuh shaw~-zhay duh plahs
How do I turn the light on / off?	**Comment éteint-on / allume-t-on les lumières?**
	koh-moh ay-teh~-toh~ / ah-luem-toh~ lay lue-mee-yayhr

Trouble In-Flight

These headphones are broken.	**Mon casque ne marche pas.** *moh~ kask nuh mahrsh pah*
Excuse me, I spilled something.	**Pardon, je me suis renversé quelque chose dessus.** *pahr-doh~ zhuh muh swee raw~-vayhr-say kehl-kuh shohz duh-sue*
My child spilled something.	**Mon enfant s'est renversé quelque chose dessus.** *moh~-naw~-faw~ say raw~-vayhr-say kehl-kuh shohz duh-sue*
My child is sick.	**Mon enfant est malade.** *moh~-naw~faw~-tay mah-lahd*
I need an airsickness bag.	**J'ai besoin d'un sac pour le mal de l'air.** *zhay buh-zweh~ duh~ sahk poohr luh mahl duh layhr*
I smell something strange.	**Je sent quelque chose bizarre.** *zhuh saw~ kehl-kuh shohz bee-zahr*
That passenger is behaving suspiciously.	**Ce passager se comporte bizzarement.** *suh pah-sah-zhay suh koh~-pohrt bee-zahr-maw~*

BAGGAGE CLAIM

Where is baggage claim for flight ____?	**Où est la zone de récupération des bagages pour le vol ____?** *oo ay lah zohn duh ray-kue-pay-rah-see-yoh~ day bah-gazh poohr luh vohl*
Would you please help me with my bags?	**Pouvez-vous m'aider à trouver mes bagages, s'il vous plaît?** *poo-vay-voo may-day ah troo-vay may bah-gazh seel voo play*
I am missing ____ bags / suitcases.	**Il me manque ____ sacs / valises.** *eel muh maw~k ____ sahk / vah-leez*

For a full list of numbers, see p7.

My bag is / was ____	**Mon sac est / était ____**
	moh~ sah-kay / sah-kay-tay
lost.	**perdu.**
	payhr-due
damaged.	**abîmé.**
	ah-bee-may
stolen.	**volé.**
	voh-lay
a suitcase.	**une valise.**
	oon vah-leez
a briefcase.	**un porte-documents.**
	uh~ pohrt-doh-kue-maw~
a carry-on.	**un bagage à main.**
	uh~ bah-gah-zhah meh~
a suit bag.	**un porte-costume.**
	uh~ pohrt-koh-stuem
a trunk.	**une malle.**
	oon mahl
golf clubs.	**des clubs de golf.**
	day klueb duh gohlf
hard.	**á coques dures.**
	ah kohk duehr
made out of ____	**en ____**
	aw~
canvas.	**toile.**
	twahl
vinyl.	**vinyle.**
	vee-neel
leather.	**cuir.**
	kweer
hard plastic.	**plastique dur.**
	plah-steek duehr
aluminum.	**aluminium.**
	ah-lue-mee-nee-uhm

For a full list of colors, see the English / French dictionary.

RENTING A VEHICLE

Is there a car rental
agency in the airport?

**Y a-t-il une agence de location de
voitures dans cet aéroport?**
*yah-teel oo-nah-zhaw~s duh loh-
kah-see-yoh~ duh vwah-tuehr
daw~ seh-tay-roh-pohr*

I have a reservation.

J'ai une réservation.
zhay oon ray-zayhr-vah-see-yoh~

VEHICLE PREFERENCES

I would like to rent ____

Je voudrais louer ____
zhuh voo-dray loo-ay

an economy car.

une voiture économie.
oon vwah-tuehr ay-koh-noh-mee

a midsize car.

une voiture intermédiaire.
*oon vwah-tuehr aw~-tayhr-may-
dee-yayhr*

a sedan.

une berline.
oon bayhr-leen

a convertible.

une décapotable.
oon day-kah-poh-tah-bluh

a van.

un fourgon.
uh~ foohr-goh~

a sports car.

une voiture de sport.
oon vwah-tuehr duh spohr

a 4-wheel-drive vehicle.

un véhicule à quatre roues motrices.
*uh~ vay-ee-kue-lah ka-truh roo
moh-trees*

a motorcycle.

une moto.
oon moh-toh

a scooter.

un scooter.
uh~ skoo-tayhr

Do you have one with ____	**En avez-vous une avec ____** *aw~-nah-vay-voo oon ah-vek*
air conditioning?	**la climatisation?** *lah klee-mah-tee-zah-see-yoh~*
a sunroof?	**un toit ouvrant?** *uh~ twah oov-raw~*
a CD player?	**un lecteur de CD?** *uh~ lek-toehr duh say-day*
satellite radio?	**la radio par satellite?** *lah rah-dee-oh pahr sah-tuh-leet*
satellite tracking?	**la télédétection?** *lah tay-lay-day-tek-see-yoh~*
an onboard map?	**un système de navigation?** *uh~ sees-tehm duh nah-vee-gah-see-yoh~*
a DVD player?	**un lecteur de DVD?** *uh~ lek-toehr duh day-vay-day*
child seats?	**des sièges pour enfant?** *day see-yehz poohr aw~-faw~*
Do you have ____	**Avez-vous ____** *ah-vay-voo*
a smaller car?	**une voiture plus petite?** *oon vwah-tuehr plue puh-teet*
a bigger car?	**une voiture plus grande?** *oon vwah-tuehr plue graw~d*
a cheaper car?	**une voiture moins chère?** *oon vwah-tuehr mweh~ shayhr*
Do you have a nonsmoking car?	**Avez-vous une voiture non fumeur?** *ah-vay-voo oon vwah-tuehr noh~-fue-moehr*
I need an automatic transmission.	**J'ai besoin d'une voiture à transmission automatique.** *zhay buh-zweh~ doon vwah-tuehr ah traw~-z-mee-shee-yoh~ ohtoh-mah-teek*

A standard transmission is okay.	**D'accord pour une boîte de vitesses** *dah-kohr poohr oon bwaht duh vee-tess*
May I have an upgrade?	**Puis-je bénéficier de la classe supérieure?** *pwee-zhuh bay-nay-fee-see-yay duh lah klahs sue-pay-ree-yoehr*

MONEY MATTERS

What's the daily / weekly / monthly rate?	**Quel est le tarif journalier / hebdomadaire / mensuel?** *keh-lay luh tah-reef zhoohr-nah-lee-yay / ehb-doh-mah-dayhr / maw~-swehl*
What is the mileage rate?	**Quel est le prix au kilomètre?** *keh-lay luh pree oh kee-loh-meh-truh*
How much is insurance?	**Combien coûte l'assurance?** *koh~-bee-yeh~ koot lah-sue-raw~-s*
Are there other fees?	**Y a-t-il d'autres coûts?** *yah-teel doh-truhs koo*
Is there a weekend rate?	**Y a-t-il un tarif spécial pour le week-end?** *yah-teel uh~ tah-reef spay-see-yahl poohr luh wee-kend*

TECHNICAL QUESTIONS

What kind of gas does it take?	**Quel type d'essence consomme-t-elle?** *kehl teep day-saw~-s koh~-som-tehl*
Do you have the manual in English?	**Avez-vous un manuel en anglais?** *ah-vay-voo uh~ maw~-nwehl aw~-naw~-glay*
Do you have an English booklet with the local traffic laws?	**Avez-vous une brochure en anglais sur le code de la route local?** *ah-vay-voo oon broh-shuehr aw~-naw~-glay suehr luh kohd duh lah root loh-kahl*

Road Signs

Vitesse limitée	Speed Limit
Stop	Stop
Céder le passage	Yield
Danger	Danger
Voie sans issue	No Exit
Voie unique	One Way
Entrée interdite	Do Not Enter
Route fermée	Road Closed
Péage	Toll
Espèces uniquement	Cash Only
Parking interdit	No Parking
Parking payant	Parking Fee
Garage couvert	Parking Garage

GETTING THERE

CAR TROUBLES

The _____ doesn't work.   _____ **ne marche pas.**
_____ *nuh mahrsh pah*

See diagram on p62 for car parts.

It is already dented.   **La carrosserie est déjà abîmée.**
lah kah-roh-seh-ree ay day-zhah
ah-bee-may

It is scratched.   **La carrosserie est rayée.**
lah kah-roh-seh-ree ay ray-ay

The windshield is cracked.   **Le pare-brise est fendu.**
luh pahr-breez ay faw~-due

The tires look low.   **Les pneus ont l'air de manquer d'air.**
lay puh-noeh oh~ layhr duh
maw~-kay dayhr

It has a flat tire.   **L'un des pneus est à plat.**
luh~ day puh-noeh ay-tah plah

Whom do I call for service?   **Qui dois-je appeler pour me faire**
dépanner?
kee dwah-zhuh ah-play poohr
muh fayhr day-pah-nay

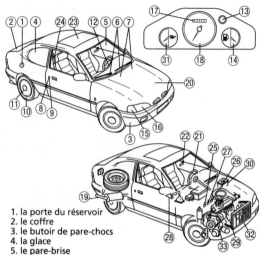

1. la porte du réservoir
2. le coffre
3. le butoir de pare-chocs
4. la glace
5. le pare-brise
6. les essuie-glaces
7. le lave-glace
8. la serrure
9. la serrure automatique
10. le pneu
11. la roue
12. l'allumage
13. les feux de détresse
14. la jauge d'essence
15. le clignotant
16. les feux avant
17. le kilométrique
18. l'indicateur de vitesse
19. le silencieux
20. le capot
21. le volant
22. le rétroviseur

23. le toit ouvrant
24. la ceinture de sécurité
25. la pédale
26. l'embrayage
27. le frein
28. le frein à main
29. le moteur
30. la batterie
31. l'indicateur de niveau d'huile (à moteur)
32. le radiator
33. la courroie de ventilateur

It won't start.	**Elle refuse de démarrer.** *ehl ruh-fuez duh day-mah-ray*
It's out of gas.	**Elle est en panne d'essence.** *ehl ay-taw~ pahn day-saw~s*
The check engine light is on.	**Le voyant de contrôle du moteur est allumé.** *luh vwah-yaw~ duh koh~-trohl due moh-toehr ay-tah-lue-may*
The oil light is on.	**Le voyant de niveau d'huile est allumé.** *luh vwah-yaw~ duh nee-voh dweel ay-tah-lue-may*
The brake light is on.	**Le voyant de contrôle des freins est allumé.** *luh vwah-yaw~ duh koh~-trohl day frehn ay-tah-lue-may*
It runs rough.	**La conduite est trop serrée.** *lah koh~-dwee-tay troh suh-ray*
The car is overheating.	**Le moteur chauffe.** *luh moh-toehr shohf*

Asking for Directions

Excuse me, please.	**Excusez-moi, s'il vous plaît.** *ehks-kue-zay mwah seel voo play*
How do I get to ____?	**Comment fais-je pour aller à ____?** *koh-moh fay-zhuh pooh-rah-lay ah*
Go straight.	**Allez tout droit.** *ah-lay too dwah*
Turn left.	**Tournez à gauche.** *toohr-nay ah gohsh*
Continue right.	**Continuez à droite.** *koh~-teen-yue-ay ah dwaht*
It's on the right.	**C'est à droite.** *say-tah dwaht*
Can you show me on the map?	**Pouvez-vous me montrer sur la carte?** *poo-vay-voo muh moh~-tray suehr lah kahrt*

Is it far from here?	**Est-ce loin d'ici?**
	ehs lweh dee-see
Is this the right way for ____?	**Est-ce que c'est la bonne route pour ____?**
	ehs kuh say lah buhn root pohr
I've lost my way.	**Je me suis perdu(e).**
	zhuh muh swee payhr-due
Could you repeat that, please?	**Est-ce que vous pouvez répéter, s'il vous plaît?**
	ehs kuh voo poo-vay ruh-puh-tay seel voo play
Thanks for your help.	**Merci pour votre aide.**
	mayhr-see pohr voh-trehd

For a full list of direction-related terms, see p5.

SORRY, OFFICER

What is the speed limit?	**Quelle est la limite de vitesse?**
	keh-lay lah lee-meet duh vee-tess
I wasn't going that fast.	**Je n'allais pas si vite.**
	zhuh nah-lay pah see veet
Where do I pay the fine?	**Où dois-je payer l'amende?**
	oo dwah-zhuh pay-ay lah-maw~d
How much is the fine?	**Combien est-ce que l'amende?**
	koh~-bee-yeh~ ehs kuh lah-maw~d
Do I have to go to court?	**Dois-je passer en justice?**
	dwah-zhuh pah-say aw~ zhues-tees
I had an accident.	**J'ai eu un accident.**
	zhay oo uh~-nahk-see-daw~
The other driver hit me.	**C'est l'autre conducteur qui m'est rentré dedans.**
	say loh-truh koh~-duek-toehr kee may raw~-tray duh-daw~
I'm at fault.	**C'est moi qui suis responsable.**
	say mwah kee swee ruh-spoh~-sah-bluh

BY TAXI

Where is the taxi stand?	**Où est la station de taxi?**
	oo ay lah stah-see-yon duh tahk-see
Is there a shuttle bus between the airport and my hotel?	**Y a-t-il une navette entre l'aéroport et mon hôtel?**
	yah-tee-loon nah-veht aw~-truh lay-roh-pohr ay moh~-noh-tel
I need to get to ____.	**Je désire aller à ____.**
	zhuh day-seer ah-lay ah
How much will that cost?	**Combien va coûter la course?**
	koh~-bee-yeh~ vah koo-tay lah koohrs
Can you take me / us to the train / bus station?	**Pouvez-vous m'emmener / nous emmener à la gare / à la gare routière?**
	poo-vay-voo maw~-m-nay / nooz-ah~-m-nay ah lah gahr / ah lah gahr roo-tee-yayhr
I am in a hurry.	**Je me suis pressé(e).**
	zhuh muh swee pruh-say
Slow down.	**Veuillez ralentir.**
	voeh-yay rah-law~-teehr
Am I close enough to walk?	**Est-ce assez près pour y aller à pied?**
	eh-sah-say pray poohr yah-lay ah pee-ay

GETTING THERE

Listen Up: Taxi Lingo

Montez!	Get in!
Laissez vos bagages. Je m'en occupe.	Leave your luggage. I got it.
C'est ____ euros par baggage.	It's ____ for each bag.
Combien de passagers?	How many passengers?
Vous êtes pressés?	Are you in a hurry?

Please let me out here.	**Laissez-moi descendre ici, s'il vous plaît.**
	leh-zay mwah duh-saw~-druh ee-see seel voo play
That's not the correct change.	**Vous ne m'avez pas rendu la bonne monnaie.**
	voo nuh mah-vay pah raw~-due lah buhn moh-nay

For a full list of numbers, see p7.

BY TRAIN

How do I get to the train station?	**Comment puis-je me rendre à la gare?**
	koh-maw~ pwee-zhuh muh raw~-drah lah gahr
Would you take me to the train station?	**Pouvez-vous m'emmener à la gare?**
	poo-vay-voo maw~-m-nay ah lah gahr
How long is the trip to ____?	**Il y a combien de kilomètres jusqu'à ____?**
	eel-yah koh~-bee-yeh~ duh kee-loh-meh-truh zhues-kah
When is the next train?	**À quelle heure part le prochain train?**
	ah keh-loehr pahr luh pro-shaw~-treh~
Do you have a schedule?	**Avez-vous un horaire des départs?**
	ah-vay-voo-zuh~-nohr-ayhr day day-pahr

Do I have to change trains?	**Dois-je changer de train?**
	dwah-zhuh shaw~-zhay duh treh~
a one-way ticket	**un aller simple**
	uh~-nah-lay seh~-pluh
a round-trip ticket	**un aller-retour**
	uh~-nah-lay ruh-toohr
Which platform does it leave from?	**De quel quai le train part-il?**
	duh kehl kay luh treh~ pahr-teel
Is there a bar car?	**Y a-t-il un service de boissons?**
	yah-teel uh~ sayhr-vees duh bwah-soh~s
Is there a dining car?	**Y a-t-il un wagon-restaurant?**
	yah-teel uh~ vah-goh~ reh-stoh-raw~
Which car is my seat in?	**Dans quel wagon se trouve ma place?**
	daw~ kehl vah-goh~ suh troov mah plahs
Is this seat taken?	**Ce siège est-il pris?**
	suh see-yehzh ey-teel pree
Where is the next stop?	**Quel est le prochain arrêt?**
	keh-lay luh proh-sheh~-nah-rey
Would you please tell me how many stops to ____?	**Pouvez-vous me dire combien d'arrêts il y a avant ____?**
	poo-vay-voo muh deer koh~-bee-yeh~ dah-rey eel-yah ah-vaw~
What's the train number and destination?	**Quel est le numéro du train et sa destination?**
	keh-lay luh nue-may-roh due treh~ ay sah deh-stee-nah-see-yoh~

BY BUS

How do I get to the bus station?	**Comment puis-je me rendre à la gare routière?** *koh-maw~ pwee-zhuh muh raw~-druh ah lah gahr roo-tee-yayhr*
Would you take me to the bus station?	**Pouvez-vous m'emmener à la gare routière?** *poo-vay-voo maw~m-nay ah lah gahr roo-tee-yayhr*
May I please have a bus schedule?	**Puis-je avoir un horaire des cars?** *pwee-zhuh ah-vwahr uh~-noh-rayhr day kahr*
Which bus goes to ____?	**Quel car va à ____?** *kehl kahr vah ah*
Where does it leave from?	**D'où part-il?** *due pahr-teel*
How long does the bus take?	**Combien de temps prend le car pour aller à ____?** *koh~-bee-yeh~ duh taw~ praw~-luh kahr poohr ah-lay ah*
How much is it?	**Combien ça coûte?** *koh~-bee-yeh~ sah koot*
Is there an express bus?	**Y a-t-il un service direct?** *yah-teel uh~ sayhr-vees dee-rekt*

| Does it make local stops? | **Dessert-il toutes les villes?** |
| | *duh-zayhr-teel toot lay veel* |

| Does it run at night? | **Fonctionne-t-il pendant la nuit?** |
| | *foh-k-see-yoh~-teel paw~-daw~ lah nwee* |

| When is the next bus? | **À quelle heure part le prochain car?** |
| | *ah keh-loehr pahr luh proh-sheh~ kahr* |

| a one-way ticket | **un aller simple** |
| | *uh~-nah-lay seh~-pluh* |

| a round-trip ticket | **un aller-retour** |
| | *uh~-nah-lay ruh-toohr* |

| How long will the bus be stopped? | **Combien de temps dure l'arrêt?** |
| | *koh~-bee-yeh~ duh taaw~ duehr lah-rey* |

| Is there an air conditioned bus? | **Y a-t-il un car climatisé?** |
| | *yah-teel uh~ kahr klee-mah-tee-zay* |

| Is this seat taken? | **Ce siège est-il pris?** |
| | *suh see-yehzh ey-teel pree* |

| Where is the next stop? | **Quel est le prochain arrêt?** |
| | *keh-lay luh proh-sheh~-nah-rey* |

| Would you please tell me when we reach ____? | **Veuillez me dire quand nous atteignons ____?** |
| | *voeh-yay muh deer kaw~ noo-zah-teh-nyoh~* |

| Would you please tell me how to get to ____? | **Pouvez-vous me dire comment aller à ____, s'il vous plaît?** |
| | *poo-vay-voo muh deer koh-maw~-ah-lay ah ___ seel voo play* |

| I'd like to get off here. | **Je voudrais descendre ici.** |
| | *zhuh voo-dray duh-saw~-druh ee-see* |

BY BOAT OR SHIP

Would you take me to the port?	**Pouvez-vous m'emmener au port?** *poo-vay-voo meh-men-ay oh pohr*
When does the boat sail?	**Quand le navire appareille-t-il?** *kaw~ luh nah-veer ah-pah-ray teel*
How long is the voyage?	**Combien de temps la traversée dure-t-elle?** *koh~-bee-yeh~duh taw~ lah trah-vayhr-say duehr-tehl*
Where are the life preservers?	**Où sont les bouées de sauvetage?** *oo soh~ lay boo-ay duh sohv-tazh*
I would like a private cabin.	**Je voudrais une cabine individuelle.** *zhuh voo-dray oon kah-been eh~-dee-vee-due-ehl*
Is the trip rough?	**Le voyage, est-il difficile?** *luh vwah-yahzh ey-teel dee-fee-seel*
I feel seasick.	**J'ai le mal de mer.** *zhay luh mahl duh mayhr*
I need some Dramamine.	**Je voudrais de la Dramamine.** *zhuh voo-dray duh lah drah-mah-meen*
Where is the bathroom?	**Où puis-je trouver des WC?** *oo pwee-zhuh troo-vay day vay-say*
Does the ship have a casino?	**Y a-t-il un casino à bord?** *yah-teel uh~ kah-zee-noh ah bohr*
Will the ship stop at ports along the way?	**Le navire fera-t-il escale dans certains ports?** *luh nah-veer fuh-rah teel ehs-kahl daw~ sayhr-teh~ pohr*

BY SUBWAY

A very convenient, fast, safe and inexpensive way to cruise through a French city is to take its **Métro**. Note that subways close at night (the Paris Métro closes from 12:50 AM to 5:30 AM), so do allocate enough time for your trip back to your hotel!

Where is the subway station?	**Où se trouve la station du métro?** *oo suh troov lah stah-see-yoh~ due meh-troh*
Where can I buy a ticket?	**Où achete-t-on des billets?** *oo ah-sheh-toh~ day bee-yay*
Could I have a map of the subway, please?	**Pouvez-vous me donner un plan métro, s'il vous plaît?** *poo-vay voo muh duh-nay uh~ plaw~ meh-troh seel voo play*
Which line should I take for _____?	**Quelle ligne prend-t-on à _____?** *kehl leen praw~ toh~ ah*
Is this the right line for _____?	**Est-ce que c'est la bonne ligne à _____?** *ehs kuh say lah buhn lee-nah*
Which stop is it for _____?	**Quel arrêt pour _____?** *keh-lah-rey poohr*
How many stops is it to _____?	**Combien d' arrêts jusqu'à _____?** *koh~-bee-yeh~ dah-rey zhues-kah*
Is the next stop _____?	**L' arrêt prochain, c'est _____?** *lah-rey proh-sheh~ say*
Where are we?	**Où sommes-nous?** *oo suhm-noo*

Where do I change to _____?	**Où est-ce que je change à _____?**
	oo ehs kuh zhuh shaw~zh ah
What time is the last train to _____?	**Á quelle heure part le dernier train à _____?**
	ah keh-loehr pahr luh dayhr-nyay treh~-nah
Where?	**Où?**
	oo

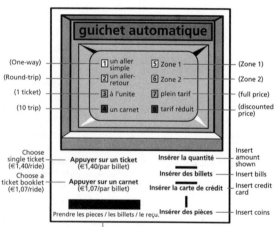

(One-way)	1 un aller simple
(Round-trip)	2 un aller-retour
(1 ticket)	3 à l'unite
(10 trip)	4 un carnet
5 Zone 1	(Zone 1)
6 Zone 2	(Zone 2)
7 plein tarif	(full price)
8 tarif réduit	(discounted price)

Choose single ticket (€1,40/ride) — **Appuyer sur un ticket** (€1,40/par billet)

Choose a ticket booklet (€1,07/ride) — **Appuyer sur un carnet** (€1,07/par billet)

Insérer la quantité — Insert amount shown

Insérer des billets — Insert bills

Insérer la carte de crédit — Insert credit card

Insérer des pièces — Insert coins

Prendre les pieces / les billets / le reçu.

Take change / tickets / receipt

TRAVELERS WITH SPECIAL NEEDS

Do you have wheelchair access?	**Ce navire est-il accessible aux personnes à mobilité réduite?** *suh nah-veer ey-teel ahk-seh-see-bluh oh payhr-suhn ah moh-bee-lee-tay ray-dweet*
Do you have elevators? Where?	**Y a-t-il des ascenseurs à bord? Où?** *yah-teel day-zah-saw~-soehrs ah bohr; oo*
Do you have ramps? Where?	**Y a-t-il des rampes à bord? Où?** *yah-teel day raw~-pah bohr; oo*
Are the restrooms handicapped accessible?	**Les toilettes sont-elles accessibles aux personnes à mobilité réduite?** *lay twah-leht soh~-tehl ahk-seh-see-bluh oh payhr-suhn ah moh-bee-lee-tay ray-dweet*
Do you have audio assistance for deaf persons?	**Offrez-vous des services audio aux malentendants?** *oh-fray-voo day sayhr-vees oh-dee-yoh oh mah-law~-taw~-daw~*
I am deaf / hearing impaired.	**Je suis sourd(e) / malentendant(e).** *zhuh swee soohr(d) / mah-law~-taw~-daw~-(t)*
May I bring my service dog?	**Puis-je emmener mon chien aidant?** *pwee-zhuh aw~m-nay moh~ shee-yeh~-nay-daw~*
I am blind / visually impaired.	**Je suis aveugle / malvoyant(e).** *zhuh swee ah-voeh-gluh / mahl-vwah-yaw~-(t)*
I need to charge my power chair.	**J'ai besoin d'assistance pour embarquer ma chaise roulante.** *zhay buh-zweh~ dah-see-staw~s poohr aw~-bahr-kay mah shehz roo-law~t*

CHAPTER THREE

LODGING

This chapter will help you find the right accomodations, at the right price—and the amenities you might need during your stay.

ROOM PREFERENCES

Would you please recommend ____	**Pourriez-vous me recommander** ____ *pooh-ree-yay-voo muh ruh-koh-maw~-day*
a clean hostel?	**une auberge propre?** *oo-noh-bayrzh proh-pruh*
a moderately priced hotel?	**un hotel au prix moyen?** *uh~ noh-tehl oh pree mwah-yaw~*
a moderately priced B&B?	**une chambre d'hôtes / un bed and breakfast au prix moyen?** *oon shaw~-bruh doht / uh~ behd ahnd brehk-fahst oh pree mwah-yaw~*
a good hotel / motel?	**un bon hôtel / motel?** *uh~ buh-noh-tehl / moh-tehl*
Does the hotel have ____	**Cet hôtel a-t-il** ____ *seh-toh-tel ah-teel*
a pool?	**une piscine?** *oon pee-seen*
a casino?	**un casino?** *uh~ kah-zee-noh*
suites?	**des suites?** *day sweet*
terraces?	**des chambres donnant sur une terrace?** *day shaw~-bruh duh-naw~ suehr oon tay-rahs*

a fitness center?	**une salle de musculation?**
	oon sahl duh mues-kue-lah-see-yoh~
a spa?	**un spa?**
	uh~ spah
a private beach?	**une plage privée?**
	oon plazh pree-vay
a tennis court?	**un court de tennis?**
	uh~ koohr duh tay-nees
I would like a room for ____ people.	**Je voudrais une chambre pour ____ personnes.**
	zhuh voo-dray oon shaw~-bruh poohr ____ payhr-suhn

For a full list of numbers, see p7.

I would like ____	**Je voudrais ____**
	zhuh voo-dray
a king-sized bed.	**une chambre à très grand lit.**
	oon shaw~-bruh ah tray graw~ lee
a double bed.	**une chambre à lit à une place.**
	oon shaw~-bruh ah lee ah oon plahs
twin beds.	**des lits jumeaux.**
	day lee zhue-moh
adjoining rooms.	**des chambres communicantes.**
	day shaw~-bruh koh-mue-neek-aw~t
a smoking room.	**une chambre fumeur**
	oon shaw~-bruh fue-moehr

LODGING

Listen Up: Reservations Lingo

Nous sommes pleins.	We have no vacancies.
Combien de nuits désirez-vous rester?	How long will you be staying?
Fumeur ou non fumeur?	Smoking or nonsmoking?

nonsmoking room.	**une chambre non fumeur.**
	oon shaw~-bruh noh~ fue-moehr
a private bathroom.	**une salle de bain privée.**
	oon sahl duh beh~ pree-vay
a room with a shower.	**une chambre avec une douche.**
	oon shaw~-bruh ah-vehk oon doosh
a room with a bathtub.	**une chambre avec une baignoire.**
	oon shaw~-bruh ah-vehk oon beh~-nwahr
air conditioning.	**climatisation.**
	klee-mah-tee-zah-see-yoh~
television.	**un poste de télévision.**
	pohst duh tay-lay-vee-zee-yoh~
cable.	**le télévision par câble.**
	luh tay-lay-vee-zee-yoh~ pahr kah-bluh
satellite TV.	**le télévision par satellite.**
	luh tay-lay-vee-zee-yoh~ pahr sah-teh-leet
a telephone.	**un téléphone.**
	un~ tay-lay-fohn
Internet access.	**accès à l'Internet.**
	ahk-say ah leh~-tayhr-neht
high-speed Internet access.	**accès haute vitesse à l'Internet.**
	ahk-say ot veet-ess ah leh~-tayhr-neht
a refrigerator.	**un réfrigérateur.**
	uh~ ray-free-zheh-rah-toehr
a beach view.	**vue sur la mer.**
	vue suehr lah mayhr
a city view.	**vue sur la rue.**
	vue suehr lah rue

a kitchenette.	**une kitchenette.**
	oon kee-shee-neht
a balcony.	**un balcon.**
	uh~ bahl-koh~
a suite.	**une suite.**
	oon sweet
a penthouse.	**une chambre terrasse.**
	oon shaw~-bruh tay-rahs
I would like a room ____	**Je voudrais une chambre ____**
	zhuh voo-dray oon shaw~-bruh
on the ground floor.	**au rez-de-chaussée.**
	oh ray duh shoh-say
near the elevator.	**à proximité d'un ascenceur.**
	ah prok-see-mee-tay duh~ ah-saw~-soehr
near the stairs.	**à proximité d'un escalier.**
	ah prok-see-mee-tay duh~ ehs-kah-lee-yay
near the pool.	**à proximité de la piscine.**
	ah prok-see-mee-tay duh lah pee-zeen
away from the street.	**à l'écart de la rue.**
	ah lay-kahr duh lah rue
I would like a corner room.	**Je voudrais une chambre d'angle.**
	zhuh voo-dray oon shaw~-bruh daw~-gluh
Do you have ____	**Avez-vous ____**
	ah-vay-voo
a crib?	**un lit d'enfant?**
	uh~ lee daw~-faw~
a foldout bed?	**un lit dépliant?**
	uh~ lee day-plee-yaw~

GUESTS WITH SPECIAL NEEDS

I need a room with _____	**J'ai besoin d'une chambre _____**
	zhay buh-zweh~ doon shaw~-bruh
wheelchair access.	**accessible en chaise roulante.**
	ahk-seh-see-bluh aw~ shehz roo-law~t
services for the visually impaired.	**équipée pour malvoyant.**
	ay-kee-pay poohr mahl-vwahy-aw~
services for the hearing impaired.	**équipée pour malentendant.**
	ay-kee-pay poohr mah-law~-taw~-daw~
I am traveling with a service dog.	**Je voyage avec un chien aidant.**
	zhuh vwah-yahzh ah-vek uh~ shee-yeh~-nay-daw~

MONEY MATTERS

I would like to make a reservation.	**Je désire faire une réservation.**
	zhuh day-zeer fayhr oon ray-zehr-vah-see-yoh~
How much per night?	**Quel est le prix par nuit?**
	keh-lay luh pree pahr nwee
Do you have a _____	**Avez-vous _____**
	ah-vay-voo
weekly rate?	**un tarif hebdomadaire?**
	uh~ tah-reef ehb-doh-mah-dayhr
monthly rate?	**un tarif mensuel?**
	uh~ tah-reef maw~-swehl
weekend rate?	**le prix de fin de semaine?**
	luh pree duh feh~ duh smehn
We will be staying for _____ days / weeks / months.	**Nous désirons rester _____ nuits / semaines / mois.**
	noo day-zeer-oh~ ruh-stay _____ nwee / smehn / mwah

For full coverage of numbers, see p7.

When is checkout time?

À quelle heure la chambre doit-elle être libérée?
ah keh-loehr lah shaw~-bruh dwah-tehl eh-truh lee-bay-ray

Do you accept credit cards / travelers' checks?

Acceptez-vous les cartes de crédit / les chèques de voyage?
ahk-sehp-tay-voo lay kahrt duh kray-dee / lay shek duh vwah-yahzh

May I see a room?

Puis-je visiter l'une de vos chambres?
pwee-zhuh vee-zee-tay loon duh voh shaw~-bruh

How much extra are taxes?

Combien ajoute-elle la taxe?
koh~-bee-yeh~ ah-zhoo-tehl lah tahks

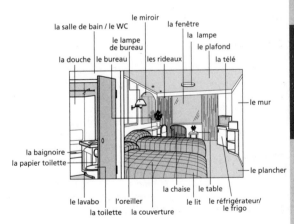

la salle de bain / le WC
le miroir
la fenêtre
le lampe de bureau
la lampe
la douche
le bureau
les rideaux
le plafond
la télé
le mur
la baignoire
la papier toilette
le mur
le plancher
le lavabo
l'oreiller
la chaise
le table
la toilette
la couverture
le lit
le réfrigérateur / le frigo

LODGING

How much is the service charge, or is it included?

Combien coûte le service, ou est-il compris?
koh~-bee-yeh~ koot luh suhr-vees oo ey-teel koh~-pree

I'd like to speak with the manager.

Je voudrais m'entretenir avec le directeur.
zhuh voo-dray maw~-truh-tuh-neer ah-vek luh dee-rehk-toehr

IN-ROOM AMENITIES

I'd like ____

Je voudrais ____
zhuh voo-dray

to place an international call.

faire un appel à l'étranger.
fayhr uh~-nah-pel ah lay-traw~-zhay

to place a long-distance call.

faire un appel longue distance.
fayhr uh~-nah-pel loh~g dee-staw~s

directory assistance in English.

les renseignements en anglais.
lay raw~-seh~-nyuh-maw~-naw~-naw~-glay

Instructions for Dialing the Hotel Phone

Pour appeler une autre chambre, composez le numéro de chambre.	To call another room, dial the room number.
Pour faire un appel local, composez d'abord le neuf.	To make a local call, first dial 9.
Pour appeler l'opératrice, composez le zéro.	To call the operator, dial 0.

room service.	**du service en chambre.** *due sayhr-vee-saw~ shaw~-bruh*
maid service.	**une femme de chambre.** *oon fahm duh shaw~-bruh*
the front desk.	**la réception.** *lah ray-sehp-see-yoh~*
Do you have room service?	**Offrez-vous du service en chambre?** *oh-fray-voo due sayhr-vees aw~* *shaw~-bruh*
When is the kitchen open?	**Quand peut-on dîner?** *kaw~ poeh-toh~ dee-nay*
Do you serve breakfast?	**Servez-vous le petit-déjeuner?** *sayhr-vay-voo luh ptee day-zhoeh-* *nay*
When is breakfast served?	**À quelle heure est le petit déjeuner?** *ah keh-loehr ey luh ptee day-* *zhuh-nay*

For a full list of time-related terms, see p12.

Do you offer massages?	**Offrez-vous un service de massage?** *oh-fray-voo uh~ sayhr-vees duh* *mah-sahzh*
Do you have a lounge?	**Y a-t-il un bar-salon dans l'hôtel?** *yah-teel uh~ bahr-sah-loh~ daw~* *loh-tehl*
Do you have a business center?	**Avez-vous un centre d'affaires?** *ah-vay-voo uh~ saw~-truh dah-fayhr*
Do you have Wi-Fi?	**Avez-vous l'accès Internet Wi-Fi?** *ah-vay-voo lahk-seh eh~-tayhr-* *neht wee-fee*

May I have a newspaper in the morning?	**Puis-je avoir un journal le matin?** *pwee-zhuh ah-vwahr uh~ zhoohr-ahl luh mah-teh~*
Do you offer a tailor service?	**Offrez-vous un service de raccommodage?** *oh-fray-voo uh~ sayhr-vees duh rah-koh-moh-dazh*
Do you offer a laundry service?	**Offrez-vous un service de lessive?** *oh-fray-voo uh~ sayhr-vees duh leh-seev*
Do you offer dry cleaning?	**Offrez-vous un service de nettoyage à sec?** *oh-fray-voo uh~ sayhr-vees duh nuh-twah-yahzh ah sek*
May we have ____	**Pourrions-nous avoir ____** *pooh-ree-yoh~-noo-zah-vwahr*
clean sheets today?	**des draps propres aujourd'hui?** *day drah proh-pruhz oh-zhoohr-dwee*
more towels?	**des serviettes supplémentaires?** *day sayhr-vee-yeht sue-play-maw~-tayhr*
more toilet paper?	**du papier toilette?** *due pah-pee-yay twah-leht*
extra pillows?	**des oreillers supplémentaires?** *day-zoh-ray-ay sue-play-maw~-tayhr*
Do you have an ice machine?	**Y a-t-il une machine à glace dans l'hôtel?** *yah-teel oon mah-sheen ah glahs daw~ loh-tehl*

Did I receive any ____	**Est-ce qu'il y a ____ pour moi?**
	ehs keel-yah ____ poohr mwah
messages?	**des messages**
	day meh-sahzh
mail?	**du courrier**
	due kooh-ree-yay
faxes?	**des télécopies**
	day tay-lay-koh-pee
May I have a spare key, please?	**Puis-je avoir une clé supplémentaire, s'il vous plaît?**
	pwee-zhuh ah-vwahr oon klay sue-play-maw~-tayhr seel voo play
May I have more hangers, please?	**Puis-je avoir des cintres supplémentaires, s'il vous plaît?**
	pwee-zhuh ah-vwahr day seh~-truh sue-play-maw~-tayhr seel voo play
I am allergic to down pillows.	**Je suis allergique aux oreillers à duvet d'oie.**
	zhuh swee-zah-layhr-zheek oh-zoh-ray-ay ah due-vay dwah
May I have a wake-up call?	**Puis-je demander un réveil téléphonique?**
	pwee-zhuh duh-maw~-day uh~-ray-vay tay-lay-foh-neek

For a full list of time-related terms, see p12.

Do you have alarm clocks?	**Avez-vous des réveils?**
	ah-vay-voo day ray-vay
Is there a safe in the room?	**Y a-t-il un coffre-fort dans la chambre?**
	yah-teel uh~ koh-fruh fohr daw~ lah shaw~-bruh
Does the room have a hair dryer?	**Y a-t-il un sèche-cheveux dans la chambre?**
	yah-teel uh~ sehsh-shuh-voeh daw~ lah shaw~-bruh

HOTEL ROOM TROUBLE

May I speak with the manager?

Puis-je parler au responsable de l'hôtel?
pwee-zhuh pahr-lay oh ruh-spoh~sah-bluh duh loh-tehl

The _____ does not work.
_____ ne marche pas.
_____ nuh mahrsh pah

television
La telévision
lah tay-lay-vee-see-yoh~

telephone line
La ligne téléphonique
lah lee-nyuh tay-lay-foh-neek

air conditioning
La climatisation
lah klee-mah-tee-zah-see-yoh~

Internet access
L'accès à l'Internet
lahk-say ah leh~-tayhr-neht

cable TV
Les chaînes câblées
lay shehn kah-blay

There is no hot water.
Il n'y a pas d'eau chaude.
eel nyah pah doh shohd

The toilet is overflowing!
Les toilettes sont débordent!
lay twah-leht soh~ day-bohrd

This room is ____	**Cette chambre est ____**
	seht shaw~-bruh ay
too loud.	**trop bruyante.**
	troh bwee-yaw~t
too cold.	**pas assez chauffée.**
	pah-zah-say shoh-fay
too warm.	**surchauffée.**
	suehr-shoh-fay
too smoky.	**trop fumeuse.**
	troh fue-moehz
This room has ____	**Il y a ____ dans cette chambre.**
	eel-yah ____ daw~ seht shaw~-bruh
bugs.	**des insectes**
	day-zeh~-sehkt
mice.	**des souris**
	day sooh-ree
May I have a different room, please?	**Puis-je avoir une autre chambre, s'il vous plaît?**
	pwee-zhuh ah-vwahr oon oh-truh shaw~-bruh seel voo play
Do you have a bigger room?	**Avez-vous une chambre plus spacieuse?**
	ah-vay-voo-zoon shaw~-bruh plue spah-see-yoehz
I locked myself out of my room.	**J'ai oublié ma clé à l'intérieur de ma chambre.**
	zhay oo-blee-yay mah klay ah leh~-tay-ree-yoehr duh mah shaw~bruh
Do you have any fans?	**Avez-vous des ventilateurs?**
	ah-vay-voo day vaw~-tee-lah-toehr
The sheets are not clean.	**Les draps de mon lit sont sales.**
	lay drah duh moh~ lee soh~ sahl

The towels are not clean.	**Les serviettes de ma salle de bains sont sales.** *lay sayhr-vee-yeht duh mah sahl duh beh~ soh~ sahl*
The room is not clean.	**Ma chambre n'a pas été nettoyée.** *mah shaw~bruh nah pah-zay-tay neh-twah-yay*
This room smells like smoke. I am allergic to smoke.	**Cette chambre sent de fumée. Je suis allergique à la fumée.** *seht shaw~-bruh saw~ duh fue-may; zhuh swee-zah-layhr-zhee-kah lah fue-may*
The guests _____ are being very loud.	**Les occupants de la chambre _____ de la mienne sont très bruyants.** *lay-zoh-kue-paw~ duh lah shaw~-bruh _____ duh lah mee-yehn soh~ trey bwee-yaw~*
next door	**à côté** *ah koh-tay*
above	**au-dessus** *oh duh-sue*
below	**en dessous** *aw~ duh-soo*

CHECKING OUT

I think this charge is a mistake.	**Je crois que ce montant-là est une erreur.** *zhuh kwah kuh se moh~taw~-lah ey-toon eh-roehr*
Would you please explain this charge to me?	**Pourriez-vous m'expliquer ce montant-là?** *poo-ree-yay-voo mehk-splee-kay suh moh~-taw~-lah*
Thank you, we have enjoyed our stay.	**Merci, nous avons passé un bon séjour.** *mayhr-see noo-zah-voh~ pah-say uh~ boh~ say-zhoohr*

The service was excellent.

Le service était excellent.
luh sayh-vee-zey-tay ehk-say-law~

Would you please call a cab for me?

Pouvez-vous m'appeler un taxi, s'il vous plaît?
poo-vay-voo mah-play uh~ tahk-see seel voo play

Would someone please get my bags?

Pouvez-vous faire amener mes bagages?
poo-vay-voo fayh-raw~m-nay may bah-gazh

HAPPY CAMPING

I'd like a site for _____

Je voudrais un emplacement pour _____
zhuh voo-dray uh~-naw~-plah-smaw~ poohr

a tent.

une tente.
oon taw~t

a camper.

un camping-car.
uh~ kaw~-peeng kahr

Are there _____

Y a-t-il _____
yah-teel

bathrooms?

des toilettes dans ce camping?
day twah-leht daw~ suh kaw~-peeng

showers?

des douches?
day doosh

Is there running water?

Y a-t-il l'eau courante?
yah-teel loh kooh-raw~t

Is the water drinkable?

L'eau est-elle potable?
loh ey-tehl poh-tah-bluh

Where is the electrical hookup?

Où est la borne de raccordement?
oo ay lah bohrn duh rah-kohrd-maw~

CHAPTER FOUR

DINING

This chapter includes a menu reader and the language you need to communicate in a range of dining establishments and food markets.

FINDING A RESTAURANT

Would you please recommend a good ____ restaurant?	**Pouvez-vous nous recommander un bon restaurant ____** *poo-vay-voo noo ruh-koh-maw~-day uh~ boh~ruh-stoh-raw~*
local	**à spécialités locales?** *ah spay-see-yah-lee-tay loh-kahl*
Italian	**italien?** *ee-tah-lee-yeh~*
French	**français?** *fraw~-say*
German	**à spécialités allemandes?** *ah spay-see-yah-lee-tay ahl-maw~d*
Spanish	**espagnoles?** *eh-spah~-nyohl*
Chinese	**chinoises?** *shee-nwahz*
Japanese	**japonaises?** *zhah-poh~-nehz*
Asian	**à spécialités asiatiques?** *ah spay-see-yah-lee-tay ah-zee-yah-teek*
steakhouse	**spécialisé dans les steaks?** *spay-see-yah-lee-zay daw~ lay stayk*

family	**familial?**
	fah-mee-lee-yahl
seafood	**de fruits de mer?**
	day fhwee duh mayhr
vegetarian	**végétarien?**
	vay-zhay-tah-ree-yeh~
buffet-style	**de style buffet?**
	duh steel bue-fay
Greek	**grec?**
	grehk
budget	**pas cher?**
	pah shayhr
Which is the best restaurant in town?	**Quel est le meilleur restaurant de la ville?**
	keh-lay luh may-yoehr ruh-stoh-raw~ duh lah veel?
Is there an all-night restaurant nearby?	**Y a-t-il un restaurant ouvert toute la nuit pas loin d'ici?**
	yah-teel uh~ ruh-stoh-raw~ oo-vayhr toot lah nwee pah lweh~ dee-see
Is there a restaurant that serves breakfast nearby?	**Y a-t-il un restaurant qui sert des petits déjeuners pas loin d'ici?**
	yah-teel uh~ ruh-stoh-raw~ kee sayhr day ptee day-zhoeh-nay pah lweh~ dee-see
Is it very expensive?	**Est-il très cher?**
	ey-teel tray shayhr
Will I need a reservation?	**Aurai-je besoin d'une réservation?**
	oh-ray-zhuh buh-zweh~ doon ray-suhr-vah-see-yoh~
Do they have a dress code?	**Y a-t-il une tenue de rigueur?**
	yah-teel oon tuh-nue duh ree-goehr

Do they also serve lunch?	**Servent-ils aussi le déjeuner?**
	sayhrv-teel oh-see luh day-
	zheuh-nay
What time do they serve dinner? For lunch?	**À quelle heure serve-t-on le dîner? Le déjeuner?**
	ah keh-loehr sayhrv-ton luh
	dee-nay; luh day-zhoeh-nay
What time do they close?	**À quelle heure ferment-ils?**
	ah keh-loehr fayhrm-teel
Do you have a take-out menu?	**Avez-vous un menu de plats à emporter?**
	ah-vay-voo uh~ muh-nue duh plah
	ah aw~-pohr-tay
Do you have a bar?	**Avez-vous un bar?**
	ah-vay-voo-zuh~ bahr
Is there a café nearby?	**Y a-t-il un café pas loin d'ici?**
	yah-teel uh~ kah-fay pah lweh~
	dee-see

GETTING SEATED

Are you still serving?	**Est-ce qu'il est encore possible de manger?**
	ehs keel ay-taw~-kohr poh-see-
	bluh duh maw~-zhay
How long is the wait?	**De combien est l'attente?**
	duh koh~-bee-yeh~ ay lah-taw~t
Do you have a non-smoking section?	**Avez-vous une section non fumeur?**
	ah-vay-voo-zoon sehk-see-yoh~
	noh~ fue-moehr
I'd like a table for ____, please.	**Je voudrais une table pour ____ personnes, s'il vous plaît.**
	zhuh voo-dray oon tah-bluh poohr
	____ payhr-suhn seel voo play

For a full list of numbers, see p7.

Do you have a quiet table?	**Avez-vous une table calme?**
	ah-vay-voo-zoon tah-bluh kahlm

Listen Up: Restaurant Lingo

Fumeur ou non fumeur? *fue-moehr oo noh~fue-moehr*	Smoking or non-smoking?
Vous devez porter une cravate et une veste. *voo duh-vay pohr-tay oon krah-vaht ay oon vehst*	You'll need a tie and a jacket.
Les shorts sont interdits. *lay shohrt soh~-teh~tayhr-dee*	No shorts are allowed.
Vous désirez quelque chose à boire? *voo day-zee-ray kehl-kuh shohz ah bwahr*	May I bring you something to drink?
Vous désirez voir la carte des vins? *voo day-zee-ray vwahr lah kahrt day veh~*	Would you like to see a wine list?
Vous désirez savoir quels sont nos plats du jour? *voo day-zee-ray sah-vwahr kehl soh~ noh plah due zhoohr*	Would you like to hear our specials?
Vous êtes prêt à / prête(s) à commander? *voo-zeht preh ah / preh-tah koh~-maw~-day*	Are you ready to order?
Je suis désolé, votre carte de crédit a été rejetée. *zhuh swee day-zoh-lay voh-truh kahrt duh kray-dee ah ay-tay ruh-zhuh-tay*	I'm sorry, your credit card was declined.

May we sit outside / inside, please?	**Pouvons-nous nous asseoir à l'extérieur / à l'intérieur?** *poo-voh~-noo noo-zah-swahr ah lehk-stay-ree-yoehr / ah leh~-tay-ree-yoehr*

May we sit at the counter?	**Pouvons-nous nous asseoir au comptoir?**
	poo-voh~-noo noo-zah-swahr oh koh~p-twahr
May I have a menu, please?	**Puis-je avoir un menu, s'il vous plaît?**
	pwee-zhuh ah-vwahr uh~ muh-nue seel voo play

ORDERING

Do you have a special tonight?	**Avez-vous un plat spécial, ce soir?**
	ah-vay-voo-zuh~ plah spay-see-yahl suh swahr
What do you recommend?	**Qu'est-ce que vous recommandez?**
	keh-skuh voo ruh-koh-maw~-day
May I see a wine list?	**Puis-je avoir la carte des vins?**
	pwee-zhuh ah-vwahr lah kahrt day veh~
Do you serve wine by the glass?	**Servez-vous du vin au verre?**
	sayhr-vay-voo due veh~-noh vayhr
May I see a drink list?	**Puis-je voir une liste des boissons?**
	pwee-zhuh vwahr oon leest day bwah-soh~
I would like it cooked ____	**Je le voudrais ____**
	zhuh luh voo-dray
rare.	**bleu.**
	bloeh
medium rare.	**à point.**
	ah pweh~
medium.	**rouge.**
	roozh
medium well.	**cuit.**
	kwee

well.	**bien cuit.**
	bee-yeh~ kwee
charred.	**cuit à fond.**
	kwee-tah foh~
Do you have a ____ menu?	**Avez-vous un menu ____**
	ah-vay-voo-zuh~ muh-nue
diabetic	**pour diabétiques?**
	poohr dee-yah-bay-teek
kosher	**kasher?**
	kah-shayhr
vegetarian	**végétarien?**
	vay-zhay-tah-ree-yeh~
children's	**pour enfants?**
	poohr aw~-faw~
Can you tell me what is in this dish?	**Pouvez-vous me dire ce qu'il y a dans ce plat?**
	poo-vay-voo muh deer suh keel-yah ah daw~ suh plah
How is it prepared?	**Comment est-il cuit?**
	koh-maw~ ey-teel kwee
What kind of oil is that cooked in?	**Avec quelle sorte d'huile est-il préparé?**
	ah-vek kehl sohrt dweel ey-teel pruh-pah-ray
I'd like some oil, please.	**Je voudrais de l'huile, s'il vous plaît.**
	zhuh voo-dray de lweel seel voo play
Do you have any low-salt dishes?	**Avez-vous des plats à faible teneur en sel?**
	ah-vay-voo day plah ah feh-bluh tuh-noehr aw~ sehl
No salt, please.	**Pas de sel, s'il vous plaît.**
	pah duh sehl seel voo play

May I have that on the side, please?	**Puis-je avoir cela sur une assiette séparée, s'il vous plaît?**
	pwee-zhuh ah-vwahr suh-lah suehr oo-nah-see-yeht say-pah-ray seel voo play
Dressing on the side, please.	**La sauce à part, s'il vous plaît.**
	lah soh-sah pahr seel voo play
May I make a substitution?	**Puis-je remplacer cela par autre chose?**
	Pwee-zhuh raw~-plah-say suh-lah pahr oh-truh shohz
I'd like to try that.	**Je voudrais essayer cela.**
	zhuh voo-dray eh-say-ay suh-lah
Is that fresh?	**C'est frais?**
	say fray
Waiter!	**Monsieur / Madame, s'il vous plaît!**
	moh~-syoehr / mah-dahm seel voo play
May I have extra butter, please?	**Puis-je avoir un peu plus de beurre, s'il vous plaît?**
	pwee-zhuh ah-vwahr uh~ poeh plue duh beur, seel voo play
More bread, please.	**Plus de pain, s'il vous plaît.**
	plue duh peh~ seel voo play
No butter, please.	**Pas de beurre, s'il vous plaît.**
	pas duh boehr seel voo play
I am lactose intolerant.	**Je suis allergique aux produits laitiers.**
	zhuh swee-zah-layhr-zheek oh proh-dwee lay-tee-yay
Would you recommend something without milk?	**Pouvez-vous me recommander quelque chose qui ne contienne pas de lait?**
	poo-vay-voo muh ruh-koh~-maw~day kehl-kuh shohz kee nuh koh~-tee-yeh~ pah duh lay

I am allergic to _____

Je suis allergique _____
zhuh swee-zah-layhr-zheek

  seafood.

  aux poissons et aux fruits de mer.
  oh pwah-soh~-nay oh fhwee duh mayhr

  shellfish.

  aux fruits de mer.
  oh fhwee duh mayhr

  nuts.

  aux noix.
  oh nwah

  peanuts.

  aux cacahuettes.
  oh kah-kah-oo-eht

Water _____, please.

De l'eau _____, s'il vous plaît.
duh loh seel voo play

  with ice

  avec des glaçons
  ah-vehk day glah-soh~

  without ice

  sans glaçons
  saw~ glah-soh~

I'm sorry, I don't think this is what I ordered.

Je suis désolée(e), mais je ne pense pas que c'est ce que j'ai commandé.
zhuh swee day-zoh-lay may zhuh nuh paw~s pah kuh say skuh zhay koh~-maw~-day

My meat is over / under cooked.

Ma viande est trop cuite / pas assez cuite.
mah vee-yahnd ay troh kweet / pahz ah-say kweet

My vegetables are a little over / under cooked.

Mes légumes sont un peu trop cuits / pas assez cuits.
may lay-guem soh~-tuh~ poeh troh kwee / pah-zah-say kwee

There's a bug in my food!

Il y a un insecte dans ma nourriture!
eel-yah uh~-neh~sekt daw~ mah nooh-ree-teuhr

May I have a refill?	**Puis-je avoir la même boisson?**
	pwee-zhuh ah-vwahr lah mehm
	bwah-soh~
A dessert menu, please?	**La carte des desserts, s'il vous plaît?**
	lah kahrt day day-zayhr seel
	voo play

DRINKS

alcoholic	**de l'alcool / une boisson alcoolisée**
	duh lahl-kool / oon bwah-soh~-
	nahl-koo-lee-zay
neat / straight	**sec**
	sehk
on the rocks	**avec des glaçons**
	ah-vehk day glah-soh~
with (seltzer or soda)	**avec du soda**
water	*ah-vehk due soh-dah*
beer	**la bière**
	lah bee-yayhr
wine	**le vin**
	luh veh~
house wine	**le vin maison**
	luh veh~ may-zoh~
sweet wine	**le vin doux**
	luh veh~ doo
dry white wine	**le vin blanc**
	luh veh~ blaw~
rosé	**le vin rosé**
	luh~ veh~ roh-zay
a light-bodied wine	**le vin léger**
	luh veh~ lay-zhay
a full-bodied wine	**le vin corsé**
	luh veh~ kohr-say
red wine	**le vin rouge**
	luh veh~ roozh
sparkling sweet wine	**le vin mousseux et doux**
	luh beh~ moo-soeh ay doo

liqueur	**une liqueur** *oon lee-koehr*
brandy	**le cognac** *luh koh~-nyak*
cognac	**le cognac** *luh koh~-nyak*
gin	**le gin** *luh zheen*
vodka	**le vodka** *luh vohd-kah*
rum	**le rhum** *luh ruhm*
non-alcoholic	**non alcoolisée / une boisson non alcoolisée** *noh~-nahl-koo-lee-zay / oon bwah-soh~ noh~-nahl-koo-lee-zay*
hot chocolate	**un chocolat chaud** *uh~ shoh-koh-lah shoh*
lemonade	**un citron pressé** *uh~ see-troh~ pruh-say*
milk	**un lait** *uh~ lay*
milkshake	**un milk-shake** *uh~ meehlk-shayk*
tea	**un thé** *uh~ tay*
coffee	**un café** *uh~ kah-fay*
latté	**un café au lait** *uh~ kah-fay oh lay*
iced coffee	**un café glacé** *uh~ kah-fay glah-say*
fruit juice	**le jus de fruits** *luh zhue duh fhwee*

For a full list of fruit, see p113.

For a full list of fruit, see p113.

DINING

SETTLING UP

Check, please.	**L'addition, s'il vous plaît!** *lah-dee-see-yoh~ seel voo play*
I'm stuffed!	**Je n'en peux plus!** *zhuh naw~ poeh plue*
The meal was excellent.	**Ce repas était excellent.** *suh ruh-pah ay-tay ehk-suh-law~*
There's a problem with my bill.	**Il y a un problème avec l'addition.** *eel-yah uh~ proh-blehm ah-vek lah-dee-see-yoh~*
Is the tip included?	**Le service est-il compris?** *luh sayhr-vees ey-teel koh~-pree*
My compliments to the chef!	**Tous mes compliments au chef!** *too may koh~-plee-maw~ oh shehf*

MENU READER

French cuisine varies broadly from region to region, but we've tried to make our list of classic dishes as encompassing as possible.

SOUPS (LES POTAGES)

crème d'asperges / de bolets / d'huîtres: cream of asparagus / mushroom / oyster soup

crème vichyssoise: cold potato-leek soup

la gratinée à l'oignon: French onion soup

potage bilibi: cream of mussel soup

potage Crécy: carrot soup

potage cressonière: watercress soup

potage parmentier: potato soup

potage printanier: mixed vegetable soup

potage Saint-Germain: puréed split pea with ham soup

soupe au pistou: pesto soup with vegetables, white beans, and pasta

soupe aux moules: mussel soup

velouté de tomates / d'asperges / de volaille / d'huîtres: rich tomato / asparagus / chicken / oyster soup

TERRINES, PÂTÉS, CONFITS, & MEAT IN ASPIC

confit de canard / d'oie / de porc: preserved duck / goose / pork

foie gras: fattened goose / duck liver

galantine: boned meat or poultry, rolled or stuffed, served cold

gelée: aspic

pâté de campagne: country-style pâté, generally with a more rustic texture

pâté de canard: duck pâté

pâté en croûte: pâté baked in puff pastry

rillettes: pot of spreadable minced meat (pork, poultry) or fish

terrine / pâté de foie de volaille: poultry liver terrine / pâté

terrine de lapin: rabbit terrine

CLASSIC BISTRO / SIDE DISHES (LES ENTRÉES)

le croque-monsieur: grilled ham and cheese sandwich on sliced bread

l'omelette aux fines herbes: omelet with minced herbs

le pizza margarita: pizza topped with cheese and herbs, without vegetables or meat

les pommes frites: French fries

le sandwich mixte: gruyère and ham on French bread

la tarte à l'oignon: onion tart

FISH / SEAFOOD (LES POISSONS / LES FRUITS DE MER)

bouillabaisse: provençal fish stew

coquilles Saint-Jacques: lightly breaded scallops sautéed or baked with lemon juice, cayenne pepper, garlic, butter, and parsley

darne de saumon: salmon filet

homard cardinal: lobster cooked with mushrooms and truffles in béchamel sauce

homard Thermidor: Lobster baked in spicy mustard sauce and gratinéed

moules à la poulette: mussels in creamy white wine sauce

moules marinière: mussels in white wine with shallots, onions, and herbs

plateau de fruits de mer: assorted seafood platter

raie au beurre noir: skate in brown butter sauce

saumon à l'oseille: salmon with sorrel sauce

sole bonne femme: sole with potatoes, shallots, parsley, and mushrooms

truite au bleu: trout cooked in hot water and vinegar very soon after gutting, causing its skin to turn blue

truite aux amandes: sautéed trout in a crème fraîche and almond sauce

truite meunière: seasoned trout rolled in flour, fried in butter, and served with butter and lemon

For a full list of fish, see p111.

BEEF (LE BŒUF)

l'assiette anglaise: potted meat

bœuf bourguignon: beef stewed in red wine with onions, mushrooms, and bacon

carbonnade: beef stew

entrecôte maître d'hôtel: steak with butter and parsley

filet de bœuf Rossini: beef filet with foie gras

fondue bourguignonne: Burgundy-style fondue (small pieces of meat cooked in boiling oil and then dipped in various sauces)

la moelle: beef marrow

steak tartare: steak tartare

LAMB (L'AGNEAU)

carré d'agneau: rack of lamb

côtelettes d'agneau: lamb chops

epaule d'agneau farcie: stuffed lamb shoulder

navarin: lamb stew

navarin de mouton: mutton stew with spring vegetables

VEAL (LE VEAU)

l'agneau de lait: milk-fed lamb

l'agneau de pré-salé: salted lamb

blanquette de veau: veal stew

escalope de veau normande: thin slices of veal in cream sauce

escalope de veau milanaise: thin slices of veal in tomato sauce

PORK (LE PORC)

cassoulet: casserole with white beans and combinations of sausages, pork, lamb, goose, or duck

choucroute: sauerkraut with ham and sausages

le cochon de lait: suckling pig

côtelettes de porc: pork chops

croque-monsieur: toasted ham and cheese sandwich

RABBIT (LE LAPIN)

gibelotte de lapin: fricasseed rabbit in red or white wine

le lapereau: young rabbit

lapin à la Lorraine: rabbit in mushroom and cream sauce

lapin à la moutarde: rabbit in mustard sauce

le lapin de garenne: wild rabbit

râble de lièvre: saddle of hare

POULTRY (LE VOLAILLE)

aspic de volaille: poultry in aspic

le blanc de canard: duck breast

canard à l'orange: duck in orange sauce

canard aux cerises: duck in cherry sauce

le canard sauvage: wild duck

le caneton: duckling

filet de canard au poivre vert: duck filet in green peppercorn sauce

coq au vin: chicken in red wine sauce

poulet à l'estragon: chicken in tarragon-cream sauce

poulet chasseur: chicken with white wine and mushrooms

le poulet fermier: free-range chicken

suprême de volaille: boneless chicken breast

VEGETABLE DISHES (LES LEGUMES, LES CRUDITÉS, ET LES SALADES)

l'assiette de crudités: raw vegetables

chou-fleur au gratin: cauliflower baked in cream, topped with gruyere

epinards à la crème: creamed spinach

gratin dauphinois: thin-sliced potatoes baked with cheese

poivron farci: stuffed green pepper

salade composée: main-course salad (with meat, cheese, and raw vegetables)

salade mixte: mixed salad

salade verte: green salad

salade de tomates: tomato salad

salade russe: diced vegetables in mayonnaise

For a full list of vegetables, see p114.

DESSERTS / PASTRIES (LES DESSERTS / LES PÂTISSERIES)

baba au rhum: small rum-soaked cake

bavaroise: custard dessert with gelatin and cream

chausson aux pommes: apple turnover

chocolat amer: dark, bitter chocolate

clafoutis: custard and fruit tart

financier: small almond cake

fondant au chocolat: chocolate dessert akin to a brownie

gâteau au fromage: cheesecake

génoise: sponge cake

les flottantes / œufs à la neige: thin custard topped with soft meringue

madeleine: lemon tea cake

mille-feuille: napoleon

mont-blanc: pastry with whipped cream, chestnut purée, and baked meringue

pain au chocolat: croissant (chocolate-filled)

pâte feuilletée: puff pastry

pêche melba: vanilla ice cream with a poached peach and raspberry sauce

petits fours: bite-sized, beautifully-decorated pastries

poire belle-Hélène: pear with chocolate sauce

profiteroles: cream puffs

religieuse: cream puffs with chocolate icing

sabayon: thin custard made with Marsala

sable: shortbread cookie

saint-Honoré: cake made with two types of pastry and cream filling

savarin: ring-shaped yeast cake in sweet syrup

soufflé au chocolat: chocolate soufflé

tarte au citron / aux fraises / aux pommes / aux abricots / aux framboises: lemon / strawberry / apple / apricot / raspberry tart

tarte tatin: upside-down apple tart

vacherin glacé: baked-Alaska-type dessert

SAUCES / METHODS OF PRESENTATION

basquaise: with ham, tomatoes, and peppers

béchamel: white sauce

bonne femme: with mushrooms and white wine

en brochette: on a skewer

aux câpres: in caper sauce

chasseur: with white wine and herbs

à la crème / à la normande: in cream sauce

au gratin: topped with cheese

jardinière: with mixed vegetables

maître d'hôtel: with butter and parsley

milanaise: in Italian-style tomato sauce

à la moutarde: in mustard sauce

à la nage: in wine and vegetable sauce

en papillote: baked in foil or parchment paper

piperade: with peppers and tomatoes

à la provençale: in olive oil (with herbs, garlic, and tomato)

sauce aurora: white sauce with tomato purée

sauce Béarnaise: hollandaise sauce (with capers)

sauce au beurre noir: dark browned butter sauce

sauce cresson: watercress sauce

sauce Mornay: white sauce with cheese

sauce noisette: light browned butter sauce

sauce à l'oseille: sorrel sauce

au vin rouge: in red wine sauce

HERBS / SPICES / CONDIMENTS

l'ail / la gousse d'ail: garlic / garlic clove
l'aneth: dill
l'anis: anise
le basilique: basil
la feuille de laurier: bay leaf
le carvi: caraway
le chervil: chervil
les ciboulettes: chives
le clou de girofle: clove
la confiture: jam
le coriandre: cilantro / coriander
l'estragon: tarragon
l'huile: oil
le laurier: bay leaf
la marjolaine: marjoram
la marjolaine sauvage: oregano
la mayonnaise: mayonnaise

le mélange d'épices: allspice
le miel: honey
la moutarde: mustard
l'origan: oregano
le persil: parsley
le poivre rose / vert: pink / green peppercorns
le romarin: rosemary
le safran: saffron
la sauge: sage
le sel / le sel marin: salt / sea salt
le sucre en poudre: sugar (granular)
le sucre en morceaux: sugar cubes
le thym: thyme
la verveine: verbena
le vinaigre: vinegar

NUTS / LEGUMES / FANCY FUNGI

les amandes: almonds
l'arachide: peanut
les haricots blancs: white beans
les haricots d'Espagne: kidney beans
les lentilles: lentils
les marrons: chestnuts
les morilles: morels

la noisette: hazelnut
la noix: walnut
la pâte d'amandes: almond paste
les pignons: pine nuts
les pistaches: pistachio nuts
les truffes: truffles

BUYING GROCERIES

In France, like most other countries, locals shop for food either at outdoor markets, specialty stores or, less commonly than in the United States, large supermarkets.

GROCERY VENUES

bakery	**la boulangerie**
	lah boo-law~-zhree
butcher	**la boucherie**
	lah boo-shree
cheese shop	**la fromagerie**
	lah froh-mahzh-ree
delicatessen	**le traiteur**
	luh treh-toehr
open-air market	**le marché en plein air**
	luh mahr-shay ehn pleh~-nayhr
pastry shop	**la pâtisserie**
	lah pah-tee-sree
pork butcher	**la charcuterie**
	la shahr-kue-tree
supermarket	**le supermarché**
	luh sue-payhr-mahr-shay

AT THE SUPERMARKET

checkout counter	**le comptoir**
	luh koh~p-twahr
cash register	**la caisse**
	lah kehs
section / aisle	**le rayon**
	luh ray-oh~
produce	**les primeurs**
	lay pree-moehr
frozen food	**les plats congelés / surgelés**
	lay plah koh~zhlay / suehr-zhlay

Which aisle has ____	**Dans quel rayon se trouvent / trouve ____**
	daw~ kehl ray-oh~ suh troov
spices?	**les épices?**
	lay-zay-pees
toiletries?	**les produits de toilette?**
	lay proh-dwee duh twah-leht
paper plates and napkins?	**les assiettes et les serviettes en papier?**
	lay-zah-see-yeht ay lay sayhr-vee-yeh-taw~ pah-pee-yay
canned goods?	**les conserves?**
	lay koh~-sayhrv
snack food?	**les amuse-gueule?**
	lay-zah-muez goehl
baby food?	**la nourriture pour bébé?**
	lah nooh-ree-teuhr poohr bay-bay
water?	**l'eau?**
	loh
juice?	**le jus de fruits?**
	luh zhues duh fhwee
bread?	**le pain?**
	luh peh~
cheese?	**le fromage?**
	luh froh-mahzh
fruit?	**le fruit?**
	luh fhwee
cookies?	**les biscuits?**
	lay bees-kwee

Bread and Rice

brown rice	**le riz brun**
	luh ree bruh~
white rice	**le riz blanc**
	luh ree blahn

wild rice	**le riz sauvage**
	luh ree sohvahzh
country-style loaf	**le pain de campagne**
	luh peh~ duh kaw~pah-nyuh
French bread: large / small	**la baguette / la flûte**
	lah bah-geht / lah fluet
rye bread	**le pain de seigle**
	luh peh~ duh seh-gluh
sourdough bread	**le pain au levain**
	luh peh~ oh luh-veh~
whole-grain bread	**le pain complet**
	luh peh~ koh~-play

Dairy

butter	**le beurre**
	luh boehr
cream	**la crème**
	lah krehm
milk, whole / skim	**le lait entier / écrémé**
	luh lay aw~-tee-yay / ay-kray-may
yogurt	**le yaourt**
	luh yah-oohr

Cheese

bleu cheese	**le fromage bleu**
	luh froh-mahzh bloeh
cream cheese	**le fromage frais**
	luh froh-mahzh fray
goat cheese	**le (fromage de) chèvre**
	luh (froh-mahzh duh) sheh-vruh
firm	**un crottin**
	uh~ kroh-teh~
semisoft cheeses	**les fromages à croûte fleurie**
	lay fro-mahzh ah kroot fleuh-ree

Eggs

free-range	**les œufs de la ferme**
	lay-zoeh duh lah fayhrm
large / extra large	**les œufs grands / très grands**
	lay-zoeh graw~ / tray graw~
small	**les œufs petits**
	lay-zoeh puhtee

AT THE BUTCHER SHOP

Is the meat fresh?	**Cette viande est-elle fraîche?**
	seht vee-yand ey-tehl frehsh
Is the fish fresh?	**Le poisson est-il frais?**
	luh pwah-soh~ ey-teel fray
Is the seafood fresh?	**Les fruits de mer sont-ils frais?**
	lay fhwee duh mayhr soh~-teel fray
Do you sell ____	**Vendez-vous de la viande de ____**
	vaw~-day-voo duh lah vee-yand duh
I would like a cut of ____	**Je voudrais un morceau ____**
	zhuh voo-dray uh~ mohr-soh
tenderloin.	**de filet.**
	duh fee-lay
T-bone.	**d'aloyau.**
	dahl-wah-yoh
brisket.	**de poitrine.**
	duh pwah-treen
rump roast.	**de rôti de croupe.**
	duh roh-tee duh kroop
pork chops.	**de côtelette de porc.**
	duh koht-leht duh pohr
filet.	**tournedos.**
	toohr-nuh-doh

I would like ____	**Je voudrais**____
	zhuh voo-dray
the breast.	**le blanc.**
	luh blahn
chops.	**la côte.**
	lah koht
free-range.	**fermier.**
	fayhr-mee-yay
liver.	**le foie.**
	luh fwah
milk-fed.	**de lait.**
	duh lay
sweetbreads.	**le ris.**
	luh ree
Would you trim the fat?	**Pouvez-vous enlever le gras?**
	poo-vay-voo aw~-luh-vay luh grah
May I smell it?	**Puis-je le / la / les sentir?**
	pwee-zhuh luh / lah / lay saw~-teer
Would you ____	**Pouvez-vous** ____
	poo-vay-voo
filet it?	**le couper en filets?**
	luh koo-pay aw~ fee-lay
debone it?	**le désosser?**
	luh day-zoh-say
remove the head and tail?	**enlever la tête et la queue?**
	aw~-luh-vay lah teht ay lah koeh

Beef (Le Bœuf)

ground beef	**le bœuf haché**
	luh boehf ah-shay
sirloin steak	**le faux-filet**
	luh foh-fee-lay
tripe	**les tripes**
	lay treep
veal	**le veau**
	luh voh

Other Meats

lamb	**l'agneau / le mouton** *lah-nyoh / luh moo-toh~*
leg of lamb	**le gigot** *luh zhee-goh*
rack of lamb	**le carré d'agneau** *luh kah-ray dah-nyoh*
horsemeat	**la viande de cheval** *lah vee-yand duh shuh-vahl*
pork	**le porc** *luh pohr*
rack of pork ribs	**le carré de porc** *luh kah-ray duh pohr*
ham	**le jambon** *luh zhahm-boh~*
bacon	**le lard** *luh lahr*
headcheese	**le fromage de tête** *luh froh-mazh duh teht*
sausage	**le saucisson** *luh soh-see-soh~*
dried sausage	**le saucisson sec** *luh soh-see-soh~ sehk*
fresh sausage	**la saucisse / le boudin** *lah soh-sees / luh boo-deh~*
rabbit	**le lapin** *luh lah-peh~*
hare	**la lièvre** *luh lee-yeh-vruh*
frog legs	**les cuisses de grenouille** *lay kwees duh gruh-nwee*
snails	**les escargots** *lay-zehs-kahr-goh*

Poultry

chicken	**le poulet** *luh poo-lay*
turkey	**la dinde** *lah deh~d*
duck	**le canard** *luh kah-nahr*
duck breast	**le blanc de canard** *luh blaw~ duh kah-nahr*
goose	**l'oie** *lwah*
pigeon / squab	**le pigeon** *luh pee-zhyoh~*
pheasant	**le faisan** *luh fay-zaw~*

Fish

catfish	**la barbotte** *lah bahr-boht*
flounder	**le flet** *luh flay*
halibut	**le flétan** *luh flay-taw~*
herring	**le hareng** *luh ah-raw~g*
mackerel	**le maquereau** *luh mah-kroh*
salmon	**le saumon** *luh soh-moh~*
sardine	**la sardine** *lah sahr-deen*
sea bass	**le bar** *luh bahr*
shark	**le requin** *luh ruh-keh~*

skate	**la raie**
	lah ray
sole	**le sole**
	luh sohl
swordfish	**l'espadon**
	leh-spah-doh~
trout	**la truite**
	lah tweet
turbot	**le turbot**
	luh tuehr-boh

Seafood

clams	**les palourdes**
	lay pah-loohrd
crab	**le crabe**
	luh krahb
crayfish	**l'écrevisse**
	lay-kray-vees
eel	**la lamproie**
	lah law~-pwah
lobster	**le homard**
	luh oh-mahr
mussels	**les moules**
	lay mool
octopus	**le poulpe**
	luh poolp
oyster	**l'huître**
	lwee-truh
scallop	**la coquille**
	lah koh-kee
shrimp	**la crevette**
	lah kruh-veht
squid	**le calmar**
	luh kahl-mahr

AT THE PRODUCE STAND / MARKET
Fruits

apple	**la pomme**
	lah puhm
apricot	**l'abricot**
	lah-bree-koh
banana	**la banane**
	lah bah-nahn
blackberries	**la mûre**
	lah muehr
blueberry	**la myrtille**
	lah meer-tee
cantaloupe	**le cantaloup**
	luh kaw~-tah-loo
cherry	**la cerise**
	lah suh-reez
coconut	**la noix de coco**
	lah nwah duh koh-koh
cranberry	**la canneberge**
	lah kah-nuh-bayhrzh
fig	**la figue**
	lah feeg
grapefruit	**le pamplemousse**
	luh paw~-pluh-moos
grapes (green, red)	**le raisin (vert, noir)**
	luh ray-zeh~ vayhr nwahr
gooseberry	**la groseille à maquereau**
	lah groh-zay ah mah-kroh
honeydew	**le melon miel**
	luh muh-loh~ mee-yehl
kiwi	**le kiwi**
	luh kee-wee
lemon	**le citron**
	luh see-troh~

lime	**le citron vert**
	luh see-troh~ vayhr
mango	**la mangue**
	lah maw~g
melon	**le melon**
	luh muh-loh~
orange	**l'orange**
	loh-raw~zh
blood orange	**la sanguine**
	lah saw~-gween
papaya	**la papaye**
	lah pah-pay
peach	**la pêche**
	lah pehsh
pear	**la poire**
	lah pwahr
pineapple	**l'ananas**
	law~-naw~-nahs
plum	**la prune**
	lah pruen
prune	**le pruneau**
	luh prue-noh
raspberry	**la framboise**
	lah fraw~-bwahz
strawberry	**la fraise**
	lah frehz
tangerine	**la mandarine**
	lah maw~-dah-reen
watermelon	**la pastèque**
	lah pah-stek

Vegetables

artichoke	**l'artichaut**
	lahr-tee-shoh
arugula	**la roquette**
	lah roh-keht

asparagus	**les asperges** *lay-zah-spayrzh*
avocado	**l'avocat** *lah-voh-kah*
beans	**les haricots** *lay-zah-ree-koh*
green beans	**les haricots verts** *lay-zah-ree-koh vayhr*
broccoli	**le brocoli** *luh broh-koh-lee*
cabbage	**le chou** *luh shoo*
carrot	**la carotte** *lah kah-roht*
cauliflower	**le chou-fleur** *luh shoo-floehr*
celery	**le céleri** *luh say-lay-ree*
corn	**le maïs** *luh may-ees*
cucumber	**le concombre** *luh koh~-koh~-bruh*
eggplant	**l'aubergine** *loh-bayhr-zheen*
endive	**la chicorée** *lah shee-koh-ray*
curly	**frisée** *free-zay*
Belgian	**l'endive** *law~-deev*
garlic	**l'ail** *lie*
leek	**le poireau** *luh pwah-roh*

lettuce	**la salade verte**
	lah sah-lahd vayhrt
romaine	**la laitue (romaine)**
	lah lay-tue
mushroom	**le champignon**
	luh shaw~-pee-nyoh~
black olives	**les olives noires**
	lay-zoh-leev nwahr
green olives	**les olives vertes**
	lay-zoh-leev vayhrt
onion	**l'oignon**
	loh-nyoh~
red pepper	**le poivron rouge**
	luh pwah-vroh roozh
green pepper	**le poivron vert**
	luh pwah-vroh vayhr
pepper (chili)	**le piment**
	luh pee-maw~
habañero pepper	**le piment habanero**
	luh pee-maw~ ah-bah-nyuh-roh
chipotle pepper	**le piment chipotle**
	luh pee-maw~ shee-poht-lay
jalapeno pepper	**le piment jalapeno**
	luh pee-maw~ yah-lah-peh-nyoh
cayenne (fresh) pepper	**le piment de cayenne**
	luh pee-maw~ duh kah-yehn
potato	**la pomme de terre**
	lah puhm duh tayhr
shallot	**l'échalote**
	lay-shah-loht
sorrel	**l'oseille**
	loh-zay
spinach	**les épinards**
	lay-zay-pee-nahr
squash	**la courge**
	lah koorzh

tomato	**la tomate** *lah toh-maht*
yam	**la patate douce** *lah pah-taht doos*
zucchini	**la courgette** *lah koohr-zheht*

AT THE DELI

What kind of salad is that?	**Quelle sorte de salade est-ce?** *kehl sohrt duh sah-lahd ehs*
What kind of cheese is that?	**Quelle sorte de fromage est-ce?** *kehl sohrt duh froh-mahzh ehs*
What kind of bread is that?	**Quelle sorte de pain est-ce?** *kehl sohrt duh peh~-nehs*
I'd like some of this, please.	**J'en voudrais celui-ci, s'il vous plaît.** *zhaw~ voo-dray seh-lwee-see seel voo play*
I'd like _____, please.	**Je voudrais _____, s'il vous plait.** *zheh voo-dray seel voo-play*
a sandwich	**un sandwich** *uh~ saw~d-weesh*
a salad	**une salade** *oon sah-lahd*
tuna salad	**au thon** *oh toh~*
chicken salad	**au poulet** *oh poo-lay*
ham	**au jambon** *oh jaw~-boh~*
roast beef	**au rosbif** *oh rohz-beef*
some cole slaw	**du céleri rémoulade** *due say-lay-ree ray-moo-lahd*
mustard	**de la moutarde** *duh lah moo-tahrd*

mayonnaise	**du mayonnaise**
	duh lah may-oh-nehz
a pickle	**un cornichon**
	uh~ kohr-nee-shoh~
about a pound	**cinq cent grammes**
	seh~k saw~ grahm
about a half-pound	**deux cent cinquante grammes**
	doeh saw~ grahm
about a quarter-pound	**cent vingt-cinq grammes**
	saw~ veh~-seh~k grahm
Is the salad fresh?	**La salade est-elle fraîche?**
	lah sah-lahd ey-tehl fresh
Is that smoked?	**C'est fumé?**
	say fue-may
May I have a package of tofu?	**Puis-je avoir du tofou?**
	pwee-zhuh ah-vwahr due toh-foo

CHAPTER FIVE

SOCIALIZING

Whether you're meeting people in a bar or a park, you'll find the language you need, in this chapter, to make new friends.

GREETINGS

Hello!	**Bonjour!**
	boh~-zhoohr
How are you?	**Comment allez-vous?** *formal /*
	Ça va? *informal*
	koh-maw~-tah-lay-voo / sah vah
Fine, thanks.	**Bien, merci.**
	bee-yeh~ mayhr-see
And you?	**Et vous?** *formal /* **Et toi?** *informal*
	ay voo / ay twah
I'm exhausted.	**Je suis épuisé(e).**
	zhuh swee-zay-pwee-zay
I have a headache.	**J'ai mal à la tête.**
	zhay mah-lah lah teht
I'm terrible.	**Je vais très mal.**
	zhuh vay treh mahl
I have a cold.	**J'ai un rhume.**
	zhay uh~ ruem
Good morning.	**Bonjour!**
	boh~-zhoohr
Good evening.	**Bonsoir!**
	boh~-swahr
Good afternoon.	**Bon après-midi!**
	boh~-nah-pray mee-dee
Good night.	**Bonne nuit!**
	buhn nwee

Listen Up: Common Greetings

Bonjour!	Hello!
boh~-zhoohr	
Ravi(e) de faire votre	It's a pleasure.
connaissance.	
rah-vee duh fayhr	
voh-truh koh~-nay-saw~-s	
Enchanté(e).	Charmed.
aw~-shaw~-tay	
Ravi(e).	Delighted.
rah-vee	
Ça va?	How's it going?
sah vah	
Au revoir!	Goodbye!
oh r'vwahr	
À la prochaine!	See you around!
ah lah proh-shen	
À bientot!	See you later!
ah bee-yeh~-toh	

THE LANGUAGE BARRIER

I'm sorry, I don't understand very well.	**Désolé(e), je ne comprends pas bien.**
	day-zoh-lay zhuh nuh koh~-praw~-pah bee-yeh~
Would you speak slower, please?	**Pouvez-vous parler plus lentement, s'il vous plaît?**
	poo-vay-voo pahr-lay plue law~-t-maw~ seel voo play
Would you speak louder, please?	**Pouvez-vous parler plus fort, s'il vous plaît?**
	poo-vay-voo pahr-lay plue fohr seel voo play
Do you speak English?	**Parlez-vous anglais?**
	pahr-lay-voo-zaw~-glay

I speak ____ better than French.	**Je parle le ____ mieux que le français.** *zhuh pahrl luh ____ mee-yoeh kuh luh fraw~-say*
I'm sorry, would you spell that, please?	**Je suis désolé(e), pouvez-vous épeler, s'il vous plaît?** *zhuh swee day-zoh-lay poo-vay-voo-zeh-play seel voo play*
Would you please repeat that?	**Pouvez-vous répéter, s'il vous plaît?** *poo-vay-voo ray-pay-tay seel voo play*
How do you say ____?	**Comment dit-on ____?** *koh-maw~ dee-toh~*
Would you show me that in this dictionary?	**Pouvez-vous me montrer cela dans ce dictionnaire?** *poo-vay-voo muh moh~-tray suh-lah daw~ suh deek-see-yoh-nayhr*

Common Curses

Merde alors! *mayhr-dah-lohr*	Oh shit!
Fils de pute! *fees duh puet*	Son of a bitch! (Son of a whore!)
Merde! *mayhrd*	Damn!
Trou du cul! *troo due kue*	Asshole!
Nous sommes foutus! *noo suhm foo-tue*	We're screwed! (We're fucked!)
Enfoiré! / Salaud! *aw~-fwah-ray / sah-loh*	Bastard!
Putain! *pue-teh~*	Fuck! / Fucker!
C'est foutu! *say foo-tue*	That's fucked up!

GETTING PERSONAL

Europeans are typically more formal than Americans. Remember to use the formal forms of speech until given permission to employ more familiar speech.

INTRODUCTIONS

What is your name?	**Comment vous appelez-vous?**
	koh-maw~ voo-zah-play-voo
My name is ____.	**Je m'appelle ____.**
	zhuh mah-pehl
I'm very pleased to meet you.	**Ravi(e) de vous rencontrer.**
	rah-vee duh voo raw~-koh~-tray
May I introduce my ____	**Laissez-moi vous présenter ____**
	leh-zay-mwah voo pray-zaw~-tay
How is your ____	**Comment va votre ____**
	koh-maw~ vah voh-truh
wife?	**ma femme?**
	mah fahm
husband?	**mon mari?**
	moh~ mah-ree
son / daughter?	**mon fils / ma fille?**
	moh~ fees / mah fee-yuh
friend?	**mon ami(e)?**
	moh~-nah-mee
boyfriend / girlfriend?	**mon petit ami / ma petite amie?**
	moh~ puh-tee-tah-mee / mah puh-tee-tah-mee
family?	**ma famille?**
	mah fah-mee
mother?	**ma mère?**
	mah mayhr
father?	**mon père?**
	moh~ payhr
brother / sister?	**mon frère / ma sœur?**
	moh~ frayhr / mah seuhr

neighbor?	**mon voisin / ma voisine?**
	moh~ vwah-zeh~ / mah vwah-zeen
boss?	**mon patron / ma patronne?**
	moh~ pah-troh~ / mah pah-truhn
cousin?	**mon cousine / ma cousine?**
	moh~ koo-zeh~ / mah koo-zeen
aunt / uncle?	**mon oncle / ma tante?**
	moh~-noh~-kluh / mah taw-t
fiancé / fiancée?	**mon fiancé / ma fiancée?**
	moh~ fee-yaw~-say / mah fee-yaw~-say
partner?	**mon partenaire?**
	moh~ pahrt-nayhr
nephew / niece?	**mon neveu / ma niece?**
	moh~-neh-voeh / mah nee-yehs
parents?	**mes parents?**
	may pah-raw~
grandparents?	**mes grand-parents?**
	may graw~-pah-raw~
Are you married / single?	**Vous êtes marié(e) / célibataire?**
	voo-zeht mah-ree-yay / say-lee-bah-tayhr
I'm married.	**Je suis marié(e).**
	zhuh swee mah-ree-yay
I'm single.	**Je suis célibataire.**
	zhuh swee say-lee-bah-tayhr
I'm divorced.	**Je suis divorcé(e).**
	zhuh swee dee-vohr-say
I'm a widow / widower.	**Je suis veuf / veuve.**
	zhuh swee voehf / voehv
We're separated.	**Nous sommes séparés.**
	noo suhm say-pah-ray

I live with my boyfriend / girlfriend.	**Je vis avec mon petit ami / ma petite amie.**
	zhuh vee ah-vek moh~ puh-tee-tah-mee / mah puh-tee-tah-mee
How old are you / your children?	**Quel âge avez vous / ont vos enfants?**
	keh-lahzh ah-vay-voo / oh~ voh-zaw~faw~
Wow, that's very young.	**Oh là, c'est très jeune.**
	oh lah say tray zhoehn
What grade are they in?	**En quelle classe sont-ils?**
	aw~ kehl klahs soh~-teel
Your wife / daughter is beautiful.	**Ta femme / fille est belle.**
	tah fahm / fee-yuh ay behl
Your husband / son is handsome.	**Ton mari / fils est beau.**
	toh~ mah-ree / fees ay boh
What a beautiful baby!	**Quel beau bébé!**
	kehl boh bay-bay
Are you here on business?	**Vous êtes ici en voyage d'affaires?**
	voo-zeht ee-see aw~ vwah-yahz dah-fayhr
I am vacationing.	**Je suis en vacances.**
	zhuh swee-zaw~ vah-kaw~s
I'm attending a conference.	**Je participe à une conférence.**
	zhuh pahr-tee-see-pah oon koh~-fay-hraw~s
How long are you staying?	**Combien de temps restez-vous ici?**
	koh~-bee-yeh~ duh taw~ ruh-stay-voo-zee-see
What are you studying?	**Vous vous spécialisez en quoi?**
	voo voo spay-see-ah-lee-zay aw~ kwah
I'm a student.	**Je suis étudiant(e).**
	zhuh swee-zay-tue-dee-yaw~(t)
Where are you from?	**D'où êtes-vous?**
	doo eht-voo

NATIONALITIES

I am ____	Je suis ____
	zhuh swee(z)
American.	**américain** *m* / **américaine** *f.*
	ah-may-ree-keh~ / ah-may-ree-kehn
Canadian.	**canadien** *m* /**canadienne** *f.*
	kah-nah-dee-yeh~ / kah-nah-dee-yehn
Chinese.	**chinois** *m* / **chinoise** *f.*
	shee-nwah / shee-nwahz
English.	**anglais** *m* / **anglaise** *f.*
	aw~-glay / aw~-glehz
French.	**français** *m* / **française** *f.*
	fraw~-say / fraw~-sehz
German.	**allemand** *m* / **allemande** *f.*
	ahl-maw~ / ahl-maw~d
Irish.	**irlandais** *m* / **irlandaise** *f.*
	eer-law~-day / eer-law~-dehz
Italian.	**italien** *m* / **italienne** *f.*
	ee-tahl-yeh~ / ee-tahl-yehn
Russian.	**russe** *m* / *f.*
	ruehs
Spanish.	**espagnol** *m* / **espagnole** *f.*
	ehs-pah-nyohl

See English / French dictionary for more nationalities.

les cheveux
les sourcils
le front
les tempes
l'oeil/les yeux
les oréilles
le nez
les joues
les dents
la bouche
les lèvres
le menton

PERSONAL DESCRIPTIONS

blond(e)	**le blond / la blonde**
	luh bloh~ / lah blohd
brunette	**le brun / la brune**
	luh bruh~ / lah bruen
redhead	**le roux / la rousse**
	luh roo / lah roos
straight hair	**Il / Elle a les cheveux raides.**
	eel / ehl ah lay shuh-voeh rayd
curly hair	**Il / Elle a les cheveux frisés.**
	eel / ehl ah lay shuh-voeh free-zay
kinky hair	**Il / Elle a les cheveux crépus.**
	eel / ehl ah lay shuh-voeh kray-pue
long hair	**Il / Elle a les cheveux longs.**
	eel / ehl ah lay shuh-voeh loh~
short hair	**Il / Elle a les cheveux courts.**
	eel / ehl ah lay shuh-voeh koohr
tanned	**Il / Elle est basané(e).**
	eel / ehl ay bah-zah-nay
pale	**Il / Elle a le teint clair.**
	eel / ehl ay luh teh~ klayhr

mocha-skinned	Il / Elle a le teint foncé. *eel / ehl ay luh teh~ foh~-say*
black	Il / Elle est noir(e). *eel / ehl ay nwahr*
white	Il / Elle est blanc / blanche. *eel / ehl ay blaw~ / blaw~sh*
Asian	Il / Elle est asiatique. *eel / ehl ay ah-see-ah-teek*
African-American	Il / Elle est afro-américain(e). *eel / ehl ay ah-froh-ah-may-ree-keh~(n)*
biracial	Il / Elle est métis / métisse. *eel / ehl ay may-tee / may-tees*
tall	Il / Elle est grand(e). *eel / ehl ay graw~(d)*
short	Il / Elle est petit(e). *eel / ehl ay puh-tee(t)*
thin	Il / Elle est mince. *eel / ehl ay meh~s*
fat	Il / Elle est gros / grosse. *eel / ehl ay groh(s)*
blue eyes	Il / Elle a les yeux bleus. *eel / ehl ah lay-zyoeh bloeh*
brown eyes	Il / Elle a les yeux bruns. *eel / ehl ah lay-zyoeh bruh~*
green eyes	Il / Elle a les yeux verts. *eel / ehl ah lay-zyoeh veyhr*
hazel eyes	Il / Elle a les yeux noisette. *eel / ehl ah lay-zyoeh nwah-zeht*
eyebrows	les sourcils *lay soohr-see*
eyelashes	les cils *lay see*

freckles	**les taches de rousseur**
	lay tash duh roo-soehr
moles	**les grains de beauté**
	lay greh~ duh boh-tay
face	**le visage**
	luh vee-zahzh

See diagram, p126, for facial features.
See diagram, p196, for body parts.

DISPOSITIONS AND MOODS

sad	**triste**
	treest
happy	**heureux** *m* / **heureuse** *f*
	oeh-roeh / oeh-roehz
angry	**fâché(e)**
	fah-shay
tired	**fatigué(e)**
	fah-tee-gay
depressed	**deprimé(e)**
	day-pree-may
stressed	**stressé(e)**
	struh-say
anxious	**anxieux** *m* / **anxieuse** *f*
	aw~k-see-yoeh / aw~k-see-yoehz
confused	**confus(e)**
	koh~-fueh / koh~-fuehz
enthusiastic	**enthousiaste**
	aw~-too-zee-ahst

PROFESSIONS

What do you do for a living?	**Quelle est votre profession?**
	keh-lay voh-truh proh-feh-see-yoh~
Here is my business card.	**Voici ma carte de visite.**
	vwah-see mah kahrt duh vee-zeet

I am ____

Je suis ____
zhuh swee

a doctor.

médecin.
may-duh-seh~

an engineer.

ingénieur.
eh~zhay-nyoehr

a lawyer.

avocat(e).
ah-voh-kah(t)

a salesperson.

représentant(e) commercial(e).
ruh-pray-saw~-taw~(t) koh-mayhr-see-yahl

a writer.

écrivain.
ay-kree-veh~

an editor.

rédacteur m / rédactrice f.
ruh-dahk-toehr / ruh-dahk-treese

a designer.

styliste.
stee-leest

an educator.

dans l'enseignement.
daw~ law~-seh~-nyuh-maw~

an artist.

artiste.
ahr-teest

a craftsperson.

artisan(e).
ahr-tee-saw~(n)

a homemaker.

femme au foyer.
fah-moh fwah-yay

an accountant.

comptable.
koh~p-tah-bluh

a nurse.

infirmier m / infirmière f.
eh~-feer-mee-yayh(r)

a musician.

musicien m / musicienne f.
mue-zee-see-yeh~(n)

a military professional.

dans l'armée.
daw~ lahr-may

a government employee.

fonctionnaire.
foh~-k-see-yoh~-nayhr

DOING BUSINESS

I'd like to make an appointment.

Je voudrais prendre rendez-vous.
zhuh voo-dray praw~-druh raw~-day-voo

I'm here to see ____.

J'ai rendez-vous avec ____.
zhay raw~-day-voo ah-vek

I need to photocopy this.

J'ai besoin de photocopier ceci.
zhay buh-zweh~ duh foh-toh-koh-pee-yay suh-see

May I use a computer here?

Puis-je utiliser un ordinateur ici?
pwee-zhuh oo-tee-lee-zay uh~-nohr-dee-nah-toehr ee-see

What's the password?

Quel est le mot de passe?
keh-lay luh moh duh pahs

May I access the Internet here?

Puis-je accéder à l'Internet d'ici?
pwee-zhuh ahk-say-day ah leh~-tayhr-neht dee-see

May I send a fax?

Puis-je envoyer une télécopie?
pwee-zhuh aw~-vwah-yay oon tay-lay-koh-pee

May I use the phone?

Puis-je faire un appel?
pwee-zhuh fayhr uh~-nah-pehl

PARTING WAYS

Keep in touch.

Restons en contact.
ruh-stoh~-naw~ koh~-tahkt

Please write or e-mail.

Correspondons par poste ou par courriel.
koh-ruh-spoh~-doh~ pahr pohst oo pahr kooh-ree-yehl

Here's my phone number. Call me!

Voici mon numéro de téléphone. Appelez-moi!
vwah-see moh~-nue-may-roh duh tay-lay-fohn; ah-play mwah

May I have your phone number / e-mail, please?

Puis-je avoir votre numéro de téléphone / adresse courriel?
pwee-zhuh ah-vwahr voh-truh nue-may-roh duh tay-lay-fohn / ah-drehs kooh-ree-yehl

May I have your card?

Puis-je avoir votre carte de visite?
pwee-zhuh ah-vwahr voh-truh kahrt duh vee-zeet

Give me your address and I'll write.

Donnez-moi votre adresse pour que je vous écrive.
duh-nay mwah voh-truh ah-drehs poohr kuh zhuh voo-zay-kreev

TOPICS OF CONVERSATION

As in the United States or anywhere in the world, the weather and current affairs are common conversation topics.

THE WEATHER

It's ____. / Is it always so ____?

sunny

Il fait beau. / Fait-il toujours si beau?
eel fay boh / fay-teel too-zhoor see boh

raining / rainy

Il pleut. / Fait-il toujours si plu-vieux?
eel ploeh / fay-teel too-zhoor see plue-vee-yoeh

cloudy

Le temps est nuageux. / Est-il toujours si nuageux?
luh taw~ ay nue-wah-zhoeh / ey-teel too-zhoor see nue-wah-zhoeh

humid	**Le temps est humide. / Est-il toujours si humide?**
	luh taw~ ay-tue-meed / ey-teel too-zhoor see oo-meed
warm	**Il fait chaud. / Fait-il toujours si chaud?**
	eel fay shoh / fay-teel too-zhoor see shoh
cool	**Il fait frais. / Fait-il toujours si frais?**
	eel fay fray / fay-teel too-zhoor see fray
windy	**Il fait du vent. / Fait-il toujours si venteux?**
	eel fay due vaw~ / fay-teel too-zhoor see vaw~-toeh
What's the forecast for tomorrow?	**Quel temps est prévu pour demain?**
	kehl taw~ ay pray-vue poohr duh-meh~

THE ISSUES

What do you think about _____	**Quelle est votre position à propos _____**
	keh-lay voh-truh poh-zee-see-yoh~ ah proh-poh
democracy?	**de la démocratie en général?**
	duh lah day-moh-krah-see aw~ zhay-nay-rahl
socialism?	**du socialisme?**
	due soh-see-yah-lee-smuh
the environment?	**de l'environnement?**
	duh leh~-vee-roh~-maw~
women's rights?	**des droits de la femme?**
	day dhwah duh lah fahm
gay rights?	**des droits des homosexuels?**
	day dhwah day-zoh-moh-sehk-sue-ehl

the French economy?	**de l'économie française?** *duh lay-koh-noh-mee fraw~-sehz*
the French / American election?	**de l'election française / americaine?** *duh lehl-ehk-see-yoh~ fraw~-sehz / ah-may-ree-kehn*
the war in _____?	**de la guerre en _____?** *duh lah guehr aw~*
What party do you belong to?	**Vous êtes membre de quel parti politique?** *voo-zeht maw~-bruh duh kehl pahr-tee poh-lee-teek*

RELIGION

Do you go to church / temple / mosque?	**Allez-vous à la messe / synagoge / mosquée?** *ah-lay-voo-zah lah mehs / see-nah-guhg / muh-skay*
Are you religious?	**Êtes-vous pratiquant(e)?** *eht-voo prah-tee-kaw~(t)*
I'm _____ / I was raised _____	**Je suis _____ / J'ai reçu une éducation _____** *zhuh swee / zhay ruh-sue oon ay-due-kah-see-yoh~*
Protestant.	**protestant(e).** *proh-teh-staw~(t)*
Catholic.	**catholique.** *kah-toh-leek*
Jewish.	**juif m / juive f.** *zhweef / zhweev*
Muslim.	**musulman(e).** *mue-suel-maw~(n)*
Buddhist.	**bouddhiste.** *boo-deest*
Orthodox Christian.	**chrétien orthodoxe.** *khreh-tee-yeh~-nohr-toh-doks*

Hindu.	**hindouiste.**
	eh~-doo-eest
agnostic.	**agnostique.**
	ahg-noh-steek
atheist.	**athée.**
	ah-tay
I'm spiritual but I don't go to church.	**Je suis spirituel** *m* **/ spirituelle** *f* **mais je ne vais pas à la messe.**
	zhuh swee spee-ree-twehl may zhuh nuh vay pah-zah lah mehs
I don't believe in that.	**Je ne crois pas en cela.**
	zhuh nuh khwah pah-zaw~ suh-lah
That's against my beliefs.	**Cela va à l'encontre de mes croyances.**
	suh-lah vah ah law~-koh~truh duh may khwah-yaw~s
I'd rather not talk about it.	**Je préfère ne pas en parler.**
	zhuh pray-fayhr nuh pah-zaw~ pahr-lay

GETTING TO KNOW SOMEONE

Following are some fun topics for you to explore with friends you meet.

MUSICAL TASTES

What kind of music do you like?	**Quel type de musique aimez-vous?**
	kehl teep duh mue-zeek ay-may-voo
I like ____	**J'aime ____**
	zhehm
rock'n'roll.	**le rock.**
	luh rohk
techno.	**la techno.**
	lah tehk-noh

disco.	**le disco.** *luh dees-koh*
classical.	**la musique classique.** *lah mue-zeek klah-seek*
jazz.	**le jazz.** *luh zhahz*
country and western.	**le country.** *luh kuhn-tree*
reggae.	**le reggae.** *luh reh-gay*
calypso.	**le calypso.** *luh kah-leep-soh*
opera.	**l'opéra.** *loh-pay-rah*
show-tunes / musicals.	**les comedies musicales.** *lay koh-may-dee mue-zee-kahl*
New Age.	**la musique New Age.** *lah mue-zeek nyue ahzh*
pop.	**la musique pop.** *lah mue-zeek pohp*

HOBBIES

What do you like to do in your spare time?	**Qu'est-ce que vous aimez faire pendant votre temps libre?** *kehs kuh voo-zay-may fayhr paw~-daw~ voh-truh taw~ lee-bruh*
I like _____	**J'aime _____** *zhehm _____*
playing the guitar.	**jouer de la guitare.** *zhoo-ay duh lah gee-tahr*
playing the piano.	**jouer du piano.** *zhoo-ay due pee-yah-noh*

For other instruments, see English / French dictionary.

painting.	**peindre.** *peh~-druh*
drawing.	**dessiner.** *deh-see-nay*

dancing.	**danser.**
	daw~-say
reading.	**lire.**
	leer
watching TV.	**regarder la télé.**
	ruh-gahr-day lah tay-lay
shopping.	**faire les magasins.**
	fayhr lay mah-gah-zeh~
going to the movies.	**aller au cinéma.**
	ah-lay oh see-nay-mah
hiking.	**faire de la marche.**
	fayhr duh lah mahrsh
camping.	**aller camper.**
	ah-lay kaw~-pay
hanging out.	**passer du temps avec mes amis.**
	pah-say due taw~ ah-vek may-zah-mee
traveling.	**voyager.**
	vwah-yah-zhay
eating out.	**manger au restaurant.**
	maw~-zhay oh ruh-stoh-raw~
cooking.	**cuisiner.**
	kwee-zee-nay
sewing.	**faire de la couture.**
	fayhr duh lah koo-tuehr
sports.	**faire du sport.**
	fayhr due spohr
Do you like to dance?	**Aimez-vous danser?**
	ay-may-voo daw~-say
Would you like to go out?	**Voulez-vous sortir avec moi?**
	voo-lay-voo sohr-teer ah-vek mwah
May I buy you dinner sometime?	**Puis-je vous inviter à dîner un de ces soirs?**
	pwee-zhuh voo-zeh~-vee-tay ah dee-nay uh~ duh say swahr

What kind of food do you like?	**Quel type de nourriture aimez-vous?** *kehl-teep duh nooh-ree-tuehr ay-may-voo*

For a full list of cuisines, see p88.

Would you like to go _____	**Voulez-vous aller _____ avec moi?** *voo-lay-voo-zah-lay _____ ah-vek mwah*
to a movie?	**au cinéma** *oh see-nay-mah*
to a concert?	**à un concert** *ah uh~ koh~-sayhr*
to the zoo?	**au zoo** *oh zoh*
to the beach?	**à la plage** *ah lah plahzh*
to a museum?	**au musée** *oh mue-zay*
for a walk in the park?	**faire une promenade au parc** *fayhr oon proh-meh-nahd oh pahr*
dancing?	**danser** *daw~-say*
Would you like to get _____	**Voulez-vous _____ avec moi?** *voo-lay-voo _____ ah-vek mwah*
lunch?	**déjeuner** *day-zhoeh-nay*
coffee?	**prendre un café** *preh~-druh uh~ kah-fay*
dinner?	**dîner** *dee-nay*

What kind of books do you like to read?	**Quel type de livres aimez-vous lire?**
	kehl teep duh lee-vruh ay-may-voo leer
I like ____	**J'aime ____**
	zhehm
mysteries.	**les romans policiers.**
	lay roh-maw~ poh-lee-see-yay
Westerns.	**les romans-western.**
	lay roh-maw~-vehs-tayhrn
dramas.	**les romans dramatiques.**
	lay roh-maw~ drah-mah-teek
novels.	**les romans.**
	lay roh-maw~
biographies.	**les biographies.**
	lay bee-yoh-grah-fee
autobiographies.	**les autobiographies.**
	lay-zoh-toh-bee-yoh-grah-fee
romance.	**les romans d'amour.**
	lay roh-maw~ dah-moohr
history.	**les livres d'histoire.**
	lay lee-vruh dees-twahr

For dating terms, see Nightlife in Chapter 10.

CHAPTER SIX

MONEY & COMMUNICATIONS

This chapter covers money, the mail, phone and Internet service, and other tools you need to connect with the outside world.

MONEY

Do you accept _____

Visa / MasterCard / Discover / American Express / Diners' Club?

credit cards?

bills?

coins?

checks?

travelers' checks?

money transfers?

May I wire transfer funds here?

Acceptez-vous _____
ahk-sehp-tay-voo

la carte Visa / MasterCard / Discover / American Express / Diners' Club?
lah kahrt vee-zah / mahs-tayhr-kahrd / dees-koh-vayhr / ah-may-ree-keh-nek-spres / day-nayhrz kloohb

les cartes de crédit?
lay kahrt duh kray-dee

les coupures / billets?
lay koo-puehr / bee-yay

les pièces?
lay pee-yes

les chèques?
lay shek

les chèques de voyage?
lay shek duh vwah-yazh

les virements?
lay veer-maw~

Puis-je virer des fonds d'ici?
pwee-zhuh vee-ray day foh~-dee-see

Would you please tell me where to find _____	**Pouvez-vous m'indiquer _____** *poo-vay-voo meh~-dee-kay*
a bank?	**un bureau de banque?** *uh~ bue-roh duh baw~k*
a credit bureau?	**une institution de crédit?** *oo-neh~-stee-tue-see-yoh~ duh kray-dee*
an ATM?	**une billeterie automatique?** *uh~ bee-yeh-tree oh-toh-mah-teek*
a currency exchange?	**un bureau de change?** *uh~ bueh-roh duh shaw~zh*
May I have a receipt, please?	**Puis-je avoir un reçu, s'il vous plaît?** *pwee-zhuh ah-vwahr uh~ reh-sue seel voo play*
Would you please tell me _____	**Pouvez-vous me dire _____** *poo-vay-voo muh deer*
today's interest rate?	**quel est le taux de change aujourd'hui?** *keh-lay luh toh duh shaw~zh oh-zhoohr-dwee*
the exchange rate for dollars to _____?	**quel est le taux de change du dollar en _____?** *keh-lay luh toh duh shaw~zh due doh-lahr en*
Is there a service charge?	**Y a-t-il des frais bancaires?** *yah-teel day frey baw~-kayhr*

En panne

Before you stick your coins or bills in a vending machine, watch out for the little sign that says *En panne* or *Hors service* (Out of Service).

Listen Up: Bank Lingo

Signez ici, s'il vous plaît. *seen-yay-zee-see seel voo play*	Please sign here.
Voici votre reçu. *vwah-see voh-truh ruh-sue*	Here is your receipt.
Puis-je voir une pièce d'identité, s'il vous plaît? *pwee-zhuh vwahr oon pee-yes dee-deh~-tee-tay seel voo play*	May I see your ID, please?
Nous acceptons les chèques de voyage. *noo-zahk-sehp-toh~ lay shek duh vwah-yahzh*	We accept travelers' checks.
Nous n'acceptons que les espèces. *noo nahk-sehp-toh~ kuh lay-zehs-pehs*	Cash only.

May I have a cash advance on my credit card?	**Puis-je retirer de l'argent sur ma carte de crédit?** *pwee-zhuh ruh-tee-ray duh lahr-zhaw~ suehr mah kahrt duh kray-dee*
Will you accept a credit card?	**Acceptez-vous les cartes de crédit?** *ahk-sehp-tay-voo lay kahrt duh kray-dee*
May I have smaller bills, please?	**Puis-je avoir des billets plus petits, s'il vous plaît?** *pwee-zhuh ah-vwahr day bee-yay plue puh-tee seel voo play*
Can you make change?	**Pouvez-vous faire de la monnaie?** *poo-vay-voo fayhr duh lah moh~-nay*

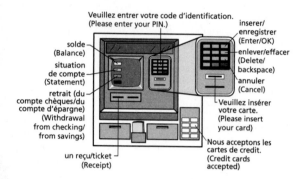

I only have bills.

Je n'ai que des billets.
zhuh nay kuh day bee-yay

May I have some coins,
please?

**Puis-je avoir quelques pièces, s'il
vous plaît?**
*pwee-zhuh ah-vwahr kehl-kuh
pee-yehs seel voo play*

PHONE SERVICE

Where can I buy or rent
a cell phone?

**Où puis-je acheter ou louer un
téléphone portable?**
*oo pwee-zhuh ahsh-tay oo loo-
way uh~ tay-lay-fohn pohr-tah-
bluh*

What rate plans do you
have?

Quels tarifs proposez-vous?
kehl tah-reef proh-poh-zay-voo

Is this good in the whole
country?

**Est-ce que c'est valable pour tout
le pays?**
*ehs-kuh say vah-lah-bluh poohr
too luh pay-ee*

| May I have a prepaid phone card? | **Puis-je avoir une carte téléphonique prépayée?** |
| | *pwee-zhuh ah-vwahr oon kahrt tay-lay-foh-neek pray-pay-ay* |

| Where can I buy a phone card? | **Où puis-je acheter une carte téléphonique?** |
| | *oo pwee-zhuh ahsh-tay oon kahrt tay-lay-foh-neek* |

| May I add more minutes to my phone card? | **Puis-je ajouter des minutes sur ma carte téléphonique?** |
| | *pwee-zhuh ah-zhoo-tay day mee-nuet suehr mah kahrt tay-lay-foh-neek* |

MAKING A CALL

| May I dial direct? | **Puis-je composer le numéro directement?** |
| | *pwee-zhuh koh~-poh-zay luh nue-may-roh dee-rehkt-maw~* |

| Operator, please. | **Je voudrais l'opératrice, s'il vous plaît.** |
| | *zhuh voo-dray loh-pay-rah-trees seel voo play* |

| I'd like to make an international call. | **Je voudrais faire un appel à l'étranger.** |
| | *zhuh voo-dray fayhr uh~-nah-peh-lah lay-traw~-zhay* |

| I'd like to make a collect call. | **Je voudrais faire un appel en PCV.** |
| | *zhuh voo-dray fayhr uh~-nah-peh-law~ pay-say-vay* |

| I'd like to use a calling card. | **Je voudrais faire un appel à l'aide d'une carte téléphonique.** |
| | *zhuh voo-dray fayhr uh~-nah-peh-lah lehd doon kahrt tay-lay-foh-neek* |

Listen Up: Phone Lingo

Bonjour.
boh~-zhoohr

Hello.

Quel numéro?
kehl nue-may-roh

What number?

**Désolé(e), la ligne
est occupée.**
*day-zoh-lay lah lee-ney-
toh-kue-pay*

I'm sorry, the line
is busy.

**Veuillez raccrocher puis
composer de nouveau le
numéro.**
*voeh-yay rah-kroh-shay
pwee koh~-poh-zay duh
noo-voh luh nue-may-roh*

Please hang up the phone and
redial.

**Désolé(e), ça ne répond
pas.**
*day-zoh-lay sah nuh
ray-poh~ pah*

I'm sorry, nobody answers.

**Il reste dix minutes sur
votre carte.**
*eel rehst dee mee-nuet
suehr voh-truh kahrt*

Your card has ten minutes left.

I'd like to bill the call to
my credit card.

**Je voudrais facturer cet appel sur
ma carte de crédit.**
*zhuh voo-dray fahk-tueh-ray seh-
tah-pehl suehr mah kahrt duh
kray-dee*

May I bill the charges to
my room?

**Puis-je ajouter cet appel à ma note
d'hôtel?**
*pwee-zhuh ah-zhoo-tay seh-tah-
pehl ah mah noht doh-tehl*

May I bill the charges to my home phone?

Puis-je facturer cet appel sur la note de téléphone de mon domicile?
pwee-zhuh fahk-tueh-ray seh-tah-pehl suehr lah noht duh tay-lay-fohn duh moh~ doh-mee-seel

Information, please.

Je voudrais les renseignements, s'il vous plaît.
zhuh voo-dray lay raw~-seh~-nyuh-maw~ seel voo play

Would you please give me the number for ____?

Je voudrais le numéro de ____, s'il vous plaît.
zhuh voo-dray luh nue-may-roh duh ____ seel voo play

I just got disconnected.

J'étais coupé(e).
zheh-tay koo-pay

The line is busy.

La ligne est occupée.
lah lee-ney-toh-kue-pay

INTERNET ACCESS

Would you tell me where to find an Internet café?

Pouvez-vous m'indiquer un cybercafé?
poo-vay-voo meh~-dee-kay uh~-see-behr-kah-fay

Is there a wireless hub / Wi-Fi access nearby?

Y a-t-il un hub Ethernet sans fil / Wi-Fi près d'ici?
yah-teel uh~-nuhb ay-tayhr-neht saw~ feel / wee-fee pray dee-see

How much do you charge per minute / hour?

Combien prenez-vous par minute / heure?

koh~-bee-yeh~ pruh-nay-voo pahr mee-nuet / oehr

Can I print here?

Puis-je imprimer des documents ici?

pwee-zhuh eh~-pree-may day doh-kue-maw~-zee-see

Can I burn a CD?

Puis-je graver un CD ici?

pwee-zhuh grah-vay uh~ say-day ee-see

Would you please help me change the preference to English?

Pouvez-vous m'aider à configurer l'anglais comme langue préférée?

poo-vay-voo may-day ah koh~-fee-gueh-ray law~-glay kohm law~g pray-fay-ray

May I scan something in here?

Puis-je scanner quelque chose ici?

pwee-zhuh skah-nay kehl-kuh shoh-zee-see

Can I upload photos from my digital camera?

Puis-je télécharger vers l'amont des photos de mon appareil photo numérique?

pwee-zhuh tay-lay-shahr-zhay vayhr law~-moh~ day foh-toh duh moh~-nah-pah-ray foh-toh nue-may-reek

Do you have a USB port so I can load some music on my MP3 player?

Avez-vous un port USB pour que je puisse importer de la musique sur mon lecteur MP3?

ah-vay-voo-zuh~ pohr oo-ehs-bay poohr kuh zhuh pwees eh~-pohr-tay duh lah mue-zeek suehr moh~-lehk-toehr ehm-pay-twhah

Do you have a machine compatible with iTunes?

Avez-vous un système compatible avec iTunes?

ah-vay-voo-zuh~ see-stehm koh~-pah-tee-bluh ah-vek ee-tuehn

Do you have a Mac?

Avez-vous un Mac?
ah-vay-voo-zuh~ mahk

Do you have a PC?

Avec-vous un compatible PC?
ah-vay-voo-zuh~ koh~-pah-tee-bluh pay-say

Do you have a newer version of this software?

Avez-vous une version plus récente de ce logiciel?
ah-vay-voo-zoon vayhr-see-yoh~ plue ray-saw~t duh suh loh-zhee-see-yehl

How fast is your connection speed here?

La vitesse d'accès est de combien de bauds ici?
lah vee-tess dahk-say ay duh koh~-bee-yeh~ duh boh-dee-see

Do you have broadband?

Avez-vous l'accès à l'Internet à large bande?
ah-vay-voo lahk-say ah leh~-tayhr-neht ah lahrzh bahnd

GETTING MAIL

Excuse me, can you tell me where to find the post office?

Excusez-moi, pouvez-vous me dire où se trouve la poste?
ek-skue-zay mwah poo-vay-voo muh deer oo suh troov lah pohst

May I send an international package?

Puis-je envoyer un colis à l'étranger d'ici?
pwee-zhuh aw~-vwah-yay uh~-koh-lee ah lay-traw~-zhay dee-see

Do I need a customs form?

Ai-je besoin de remplir un formulaire de douane?
ay-zhuh buh-zweh~ duh raw~-pleer uh~ fohr-mue-layhr duh doo-wahn

Do you sell insurance?

Offrez-vous une formule assurance?
oh-fray-voo-zoon fohr-muel ah-sueh-raw~s

Please, mark it fragile.

Apposez un tampon "Fragile", s'il vous plaît.
ah-poh-zay uh~ taw~-poh~ frah-zheel seel voo play

Please, handle with care.

Manipulez-le doucement, s'il vous plaît.
mah-nee-pue-lay-luh doos-maw~ seel voo play

Do you have more twine?

Avez-vous de la ficelle, s'il vous plaît?
ah-vay-voo duh lah fee-sehl seel voo play

Would you please tell me where to find a DHL office?

Pouvez-vous me dire où se trouve l'agence DHL la plus proche?
poo-vay-voo muh deer oo suh troov lah-zhaw~s day-ahsh-ehl lah plue prohsh

Do you sell stamps?

Est-ce que vous vendez des timbres?
ehs kuh voo vaw~-day day taw~-bruh

Do you sell postcards?

Est-ce que vous vendez des cartes postales?
ehs kuh voo vaw~-day day kahrt poh-stahl

Listen Up: Postal Lingo

Au suivant!	Next!
oh swee-vaw~	
Veuillez le poser ici.	Set it here.
voeh-yay luh poh-zay	
ee-see	
Quelle classe?	Which class?
kehl klahs	
Vous désirez?	What kind of service would you
voo day-zee-ray	like?
En quoi puis-je vous être	How can I help you?
utile?	
aw~ kwah pwee-zhuh	
voo-zeh-truh oo-teel	
le guichet de dépôt	dropoff window
luh gee-shay duh day-poh	
le guichet de récupération	pickup window
luh gee-shay duh ray-kue-	
pay-rah-see-yoh~	

I'd like to send this first class / priority mail.	**Je voudrais le service rapide / prioritaire.**
	zhuh voo-dray luh sayhr-vees rah-peed / pree-oh-ree-tayhr
How much to send that express / air mail?	**Combien coûte l'envoi accéléré / par avion?**
	koh~-bee-yeh~ koot law~-vwah ahk-say-lay-ray / pahr ah-vee-yoh~
Do you offer overnight delivery?	**Offrez-vous un service de livraison sous 24 heures?**
	oh-fray-voo-zuh~ sayhr-vees duh lee-vray-zoh~ soo vaw~-kah-truh oehr

How long will that take?	**Combien de jours est-ce que l'envoi prendra?** *koh~-bee-yeh~ duh zhoohr ehs kuh law~-vwah praw~-drah*
I'd like to buy an envelope, please.	**Je voudrais acheter une enveloppe, s'il vous plaît.** *zhuh voo-dray ahsh-tay oo-naw~-vuh-lohp seel voo play*
May I send it airmail?	**Puis-je l'envoyer par avion?** *pwee-zhuh law~-vwah-yay pahr ah-vee-yoh~*
I'd like to send it certified / registered mail.	**Je voudrais l'envoyer en recommandé.** *zhuh voo-dray law~-vwah-yay aw~-ruh-koh-maw~-day*

CINEMA

Is there a movie theater nearby?

Y a-t-il un cinéma près d'ici?
yah-teel uh~ see-nay-mah pray dee-see

Would you please tell me what's playing tonight?

Pouvez-vous me dire quels films passent ce soir?
poo-vay-voo muh deer kehl feelm pahs suh swahr

Is that in English or French?

Est-ce un film en français ou en anglais?
ehs uh~ feelm aw~ fraw~-say oo aw~-naw~-glay

Are there English subtitles?

Y a-t-il des soustitres en anglais?
yah-teel day soo-tee-truh aw~-naw~-glay

Is the theater air conditioned?

La salle est-elle climatisée?
lah sahl ey-tehl klee-mah-tee-zay

How much is a ticket?

Combien coûte un billet?
koh~-bee-yeh~ koo-tuh~ bee-yay

Do you have a discount for ____

Offrez-vous une réduction aux ____
oh-fray-voo-zoon ray-duek-see-yoh~-noh

seniors?

personnes âgées?
payhr-suh-nah-zhay

students?

étudiants?
zay-tue-dee-yaw~

children?

enfants?
zaw~-faw~

What time is the next showing?	**À quelle heure commence la prochaine séance?**
	ah keh-loehr koh~-maw~s lah proh-shen say-aw~s
How long is the movie?	**Combien de temps dure ce film?**
	koh~-bee-yeh~ duh taw~ duehr suh feelm
May I buy tickets in advance?	**Puis-je acheter des billets à l'avance?**
	pwee-zhuh ahsh-tay day bee-yay ah lah-vaw~s
Is it sold out?	**C'est complet?**
	say koh~-play
When does it begin?	**Quand commence-t-il?**
	kaw~ koh-maw~-steel

PERFORMANCES

Do you have ballroom dancing?	**Y a-t-il de la danse de salon ici?**
	yah-teel duh lah daw~s duh sah-loh~-nee-see
Are there any plays showing right now?	**Quelle pièce avez-vous en ce moment?**
	kehl pee-yehs ah-vay-voo-zaw~ suh moh~-maw~
Is there a dinner theater?	**Y a-t-il une salle de dîner théâtre?**
	yah-teel oon sahl duh dee-nay tay-ah-truh
Where can I buy tickets?	**Où achete-t-on des billets?**
	oo ah-sheh-toh~ day bee-yay
Do you offer a student discount?	**Offrez-vous un tarif réduit aux étudiants?**
	oh-fray-voo-zuh~ tah-reef ray-dwee oh-zay-tue-dee-yaw~

Listen Up: Box Office Lingo

Quel film désirez-vous voir?
kehl feelm day-zee-ray-voo vwahr

What would you like to see?

Combien de personnes?
koh~-bee-yeh~ duh payhr-suhn

How many?

Deux adultes?
doeh-zah-duelt

For two adults?

Avec du beurre? Du sel?
ah-vek due boehr; due sehl

With butter? Salt?

Désirez-vous autre chose?
day-zee-ray-voo-zoh-truh shohz

Would you like anything else?

I need ____ seats.	**J'ai besoin de places ____** *zhay buh-zweh~ duh plahs*
aisle	**côté couloir.** *koh-tay kool-wahr*
orchestra	**parterre.** *pahr-tayhr*
What time does the play start?	**À quelle heure la pièce commence-t-elle?** *ah keh-loehr lah pee-yes koh~-maw~-s-tehl*
Is there an intermission?	**Y a-t-il un entracte?** *yah-teel uh~-naw~-trahkt*
Is there an opera house?	**Y a-t-il une salle d'opéra?** *yah-teel oon sahl doh-pay-rah*

CULTURE

Is there a local symphony?

Y a-t-il un orchestre philharmonique local?

yah-teel uh~-nohr-keh-struh fee-lahr-moh~-neek loh-kahl

May I purchase tickets over the phone?

Puis-je acheter des billets par téléphone?

pwee-zhuh ahsh-tay day bee-yay pahr tay-lay-fohn

What time is the box office open?

À quelle heure le bureau de location ouvre-t-il?

ah keh-loehr luh bueh-roh duh loh-kah-see-yoh~ oo-vruh-teel

I need space for a wheelchair.

J'ai besoin de suffisamment d'espace pour une chaise roulante.

zhay buh-zweh~ duh sue-fee-zah-maw~ day-spahs poohr oon shez roo-law~t

Do you have private boxes available?

Avez-vous des loges privés de libres?

ah-vay-voo day lohzh pree-vay duh lee-bruh

I'd like a program, please.

Je voudrais un programme, s'il vous plaît.

zhuh voo-dray uh~ proh-grahm seel voo play

Could you please show us our seats?

Pouvez-vous nous montrer où sont nos places?

poo-vay-voo noo moh~-tray oo soh~ noh plahs

MUSEUMS, GALLERIES & SIGHTS

Do you have a museum guide?	**Avez-vous un guide des musées de la ville?** *ah-vay-voo-zuh~ geed day mue-zay duh lah veel*
Do you have guided tours?	**Offrez-vous des excursions?** *oh-fray-voo day-zhek-skuehr-see-yoh~*
What are the museum hours?	**Quelles sont les heures d'ouverture de ce musée?** *kehl soh~ lay-zoehr doo-vayhr-tuehr duh suh mue-zay*
Do I need to make an appointment?	**Ai-je besoin de m'inscrire à l'avance?** *ay-zhuh buh-zweh~ duh meh~-skreer ah lah-vaw~s*
Is there an admission fee?	**L'entrée est-elle payante?** *law~-tray ey-tehl pay-aw~t*
Do you offer _____	**Offrez-vous** _____ *oh-fray-voo*
student discounts?	**des tarifs réduit aux étudiants?** *day tah-reef ray-dwee oh-zay-tue-dee-yaw~*
senior discounts?	**des tarifs réduits aux personnes âgées?** *day tah-reef ray-dwee oh payhr-suh-nah-zhay*
services for the hearing impaired?	**des services pour malentendants?** *day sayhr-vees poohr mah-law~-taw~-daw~*
audio tours in English?	**une visite audioguidée en anglais?** *oon vee-zeet oh-toh-gee-day aw~-naw~-glay*

CHAPTER EIGHT

SHOPPING

This chapter covers the phrases you'll need for shopping in a variety of settings: from the mall to the town square artisan market. We also throw in the terminology you'll need to visit the barber or hairdresser.

For coverage of food and grocery shopping, see Chapter 4, Dining.

GENERAL SHOPPING TERMS

Would you please tell me ____	**S'il vous plaît, pouvez-vous m'indiquer ____** *seel voo play poo-vay-voo meh~-dee-kay*
how to get to a mall?	**comment aller au centre commercial le plus près?** *koh~-maw~-tah-lay oh saw~-truh koh~-mayhr-see-yahl luh plue pray*
the best place for shopping?	**le meilleur endroit pour faire des courses?** *luh may-yoehr aw~-dhwah poohr fayhr day koohrs*
how to get downtown?	**comment aller au centre-ville?** *koh~-maw~-tah-lay oh saw~-truh veel*
Where can I find a ____	**Où puis-je trouver ____** *oo pwee-zhuh troo-vay*
shoe store?	**un magasin qui vende des chaussures?** *uh~ mah-gah-zeh~ kee vaw~d day shoh-suehr*
clothing store?	**un magasin qui vende des vêtements?** *uh~ mah-gah-zeh~ kee vaw~d day veht-maw~*

designer fashion boutique?	**une boutique haute couture?**
	oon boo-teek oht koo-tuehr
vintage clothing store?	**une friperie?**
	oon fhree-pay-ree
jewelry store?	**une bijouxterie?**
	oon bee-zhoo-tree
bookstore?	**une librairie?**
	oon lee-bray-ree
toy store?	**un magasin des jouets?**
	uh~ mah-gah-zeh~ day zhoo-ay
stationery store?	**une papeterie?**
	oon pah-pay-tree
cigar store / tobacco shop?	**un magasin qui vende des cigares / un tabac?**
	uh~ mah-gah-zeh~ kee vaw~d day day see-gahr / uh~ tah-bahk
antique shop?	**un antiquaire?**
	uh~-naw~-tee-kwayhr
souvenir shop?	**un magasin qui vende des souvenirs?**
	uh~ mah-gah-zeh~ kee vaw~d day soov-neer
flea market?	**un marché à puces?**
	uh~ mahr-shay ah pues

CLOTHES SHOPPING

I'd like to buy _____	**Je voudrais acheter _____**
	zhuh voo-dray ahsh-tay
some men's shirts.	**des chemises pour homme.**
	day shmeez pooh-ruhm
some women's shoes.	**des chaussures pour femme.**
	day shoh-suehr poohr fahm
some children's clothes.	**des vêtements pour enfant.**
	day veht-maw~ pooh-raw~-faw~
some toys for my kids.	**des jouets pour mes enfants.**
	day zhoo-ay poohr may-zaw~-faw~

les boucles d'oreille
le collier
la robe
la montre

la chemise
la cravate
le veston
la ceinture
le pantalon
les chaussures

I'm looking for a size ____	**Je cherche une taille ____** *zhuh shayhrsh oon tie*

For a full list of numbers, see p7.

small.	**petit.** *puh-tee*
medium.	**moyen.** *mwah-yeh~*
large.	**large.** *lahrzh*
extra-large.	**extra-large.** *ehk-strah-lahrzh*
I'm looking for ____	**Je suis à la recherche ____** *zhuh sweez ah lah ruh-shayhrsh*
a silk blouse.	**d'un chemisier en soie.** *duh~ shmee-zee-yay aw~ swah*
cotton pants.	**d'une paire de pantalons en coton.** *doon payhr duh paw~-tah-loh~-naw~ koh-toh~*

— les lunettes

— le tee-shirt

— le jean

— les chaussures de tennis

a hat.	**d'un chapeau.**
	duh~ shah-poh
sunglasses.	**de lunettes de soleil.**
	duh lue-neht duh soh-lay
some underwear.	**de sous-vêtements.**
	duh soo veht-maw~
socks.	**de chausettes.**
	duh shoh-seht
a sweater.	**d'un pull.**
	duh~ puehl
a swimsuit.	**d'un maillot de bain.**
	duh~ mie-yoh duh beh~
a coat.	**d'un manteau.**
	duh~ maw~-toh
May I try it on?	**Puis-je l'essayer?**
	pwee-zhuh leh-say-yay
Do you have fitting rooms?	**Avez-vous des cabines d'essayage?**
	ah-vay-voo day kah-been deh-say-yazh

This is ____	**C'est ____**
	say
too tight.	**trop étroit.**
	troh ay-twah
too loose.	**trop flou.**
	troh floo
too long.	**trop long.**
	troh loh~g
too short.	**trop court.**
	troh koohr
This fits great!	**C'est parfait comme taille!**
	say pahr-fay kohm tie
Thanks, I'll take it.	**Merci, je le m / la f prends.**
	mayhrsee zhuh luh / lah praw~
Do you have that ____	**Est-ce que vous avez cet article**
	____
	ehs kuh voo-zah-vay seh-tahr-tee-kluh
in a smaller / larger size?	**dans une taille plus petite / grande?**
	daw~-zoon tie plue puh-teet / graw~d
in a different color?	**dans une autre couleur?**
	daw~-zoo-noh-truh koo-loehr
How much is it?	**Ça coûte combien?**
	sah koot koh~-bee-yeh~

ARTISAN MARKET SHOPPING

Is there a craft / artisans market?	**Y a-t-il un marché d'artisans?**
	yah-teel uh~ mahr-shay dahr-tee-zaw~
That's beautiful. May I take a look at it?	**C'est très beau. Puis-je le regarder de plus près?**
	say tray boh; pwee-zhuh luh ruh-gahr-day duh plue pray

When is the farmers' market open?	**Quelles sont les heures d'ouverture du marché de producteurs?** *kehl soh~ lay-zoehr doo-vayhr-tuehr due mahr-shay duh proh-duek-toehr*
Is that open every day of the week?	**Est-il ouvert tous les jours de la semaine?** *ey-teel oo-vayhr too lay zhoohr duh lah smehn*
How much does that cost?	**Combien est-ce que cela coûte?** *koh~-bee-yeh~ ehs kuh suh-lah koot*
Oh, that's too expensive!	**Oh là, c'est trop cher m / chère f!** *oh lah say troh shayhr*
How much for both?	**Combien coûte tous les deux?** *koh~-bee-yeh~ koot too lay doeh*
Is there a cash discount?	**Y a-t-il un escompte de caisse?** *yah-teel uh~-nuh-skoh~t duh kehs*
No thanks. Maybe I'll come back.	**Non, merci. Peut-être je reviens.** *noh~ mayhr-see; poeh-teh-truh zhuh ruh-vee-yeh~*
Would you take €_____?	**Accepteriez-vous _____ euros?** *ahk-sehp-tay-ree-yay-voo _____ oeh-roh*

For a full list of numbers, see p7.

Okay, it's a deal. I'll take it / them!	**D'accord. Je le m / la f / les pl prends!** *dah-kohr; zhuh luh / lah / lay praw~*
Do you have a less expensive one?	**Est-ce que vous en avez moins cher m / chère f?** *ehs kuh voo-zaw~-nah-vay mweh~ shayhr*
Is tax included?	**La taxe est-elle comprise?** *lah tahks ey-tehl koh~-preez*
May I have a VAT form?	**Puis-je avoir un formulaire TVA?** *pwee-zhuh ah-vwahr uh~ fohr-mue-layhr tay-vay-ah*

BOOKSTORE / NEWSSTAND SHOPPING

Is there a bookstore / newsstand nearby?	**Y a-t-il un libraire / kiosque à journaux près d'ici?** *yah-teel uh~ lee-brayhr / kee-ohsk ah zhoohr-noh pray dee-see*
Do you have ____	**Avez-vous ____** *ah-vay-voo*
books in English?	**des livres en anglais?** *day lee-vruh-zaw~-naw~-glay*
current newspapers?	**des journaux récents?** *day zhoohr-noh ray-saw~*
international newspapers?	**des journaux internationaux?** *day zhoohr-noh eh~-tayhr-nah-see-yoh~-noh*
magazines?	**des magazines?** *day mah-gah-zeen*
books about local history?	**des livres sur l'histoire de cette région?** *day lee-vruh suehr lees-twahr duh seht ray-zhee-yoh~*
picture books?	**des livres d'image?** *day lee-vruh dee-mahzh*

SHOPPING FOR ELECTRONICS

With some exceptions, shopping for electronic goods in France is generally not recommended. Many DVDs, CDs, and other products contain different signal coding than what is used in the United States and Canada to help deter piracy. Radios are probably the biggest exception, though, and lots of U.S. market goods are available.

Can I play this in the United States?	**Est-ce que cela va marcher aux États-Unis?** *ehs kuh suh-lah vah mahr-shay oh-zay-tah-zue-nee*

Will this game work on my game console in the United States?	**Est-ce que ce jeu va marcher sur ma console de jeu aux États-Unis?** *ehs kuh suh zhoeh vah mahr-shay suehr mah koh~-sohl duh zhoeh oh-zay-tah-zue-nee*
Do you have this in a U.S. market format?	**Avez-vous cela en format américain?** *ah-vay-voo suh-lah aw~ fohr-mah ah-may-ree-keh~*
Can you convert this to a U.S. market format?	**Pouvez-vous convertir cela au format américain?** *poo-vay-voo koh~-vayhr-teer suh-lah oh fohr-mah ah-may-ree-keh~*
Will this work with a 110 VAC adapter?	**Est-ce que cela va marcher avec un adaptateur 110 VCA?** *ehs kuh suh-lah vah mahr-shay ah-vek uh~-nah-dahp-toehr saw~-dees vay-say-ah*
Do you have an adapter plug for 110 to 220?	**Est-ce que vous avez un adaptateur 110 à 220?** *ehs kuh voo-zah-vay-zuh~-nah-dahp-toehr saw~-dee-zah saw~-veh~*
Do you sell electronics adapters here?	**Est-ce que vous vendez des adaptateurs pour appareils électroniques?** *ehs kuh voo vaw~-day day-zah-dahp-toehr poohr ah-pah-ray ay-lehk-troh-neek*
Is it safe to use my laptop with this adapter?	**Est-ce sans risque d'utiliser mon ordinateur portable avec cet adaptateur?** *ehs saw~ reesk due-tee-lee-zay moh~-nohr-dee-nah-toehr pohr-tah-bluh ah-vek seh-tah-dahp-toehr*

If it doesn't work, may I return it?	**Si cela ne marche pas, puis-je le ramener?**
	see suh-lah nuh mahrsh pah pwee-zhuh luh rah-mnay
May I try it here in the store?	**Puis-je l'essayer ici, dans le magasin?**
	pwee-zhuh leh-say-ay ee-see daw~-luh mah-gah-zeh~

AT THE BARBER / HAIRDRESSER

Do you have a style guide?	**Avez-vous des photos avec les différents styles?**
	ah-vay-voo day foh-toh ah-vek lay dee-fay-raw~ steel
I'd like a trim.	**Je voudrais une coupe.**
	zhuh voo-dray-zoon koop
I'd like it bleached.	**Je voudrais une couleur.**
	zhuh voo-dray-zoon koo-loehr
Would you change the color?	**Pouvez-vous changer ma couleur?**
	poo-vay-voo shaw~-zhay mah koo-loehr
I'd like it darker.	**Je la voudrais plus foncée.**
	zhuh lah voo-dray plue foh~-say
I'd like it lighter.	**Je la voudrais plus claire.**
	zhuh lah voo-dray plue klayhr
Would you just touch it up a little?	**Pouvez-vous faire une simple retouche?**
	poo-vay-voo fayhr oon seh~-pluh ruh-toosh
I'd like it curled.	**Je voudrais une mise en plis.**
	zhuh voo-dray-zoon mee-zaw~-plee
Do I need an appointment?	**Ai-je besoin d'un rendez-vous?**
	ay-zhuh buh-zweh~ duh~ raw~-day-voo

Wash, dry, and set.

Je voudrais un shampooing et un brushing, s'il vous plaît.
zhuh voo-dray uh~ shaw~-poo-een ay uh~ bruh-sheen seel voo play

Do you do perms?

Faites-vous des permanentes?
feht-voo day payhr-maw~-naw~t

Please use low heat.

Vérifiez que le séchoir ne soit pas trop chaud, s'il vous plaît.
vay-ree-fee-yay kuh luh say-shwahr nuh swah pah troh shoh seel voo play

Please don't blow dry it.

Pas de brushing, s'il vous plaît.
pah duh bruh-sheen seel voo play

Please dry it curly.

Faites-les boucler, s'il vous plaît.
feht-lay boo-klay seel voo play

Please dry it straight.

Lissez-les, s'il vous plaît.
lee-say lay seel voo play

Would you fix my braids?

Pouvez-vous me refaire mes nattes?
poo-vay-voo muh ruh-fayhr may naht

Would you fix my highlights?

Pouvez-vous me refaire mes mèches?
poo-vay-voo muh ruh-fayhr may mehsh

Do you wax?

Est-ce que vous faites des épilations à la cire?
ehs kuh voo feht day-zay-pee-lah-see-yoh~ ah lah seer

Please wax my _____

Épilez-moi _____ à la cire, s'il vous plaît.
ay-pee-lay mwah _____ ah lah seer seel voo play

legs.

les jambes
lay zhahmb

bikini line.

le maillot
luh mah-yoh

eyebrows.	**les sourcils**
	lay soohr-seel
under my nose.	**sous le nez**
	soo luh nay
Please trim my beard.	**Raccourcissez-moi un peu la barbe, s'il vous plaît.**
	rah-koohr-see-say mwah uh~ poeh lah bahrb seel voo play
May I have a shave, please?	**Puis-je me faire raser, s'il vous plaît?**
	pwee-zhuh muh fayhr rah-zay seel voo play
Use a fresh blade, please.	**Utilisez une lame neuve, s'il vous plaît.**
	oo-tee-lee-zay oon lahm noehv seel voo play
Sure, cut it all off.	**D'accord, coupez-la f / coupez-les pl complètement.**
	dah-kohr koo-pay lah / les koh~-pleht-maw~

GETTING FIT

Is there a gymnasium nearby?

Y a-t-il un gymnase près d'ici?
yah-teel uh~ zheem-nahz prey dee-see

Do you have free weights?

Avez-vous des altères?
ah-vay-voo day-zahl-tayhr

I'd like to go for a swim.

Je voudrais aller nager.
zhuh voo-dray-zah-lay nah-zhay

Do I have to be a member?

L'entrée est-elle réservée aux membres?
law~-tray ey-tehl ray-zehr-vay oh maw~-bruh

May I come here for one day?

Puis-je entrer pour un séance à l'unité?
pwee-zhuh aw~-tray poohr uh~ say-aw~s ah lue-nee-tay

How much does a membership cost?

Combien coûte l'abonnement?
koh~-bee-yeh~ koot lah-buhn-maw~

I need to get a locker, please.	**Je voudrais un casier, s'il vous plaît.**
	zhuh voo-dray uh~ kahz-yay seel voo play
Do you have locks for those?	**Avez-vous des cadenas pour les casiers?**
	ah-vay-voo day kahd-nah poohr lay kahz-yay
Do you have a treadmill?	**Y a-t-il un tapis roulant ici?**
	yah-teel uh~ tah-pee roo-law~ ee-see
Do you have a stationary bike?	**Y a-t-il un vélo d'exercice?**
	yah-teel uh~ vaylo dehk-sayhr-sees
Do you have a handball / squash court?	**Avez-vous un terrain de jeu de hand-ball / squash?**
	ah-vay-voo-zuh~ tuh-reh~ duh zhoeh duh ahnd bahl / skwahsh
Are they indoors?	**Sont-ils couverts?**
	soh~-teel koo-vayhr
I'd like to play tennis.	**J'aime jouer au tennis.**
	zhehm zhoo-ay oh teh-nees
Would you like to play?	**Voulez-vous jouer avec moi?**
	voo-lay-voo zhoo-ay ah-vek mwah
I'd like to rent a racquet.	**Je voudrais louer une raquette.**
	zhuh voo-dray loo-ay oon rah-keht
I need to buy some new balls.	**Je voudrais acheter des balles neuves.**
	zhuh voo-dray ahsh-tay day bahl noehv
I lost my safety glasses.	**J'ai perdu mes lunettes protectrices.**
	zhay payhr-due may lue-neht proh-tehk-trees
May I rent a court for tomorrow?	**Puis-je louer un court pour demain?**
	pwee-zhuh loo-ay uh~ koohr poohr duh-meh~

Do you have clean towels?	**Avez-vous des serviettes propres?**
	ah-vay-voo day sayhr-vee-yeht proh-pruh
Where are the showers / locker rooms?	**Où sont les douches / vestiaires, s'il vous plaît?**
	oo soh~ lay doosh / vehs-tee-yayhr seel voo play
Do you have a workout room for women only?	**Avez-vous une salle d'entraîne-ment réservée aux femmes?**
	ah-vay-voo-zoon sahl daw~-treh~-maw~ ray-zehr-vay oh fahm
Do you have aerobics classes?	**Avez-vous des cours d'aérobic?**
	ah-vay-voo day koohr dah-eyh-roh-beek
Do you have a women's pool?	**Avez-vous une piscine réservée aux femmes?**
	ah-vay-voo-zoon pee-seen ray-sehr-vay oh fahm
Let's go for a jog.	**Allons faire un jogging.**
	ah-loh~ fayhr uh~ zhoh-gheeng
That was a great workout.	**Je me suis bien entraîné(e).**
	zhuh muh swee bee-yeh~ aw~-treh~-nay

CATCHING A GAME

Where is the stadium?	**Où se trouve le stade?**
	oo suh troov luh stahd
Who is the best goalie?	**Qui est le meilleur gardien de but?**
	kee ay luh may-yoehr gahr-dee-yeh~ duh bue
Is there a women's team?	**Y a-t-il une équipe féminine?**
	yah-teel oon ay-keep fay-mee-neen

Do you have any amateur / professional teams?	**Avez-vous des équipes amateurs / professionnelles?** *ah-vay-voo day-zay-keep ah-mah-toehr / proh-feh-see-yoh-nehl*
Is there a game I could play in?	**Y a-t-il un événement sportif auquel je pourrais participer?** *yah-teel uh~-nay-vay-nuh-maw~-spohr-teef oh-kehl zhuh pooh-ray pahr-tee-see-pay*
Which is the best team?	**Quelle est la meilleure équipe?** *keh-lay lah may-yoehr ay-keep*
Will the game be on television?	**Le match va-t-il passer à la télévision?** *luh mahtch vah-teel pah-say ah lah tay-lay-veez-yoh~*
Where can I buy tickets?	**Où puis-je acheter des places?** *oo pwee-zhuh ahsh-tay day plahs*
The best seats, please.	**Les meilleures places, s'il vous plaît.** *lay may-yoehrs plahs seel voo play*
The cheapest seats, please.	**Les places les moins chères, s'il vous plaît.** *lay plahs lay mweh~ shayhr seel voo play*

How close are these seats?	**Ces places sont-elles près du terrain?**
	say plahs soh~-tehl pray due tuh-reh~
May I have a private box?	**Puis-je avoir un box privé?**
	pwee-zhuh ah-vwahr uh~ bohks pree-vay
Wow! What a game!	**Quel match!**
	kehl mahtch
Go! Go! Go!	**On va gagner!** *repeat several times*
	oh~ vah gah-nyay
Oh no!	**Oh non!**
	oh noh~
Give it to them!	**Montrez leur!**
	moh~-tray loehr
Go for it!	**Vas-y!**
	vah-zee
Score!	**Marque un but!**
	mahrk uh~ bue
What's the score?	**Quel est le score?**
	keh-lay luh skohr
Who's winning?	**Qui est en train de gagner?**
	kee eh-taw~ treh~ duh gah-nyay

HIKING

Where can I find a guide to hiking trails?	**Où puis-je trouver un guide des randonnées régionales?**
	oo pwee-zhuh troo-vay uh~ gheed day raw~-doh~-nay ray-zhee-oh~-nahl
Do we need to hire a guide?	**Est-il nécessaire d'embaucher un guide?**
	ey-teel nay-suh-sayhr daw~-boh-shay uh~ gheed

Where can I rent equipment?

Où puis-je louer du matériel d'escalade?
oo pwee-zhuh loo-ay due mah-tayh-ree-yehl dehs-kah-lahd

Do they have rock climbing there?

Y a-t-il des endroits où on peut faire de la varappe?
yah-teel day-zaw~-dhwah oo oh~-poeh fayhr duh lah vah-rahp

We need to get more ropes and carabiners.

Nous avons besoin de cordes et de mousquetons supplémentaires.
noo-zah-voh~ buh-zweh~ duh kohrd ay duh moos-kuh-toh~ sue-play-maw~-tayhr

Where can we go mountain climbing?

Où est-il possible de faire de l'escalade?
oo ey-teel poh-see-bluh duh fayhr duh lehs-kah-lahd

Are the routes well marked?

Les routes sont-elles bien signa-lisées?
lay root soh~-tehl bee-yeh~ see-nyah-lee-zay

Are the routes in good condition?

Les chemins sont-ils en bon état?
lay shuh-meh~ soh~-teel aw~ boh~-nay-tah

What is the altitude there?

Quelle est l'altitude là-bas?
keh-lay lahl-tee-tued lah bah

How long will it take?

Combien de temps cela prendra-t-il?
koh~-bee-yeh~ duh taw~ suh-lah praw~-drah-teel

Is it very difficult?

Est-ce très difficile?
ehs tray dee-fee-seel

I'd like a challenging climb, but I don't want to take oxygen.

Je voudrais une escalade ambitieuse, mais je ne veux pas porter de l'oxygène.
zhuh voo-dray oo-neh-skah-lahd aw~-bee-see-yoehz may zhuh nuh voeh pah pohr-tay duh lohk-see-zhehn

I want to hire someone to carry my excess gear.

Je voudrais embaucher quelqu'un qui puisse porter mon excédent de matériel.
zhuh voo-dray aw~boh-shay kehl-kuh~ kee pwees pohr-tay moh~ ehk-say-daw~ duh mah-tayh-ree-yehl

We don't have time for a long route.

Nous n'avons pas le temps de faire une longue sortie.
noo nah-voh~ pah luh taw~ duh fayhr oon loh~g sohr-tee

I don't think it's safe to proceed.

Je ne pense pas qu'il soit prudent de continuer.
zhuh nuh paw~s pah keel swah prue-daw~ duh koh~-tee-nue-ay

Do we have a backup plan?

Avons-nous un plan en cas de problème?
ah-voh~-noo-zuh~ plaw~ aw~ kah duh proh-blehm

If we're not back by tomorrow, send a search party.	**Si nous ne sommes pas revenus demain, envoyez quelqu'un à notre recherche.**
	see noo nuh sohm pah ruhv-noo duh-meh~ aw~vwah-yay kehl-kuh~ ah noh-truh ruh-shersh
Are the campsites marked?	**Les emplacements de camping sont-ils balisés?**
	layz aw~-plahs-maw~ duh kaw~-peeng soh~-teel bah-lee-zay
Can we camp off the trail?	**Est-il possible de camper en pleine nature?**
	ey-teel poh-see-bluh duh kaw~-pay aw~ plehn nah-tuehr
Is it okay to build fires here?	**A-t-on le droit de faire des feux de camp ici?**
	ah-toh~ luh dhwah duh fayhr day foeh duh kaw~ ee- see
Do we need permits?	**A-t-on besoin d'une autorisation?**
	ah-toh~ buh-zweh~ doon oh-toh-ree-zah-see-yoh~

For more camping terms, see p87.

BOATING OR FISHING

When do we sail?	**À quelle heure appareillons-nous?**
	ah keh-loehr ah-pah-ray-oh~-noo
Where are the life preservers / vests?	**Où sont les bouées / gilets de sauvetage?**
	oo soh~ lay boo-ay / zhee-lay duh sohv-tazh
Can I purchase bait?	**Puis-je acheter de l'appâts?**
	pwee-zhuh ahsh-tay duh lah-pah

Can I rent a pole?	**Puis-je louer une canne?** *pwee-zhuh loo-ay oon kahn*
How long is the voyage?	**Combien de temps dure la sortie?** *koh~-bee-yeh~ duh taw~ duehr* *lah sohr-tee*
Are we going up river or down?	**Remontons-nous ou descendons-nous la rivière?** *ruh-moh~-toh~-noo oo duh-saw~-doh~-noo lah ree-vee-yayhr*
How far out are we going?	**Jusqu'où allons-nous aller?** *zhues-koo ah-loh~-noo-zah-lay*
How fast are we going?	**On va à quelle vitesse?** *oh~ vah ah kehl vee-tehs*
How deep is the water here?	**Quelle est la profondeur de l'eau ici?** *keh-lay lah proh-foh~-doehr duh loh ee-see*
I got one!	**J'ai attrapé un poisson!** *zhay ah-trah-pay uh~ pwah-soh~*
I can't swim.	**Je ne sais pas nager.** *zhuh nuh say pah nah-zhay*
Can we go ashore?	**Pouvons-nous aller à terre?** *poo-voh~-noo-zah-lay ah tayhr*

For more boating terms, see p70.

DIVING

I'd like to go snorkeling.	**Je voudrais faire de la plongée avec masque et tuba.** *zhuh voo-dray fayhr duh lah ploh~-zhay ah-vek mahsk ay tue-bah*
I'd like to go scuba diving.	**Je voudrais faire de la plongée sous-marine.** *zhuh voo-dray fayhr duh lah ploh~-zhay soo mah-reen*

I have a NAUI / PADI certification.

J'ai le brevet de plongeur NAUI / PADI.
zhay luh bruh-vay duh ploh~-zhoehr enn-ah-oo-ee / pay-ah-day-ee

I need to rent gear.

Je voudrais louer du matériel de plongée.
zhuh voo-dray loo-ay due mah-tayh-ree-yehl duh ploh~-zhay

We'd like to see some shipwrecks if we can.

Nous aimerions si possible voir des épaves.
noo-zeh-meh-ree-yoh~ see poh-see-bluh vwahr day-zay-pahv

Are there any good cave / reef dives?

Y a-t-il des bonnes plongées aux grottes / récifs?
yah-teel day buhn ploh~-zhay oh groht / ray-seef

I'd like to see a lot of diverse sea-life.

Je voudrais voir un milieu sous-marin diversifié.
zhuh voo-dray vwahr uh~ meel-yoeh soo-mah-reh~ dee-vayhr-see-fee-yay

Are the currents strong?

Le courant est-il fort?
luh kooh-raw~ ey-teel fohr

How is the clarity?

Les eaux sont-elles claires?
lay-zoh soh~-tehl klayhr

I want / don't want to go with a group.

Je voudrais / je ne veux pas me joindre avec une groupe.
zhuh voo-dray / zhuh nuh voeh pah muh zhweh~-druh ah-vek oon groohp

Do we have to go with a group, or can we charter our own boat?

Devons-nous nous joindre à un groupe, ou pouvons-nous louer notre propre bateau?
duh-voh~-noo noo zhweh~druh ah uh~ groop oo poo-voh~-noo loo-ay noh-truh proh-pruh bah-toh

SURFING

I'd like to go surfing.

Je voudrais aller faire du surf.
zhuh voo-dray ah-lay fayhr due suehrf

Are there any good beaches?

Y a-t-il de bonnes plages à surf?
yah-teel duh buhn plahzh ah suehrf

Can I rent a board?

Puis-je louer une planche?
pwee-zhuh loo-ay oon plaw~sh

How are the currents?

Y a-t-il beaucoup de courant?
yah-teel boh-koo duh kooh-raw~

How high are the waves?

Les vagues sont de quelle hauteur?
lay vahg soh~ duh kehl oh-toehr

Is it usually crowded?

Y a-t-il du monde d'habitude sur la plage?
yah-teel due moh~d dah-bee-tued suehr lah plahzh

Are there facilities on that beach?

Y a-t-il des infrastructures sur la plage?
yah-teel day-zeh~-frah-struek-tuehr suehr lah plahzh

Is there wind surfing there also?

Est-il possible de faire de la planche à voile?
ey-teel poh-seeb-luh duh fayhr duh lah plaw~sh ah vwahl

GOLFING

I'd like to reserve a tee-time, please.
Je voudrais réserver une heure de départ, s'il vous plaît.
zhuh voo-dray ray-zehr-vay oo-noehr duh day-pahr seel voo play

Do we need to be members to play your course?
Ce terrain de golf est-il réservé aux membres?
suh tuh-reh~ duh gohlf ey-teel ray-zehr-vay oh maw~-bruh

How many holes is your course?
C'est un golf à combien de trous?
seht uh~ gohlf ah koh~-bee-yeh~ duh troo

What is par for the course?
Combien est par pour ce terrain?
koh~-bee-yeh~ ay pahr poohr suh teh-reh~

I need to rent clubs.
J'ai besoin de louer des bâtons de golf.
zhay buh-zweh~ duh loo-ay day bah-toh~ duh gohlf

I need to purchase some balls.
J'ai besoin d'acheter des balles de golf.
zhay buh-zweh~ dahsh-tay day bahl duh gohlf

I need a glove.
J'ai besoin d'un gant.
zhay buh-zweh~ duh~ gaw~

I need a new hat.
J'ai besoin d'une nouvelle casquette.
zhay buh-zweh~ doon noo-vehl kahs-keht

Do you require soft spikes?	**Exigez-vous des crampons mous?** *ek-zee-zhay-voo day kraw~-poh~ moo*
Do you have carts?	**Avez-vous des voiturettes?** *ah-vay-voo day vwah-tueh-reht*
I'd like to hire a caddie.	**Je voudrais embaucher un cadet.** *zhuh voo-dray aw~-boh-shay uh~ kah-day*
Do you have a driving range?	**Avez-vous un terrain d'exercice?** *ah-vay-voo-zuh~ tuh-reh~ dayk- sayhr-sees*
How much are the greens fees?	**Combien coûte le droit d'entrée?** *koh~-bee-yeh~ koot luh dwah daw~-tray*
Can I book a lesson with the pro?	**Puis-je prendre rendez-vous pour une leçon avec un professionnel?** *pwee-zhuh praw~-druh raw~-day- voo poohr oon leh-soh~ ah-vek uh~ proh-feh-see-yoh-nehl*
I need to have a club repaired.	**J'ai besoin de faire réparer l'un de mes bâtons.** *zhay buh-zweh~ duh fayhr ray- pah-ray luh~ duh may bah-toh~*
Is the course dry?	**L'herbe du golf est-elle sèche?** *layhrb due gohlf ey-tehl sehsh*
Are there any wildlife hazards?	**Est-ce qu'on risque de rencontrer des animaux sauvages?** *ehs koh~ reesk duh raw~-koh~- tray day-zah-nee-moh soh-vahzh*
How many total meters is the course?	**Quelle est la longueur totale du golf?** *keh-lay lah loh~-goehr toh-tahl due gohlf*
Is it very hilly?	**Le terrain est-il très onduleux?** *luh tuh-reh~-ney-teel tray-zoh~- due-loeh*

CHAPTER TEN

NIGHTLIFE

For coverage of movies and cultural events, see Chapter 7, Culture.

NIGHTCLUBBING

Would you please tell me where to find ____

Pourriez-vous m'indiquer ____, s'il vous plaît?
poo-vay-voo meh~-dee-kay ___ seel voo play

a good nightclub?
une bonne boîte de nuit
oon buhn bwaht duh nwee

a club with a live band?
une boîte où une groupe joue de la musique
oon bwaht oo oon groop zhoo duh lah mue-zeek

a reggae club?
une boîte où l'on joue du reggae
oon bwaht oo loh~ zhoo due reh-gay

a hip hop club?
une boîte de hip-hop
oon bwaht duh eep-ohp

a techno club?
une boîte de la musique techno
oon bwaht duh lah mue-zeek tehk-noh

a jazz club?
une boîte de le jazz
oon bwaht duh luh zhahz

a country / western club?
une boîte de la country
oon bwaht duh lah kuhn-tree

a gay / lesbian club?
une boîte pour homosexuels / lesbiennes
oon bwaht poohr oh-moh-sehk-sue-ehl / lehz-bee-yehn

a club where I can dance?	**une boîte où l'on danse vraiment** *oon bwaht oo loh~ daw~s vray-maw~*
a club with French music?	**une boîte de la musique française** *oon bwaht duh lah mue-zeek fraw~-sehz*
the most popular club in town?	**la boîte la plus chaude du quartier** *lah bwaht lah plue shohd due kahr-tee-yay*
a singles bar?	**une boîte célibataire** *(unmarried)* *oon bwaht say-lee-bah-tayhr*
a piano bar?	**un piano-bar** *oon pee-yah-noh-bahr*
the most upscale bar?	**le bar le plus classieux / luxe** *luh bahr luh plue klah-syoeh / lueks*
What's the hottest bar these days?	**Quel est le bar le plus chaud maintenant?** *keh-lay luh bahr luh plue shohd meh~-t-naw~*
What's the cover charge?	**Combien est le prix d'entrée?** *koh~-bee-yeh~ ay luh pree daw~-tray*
Do they have a dress code?	**Y a-t-il une tenue de rigueur?** *yah-teel oon teh-nue duh ree-goehr*
Is that an expensive club?	**Est-ce une boîte chère?** *es oon bwaht shayhr*
What's the best time to get there?	**Quelle est la meilleure heure d'arriver?** *keh-lay lah may-yoeh-roehr dah-ree-vay*

Do You Mind If I Smoke?

Est-ce qu'on a le droit d'y fumer? *ehs-koh~ ah luh dhwah dee fue-may*	May I smoke?
Avez-vous _____, s'il vous plaît? *ah-vay-voo _____ seel voo play*	Do you have _____
une cigarette *oon see-gah-reht*	a cigarette?
du feu *due foeh*	a light?
Puis-je vous offrir du feu? *pwee-zhuh voo-zoh-freer due foeh*	May I offer you a light?

What kind of music do they play there?	**Quel type de musique y joue-t-on?** *kehl teep duh mue-zeek ee zhoo-toh~*
May I smoke here?	**Est-ce qu'on a le droit d'y fumer?** *ehs-koh~ ah luh dhwah dee fue-may*
I'm looking for _____	**Je cherche _____** *zhuh shayhrsh*
a good cigar shop.	**un bon magasin de cigares.** *uh~ boh mah-gah-zaw~ duh see-gahr*
a pack of cigarettes.	**un paquet de cigarettes.** *uh~ pah-kay duh see-gah-reht*

I'd like ____	**Je voudrais ____**
	zhuh voo-dray
a drink, please!	**à boire, s'il vous plaît!**
	ah bwahr seel voo play
a bottle of beer, please!	**une bouteille de bière, s'il vous plaît!**
	oon boo-tay duh bee-yayhr seel voo play
a beer on tap, please.	**une bière pression, s'il vous plaît.**
	oon bee-yayhr pruh-syoh~ seel voo play
a shot of ____, please.	**un verre de ____, s'il vous plaît.**
	uh~ vayhr duh ____ seel voo play

For a full list of beverages, see p96.

Make it a double, please!	**Un double verre de ____, s'il vous plaît!**
	uh~ doo-bluh vayhr duh ____ seel voo play
May I have that with ice, please?	**Avec des glaçons, s'il vous plaît?**
	ah-vek day glah-soh~ seel voo play
I'd like to buy a drink for that girl / guy over there.	**Je voudrais offrir un verre à la jeune fille / au jeune homme là-bas.**
	zhuh voo-dray oh-freer uh~ vayhr ah lah zhoehn fee / oh zhoeh-nuhm lah-bah
How much for a bottle / glass of beer?	**Combien coûte une bouteille / un verre de bière?**
	koh~-bee-yeh~ koot oon boo-tay / uh~ vayhr duh bee-yayhr
May I have a pack of cigarettes, please?	**Puis-je avoir un paquet de cigarettes, s'il vous plaît?**
	pwee-zhuh ah-vwahr uh~ pah-kay duh seeg-ah-reht, seel voo play

NIGHTLIFE

Do you have a lighter or matches?	**Avez-vous un briquet ou des allumettes?**
	ah-vay-voo uh~ bree-kay oo day-zah-lue-meht
Do you smoke?	**Vous fumez?**
	voo fue-may
Would you like a cigarette?	**Voulez-vous une cigarette?**
	voo-lay-voo-zoon see-gah-reht
May I run a tab?	**Puis-je mettre cela sur une addition?**
	pwee-zhuh meht-ruh suh-lah suehr oo-nah-dee-see-yoh~
What's the cover?	**Quel est le prix à l'entrée?**
	keh-lay luh pree ah law~-tray

ACROSS A CROWDED ROOM

You look like the most interesting person in the room.	**Tu me semble comme la personne la plus intèressante ici.**
	tueh muh saw~-bluh koh~m lah payhr-suhn lah plue-zeh~-tay-ray-saw~t ee-see
Excuse me, may I buy you a drink?	**Pardon, puis-je vous offrir un verre?**
	pahr-doh~ pwee-zhuh voo-zoh-freer uh~ vayhr

You look amazing!	**Vous avez l'air fantastique!**
	voo-zah-vay layhr faw~-tahs-teek
Would you like to dance?	**Voulez-vous danser avec moi?**
	voo-lay-voo daw~-say ah-vek mwah
Do you like to dance fast or slow?	**Aimez-vous danser le rock ou le slow?**
	ey-may-voo daw~-say luh rohk oo luh sloh
Here, give me your hand.	**Alors, donne-moi la main.**
	ah-lohr duhn-mwah lah meh~
What would you like to drink?	**Qu'est-ce que vous voulez boire?**
	kehs-kuh voo voo-lay bwahr
You're a great dancer!	**Vous dansez très bien!**
	voo daw~-say tray bee-yeh~
I don't know that dance.	**Je ne sais pas cette danse.**
	zhuh nuh say pah seht daw~s
Do you like this song?	**Vous aimez cette chanson?**
	voo-zey-may seht shaw~-soh~
You have nice eyes!	**Vous avez de beaux yeux!**
	voo-zah-vay duh bohz yoeh

For a full list of features, see p126.

May I have your phone number?	**Puis-je avoir votre numéro de téléphone?**
	pwee-zhuh ah-vwahr voh-truh nue-may-roh duh tay-lay-fohn

GETTING CLOSER

You're very attractive.

Tu es très séduisant m / très jolie f.
tueh ay tray say-dwee-zaw~ / tray
zhoh-ee

I like being with you.

Je me sens bien avec toi.
zhuh muh saw~ bee-yeh~ ah-vek
twah

I like you.

Tu me plaît beaucoup.
tueh muh play boh-koo

I want to hold you.

Je veux te serrer dans les bras.
zhuh voeh tuh suh-ray daw~ lay
brah-s

Kiss me.

Embrassez-moi.
aw~-brah-say mwah

May I give you a kiss?

Puis-je t'embrasser?
pwee-zhuh taw~-brah-say

Would you like a massage /
a back rub?

**Veux-tu un massage / que je te
masse le dos?**
voeh-tueh uh~ mah-sazh / kuh
zhuh tuh mahs luh doh

GETTING INTIMATE

Would you like to come inside?	**Veux-tu entrer?**
	voeh-tueh aw~-tray
May I come inside?	**Puis-je entrer?**
	pwee-zhuh aw~-tray
Let me help you out of that.	**Laissez-moi l'enlever pour toi.**
	leh-say mwah law~-luh-vay poohr twah
Would you help me out of this?	**Peux-tu m'aider à l'enlever?**
	poeh-tueh may-day ah law~-luh-vay
You smell so good.	**Tu sens si bon.**
	tueh saw~ see boh~
You're handsome / beautiful.	**Tu es très beau** *m* / **très belle** *f.*
	tueh ay tray boh / tray bell
May I?	**Puis-je?**
	pwee-zhuh
OK?	**Tu es d'accord?**
	tueh ay dah-kohr
Like this?	**Comme cela?**
	kohm suh-lah
How?	**Comment?**
	koh-maw~

HOLD ON A SECOND

Please, don't do that.	**S'il te plaît, arrête de faire cela.**
	seel tuh play ah-reht duh fayhr suh-lah
Stop, please.	**S'il te plaît, arrête.**
	seel tuh play ah-reht
Do you want me to stop?	**Tu veux que j'arrête?**
	tueh voeh kuh zhah-reht
Let's just be friends.	**Soyons amis, sans plus.**
	swah-yoh~-zah-mee saw~ plues

For a full list of features, see p126.
For a full list of body parts, see p196.

NIGHTLIFE

Do you have a condom?	**Est-ce que tu as un préservatif?**
	ehs-kuh tueh ah uh~ prey-zehr-
	vah-teef
Are you on birth control?	**Est-ce que tu prends la pillule?**
	ehs-kuh tueh praw~ lah peel-uel
Hold on, I have a condom here.	**Attends, laisse-moi prendre un préservatif.**
	ah-taw~ lehs-mwah praw~druh uh
	prey-zehhr-vah-teef
You don't have anything you want to tell me first, do you?	**Y a-t-il quelque chose dont tu voudrais me parler?**
	yah-teel kehl-kuh shohz doh~ tueh
	voo-dray muh pahr-lay

BACK TO IT

That's it!	**Oui, comme ça!**
	wee kohm sah
That's not it!	**Non, pas comme ça!**
	noh~ pah kohm sah
Here.	**Voici.**
	vwah-see
There.	**Voilà.**
	vwah-lah
More!	**Continue comme ça!**
	koh~-tee-nue kohm sah
Harder!	**Plus fort!**
	plue fohr
Faster!	**Plus vite!**
	plue veet
Deeper!	**Va plus loin!**
	vah plue lweh~
Slower!	**Moins vite!**
	mweh~ veet
Easier!	**Plus doucement!**
	plue doos-maw~

COOLDOWN

You're great!

Tu as été formidable!
tueh ah ay-tay fohr-mee-dah-bluh

That was great.

C'était magnifique.
seh-tay mah-nyee-feek

Would you like ____

Tu veux ____
tueh voeh

a drink?

quelque chose à boire?
kehl-kuh shohz ah bwahr

a snack?

manger quelque chose?
maw~-zhay kehl-kuh shohz

a shower?

prendre une douche?
praw~-druh oon doosh

May I stay here?

Puis-je passer la nuit ici?
pwee-zhuh pah-say lah nwee ee-see

Would you like to stay here?

Veux-tu passer la nuit ici?
voeh-tueh pah-say lah nwee ee-see

I'm sorry, I have to go now.

Je suis désolé(e), je dois m'en aller maintenant.
zhuh swee day-zoh-lay zhuh dwah maw~-nah-lay meh~-t-naw~

Where are you going?

Où vas-tu?
oo vah-tueh

I have to work early.

Je dois me lever tôt pour mon travail.
zhuh dwah muh leh-vay toh poohr moh~ trah-vie

I'm flying home in the morning.

Je prends l'avion demain matin.
zhuh praw~ lah-vee-yon duh-meh~ mah-teh~

I have an early flight.

Mon vol part très tôt.
moh~ vohl pahr tray toh

I think this was a mistake.	**Nous n'aurions pas dû.**
	noo noh-ree-yoh~ pah due
Will you make me breakfast?	**Peux-tu me préparer un petit déjeuner?**
	poeh-tueh muh pray-pah-ray uh~ puh-tee day-zhoeh-nay
Stay, I'll make you breakfast.	**Reste, je te sert de petit déjeuner.**
	rehst zhuh tuh sayhr duh puh-tee day-zhoeh-nay

IN THE CASINO

How much is this table?	**Combien sont les mises à cette table?**
	koh~-bee-yeh~ soh~ lay meez ah seht tah-bluh
Deal me in.	**Donnez-moi des cartes, s'il vous plaît.**
	doh-nay mwah day kahrt seel voo play
Put it on red!	**Sur le rouge, s'il vous plaît!**
	suehr luh roozh seel voo play
Put it on black!	**Sur le noir, s'il vous plaît!**
	suehr luh nwahr seel voo play
Let it ride!	**Je garde ma mise sur la table!**
	zhuh gahrd mah meez suehr lah tah-bluh
21!	**Vingt-et-un!**
	veh~-tay-uh~
Snake-eyes!	**Paire d'as!**
	payhr dahs
Seven.	**Sept.**
	seht

For a full list of numbers, see p7.

Damn, eleven.	**Mince, c'est le onze.** *meh~s say loh~z*
I'll pass.	**Passe.** *pahs*
Hit me!	**Donne!** *duhn*
Split.	**Le split.** *luh spleet*
Are the drinks complimentary?	**Les boissons sont-elles gratuites?** *lay bwah-soh~ soh~-tehl grah-tweet*
May I bill it to my room?	**Puis-je mettre cela sur ma note?** *pwee-zhuh meh-truh seh-lah suehr mah noht*
I'd like to cash out.	**Je voudrais faire les comptes.** *zhuh voo-dray fayhr lay koh~t*
I'll hold.	**Je reste.** *zhuh rehst*
I'll see your bet.	**Je relance ta mise.** *zhuh ruh-law~s tah meez*
I call.	**J'abandonne.** *zhah-baw~-duhn*
Full house!	**Full!** *fuehl*
Royal flush!	**Quinte flush royale!** *keh~t fluesh rwah-yahl*
Straight!	**Quinte!** *keh~t*

CHAPTER ELEVEN

HEALTH & SAFETY

This chapter covers the terms you'll need to maintain your health
and safety—including the most useful phrases for the pharmacy,
doctor's office, and police station.

AT THE PHARMACY

Would you please fill this
prescription?

**Pouvez-vous exécuter cette
ordonnance, s'il vous plaît?**
*poo-vay-voo-zehk-say-kue-tay seht
ohr-duh-naw~s seel voo play*

Do you have anything for
a cold?

**Avez-vous quelque chose contre
le rhume?**
*ah-vay-voo kehl-kuh
shohz koh~-truh luh ruem*

I have a cough.

Je tousse.
zhuh toos

I need something to help
me sleep.

**J'ai besoin de quelque chose pour
m'aider à dormir.**
*zhay buh-zweh~ duh kehl-kuh
shohz poohr may-day ah dohr-meer*

I need something to help
me relax.

**J'ai besoin de quelque chose pour
m'aider à me détendre.**
*zhay buh-zweh~ duh kehl-kuh
shohz poohr may-day ah muh day-
taw~-druh*

I want to buy ____

Je voudrais acheter ____
zhuh voo-dray ahsh-tay

condoms.

des préservatifs.
day prey-zayhr-vah-teef

an antihistimine.

de l'antihistamique.
duh law~-tee-ees-tah-meek

antibiotic cream.

de l'antibiotique.
duh law~-tee-bee-oh-teek

192

aspirin.	**de l'aspirine.**
	duh lah-spreen
nonaspirin pain reliever.	**de l'analgésique.**
	duh law~-nahl-zhay-zeek
medicine with codeine.	**du médicament avec du codéine.**
	due may-deek-maw~ ah-vehk
	due koh-deen
insect repellant.	**de l'insectifuge.**
	duh leh~-sehk-tee-fuezh
I need something for ____	**J'ai besoin de quelque chose pour**
	____
	zhay buh-zweh~ duh kehl-kuh
	shohz poohr
corns.	**le cor au pied.**
	luh kohr oh pee-yay
congestion.	**la congestion.**
	lah koh~-zhay-stee-yoh~
warts.	**la vernie.**
	lah vayhr-nee
constipation.	**la constipation.**
	lah koh~-stee-pah-see-yoh~
diarrhea.	**la diarrhée.**
	lah dee-yah-ray
indigestion.	**l'indigestion.**
	leh~-dee-zhay-stee-yoh~
nausea.	**la nausée.**
	lah noh-zay
motion sickness.	**le mal de transports.**
	luh mahl duh traw~-spohr
seasickness.	**le mal de mer.**
	luh mahl duh mayhr
acne.	**l'acné.**
	lahk-nay
I need a band-aid.	**J'ai besoin d'un pansement.**
	zhay buh-zweh~ duh~ paw~-s-maw~

AT THE DOCTOR'S OFFICE

I would like to see ____	**Je voudrais consulter ____** *zhuh voo-dray koh~-suel-tay*
a doctor.	**un médecin.** *uh~ may-duh-seh~*
a chiropractor.	**un chiropracticien.** *uh~ kee-roh-prahk-tees-yeh~*
a gynecologist.	**un gynécologue.** *uh~ zhee-nay-koh-lohg*
an eye specialist / an ear, nose, and throat (ENT) specialist.	**un oculiste / un oto-rhino-laryngologiste (ORL).** *un~-noh-kue-leest / uh~-noh-toh-ree-noh-lah-ree-goh-loh-zheest (oh-ayhr-ehl)*
a dentist.	**un dentiste.** *uh~ daw~-teest*
an optometrist.	**un optométriste.** *uh~ ohp-toh-may-treest*
a dermatologist.	**un dermatologue.** *uh~ dayhr-mah-toh-lohg*
Do I need an appointment?	**Ai-je besoin d'un rendez-vous?** *ay-zhuh buh-zweh~ duh~ raw~-day-voo*
I have an emergency.	**C'est une urgence.** *seh-toon oohr-zhaw~s*
I need an emergency prescription refill.	**J'ai besoin de faire renouveler mon ordonnance d'urgence.** *zhay buh-zweh~ duh fayhr ruh-noov-lay moh~-nohr-doh-naw~s duehr-zhaw~s*
Please call the doctor.	**Appelez un médecin, s'il vous plaît.** *ah-play uh~ may-duh-seh~ seel voo play*
I need an ambulance.	**Faites venir une ambulance.** *feht veh-neer oon aw~-bue-law~s*

SYMPTOMS

My _____ hurts.

J'ai mal au *m* **/ à la** *f* **/ aux** *pl* _____.
zhay mahl oh / ah lah / oh

My _____ is stiff.

Le *m* **/ La** *f* _____ **est raide.**
luh / lah _____ ay rehd

I think I'm having a heart attack.

Je crois que je vais faire une crise cardiaque.
zhuh kwah kuh zhuh vay fayhr oon kreez kahr-dee-yahk

I can't move.

Je ne peux pas bouger.
zhuh nuh poeh pah boo-zhay

I fell.

Je suis tombé(e).
zhuh swee toh~bay

I fainted.

J'ai perdu connaissance.
zhay payhr-due koh~nay-saw~s

I have a cut on my _____.

Je me suis coupé(e) le *m* **/ la** *f* _____.
zhuh muh swee koo-pay luh / lah

I have a headache.

J'ai mal à la tête.
zhay mahl ah lah teht

My vision is blurry.

Je vois trouble.
zhuh vwah troo-bluh

I feel dizzy.

J'ai des vertiges.
zhay day vayhr-teezh

I think I'm pregnant.

Je crois que je suis enceinte.
zhuh kwah kuh zhuh swee-zaw~sehnt

I don't think I'm pregnant.

Je ne crois pas que je suis enceinte.
zhuh nuh kwah pah kuh zhuh swee-zaw~sehnt

I'm having trouble walking.

J'ai du mal à marcher.
zhay due mahl ah mahr-shay

My back hurts.

J'ai mal au dos.
zhay mahl oh doh

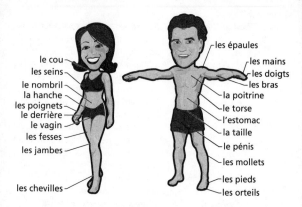

les épaules
le cou
les mains
les seins
les doigts
le nombril
les bras
la hanche
la poitrine
les poignets
le torse
le derrière
l'estomac
le vagin
la taille
les fesses
le pénis
les jambes
les mollets
les pieds
les chevilles
les orteils

I can't get up.	**Je ne peux pas me lever.**
	zhuh nuh poeh pah muh luh-vay
I was mugged.	**J'ai été attaqué(e) par des voleurs.**
	zhay ay-tay ah-tah-kay pahr day
	voh-loehr
I was raped.	**J'ai été violé(e).**
	zheh-tay vee-yoh-lay
A dog attacked me.	**J'ai été attaqué(e) par un chien.**
	zhay ay-tay ah-tahk-ay pahr uh
	shee-yeh~
A snake bit me.	**J'ai été mordu(e) par un serpent.**
	zhay ay-tay mohr-due pahr uh~
	sayhr-paw~
I can't move my ____ without pain.	**Cela fait mal lorsque je bouge le m / la f ____.**
	suh-lah fay mahl lohr-skuh zhuh
	boozh luh l lah
I think I sprained my ankle.	**Je crois que j'ai la cheville foulée.**
	zhuh kwah kuh zhay lah shuh-vee foo-lay

MEDICATIONS

I need morning-after pills.

J'ai besoin des pilules de lendemain.
zhay buh-zweh~ day peel-uel duh law~-d-meh~

I need birth control pills.

J'ai besoin des pilules contraceptives.
zhay buh-zweh~ day peel-uel koh~-trah-sehp-teev

I lost my eyeglasses and need new ones.

J'ai perdu mes lunettes et j'en ai besoin de nouvelles.
zhay payhr-due may lue-neh-tay zhaw~-nay buh-zweh~ duh noo-vehl

I lost a contact lens.

J'ai perdu une lentille de contact.
zhay payhr-due oon law~-tee duh koh~-tahkt

I need erectile dysfunction pills.

J'ai besoin des pilules d'érectile-dysfonctionnent.
zhay buh-zweh~ day peel-uel day-rukh-teel dees-foh~-k-see-yoh~-n-maw~

It's cold in here!

Il fait froid ici!
eel fay fwah ee-see

I am allergic to _____

Je suis allergique _____
zhuh swee-zah-layhr-zheek

  penicillin.

  à la pénicilline.
  ah lah pay-nee-see-leen

  antibiotics.

  aux antibiotiques.
  oh-zaw~-tee-bee-yoh-teek

  sulfa drugs.

  aux sulfamides.
  oh suel-fah-meed

  steroids.

  aux stéroïdes.
  oh stay-roh-eed

I have asthma.

Je suis asthmatique.
zhuh swee-zahst-mah-teek

DENTAL PROBLEMS

I have a sore tooth.

J'ai mal à une dent.
zhay mahl ah oon daw~

I chipped a tooth.

J'ai une dent d'ébréchée.
zhay oon daw~ day-bray-shay

My bridge came loose.

Mon bridge s'est défait.
moh~ breedzh say day-fay

I lost a crown.

J'ai perdu une couronne.
zhay payhr-due oon koo-rohn

I lost a denture plate.

J'ai perdu une plaque de prothèse.
zhay payhr-due oon plak duh proh-tehz

DEALING WITH POLICE

I'm sorry, did I do something wrong?

Pardon, j'ai fait quelque chose de mal?
pahr-doh~ zhay fay kehl-kuh shohz duh mahl

I am _____

Je suis _____
zhuh swee

American.

américain m / américaine f.
ah-may-ree-kah / ah-may-ree-kehn

Canadian.

canadien m / canadienne f.
kah-nah-dee-eh~ / kah-nah-dee-ehn

Irish.

irlandais m / irlandaise f.
eer-law~-day / eer-law~-dehz

English.

anglais m / anglaise f.
aw~-glay / aw~-glehz

Australian.

australien m / australienne f.
oh-strah-lee-eh~ / oh-strah-lee-ehn

New Zealander.

néo-zélandais m / néozélandaise f.
nay-oh-zay-law~dey / nay-oh-zay-law~-dehz

For more languages and nationalities, see the English / French dictionary.

Listen Up: Police Lingo

Permis de conduire et carte grise, s'il vous plaît. *payhr-mee duh koh~-dweer ay kahrt greez seel voo play*	Your license, registration, and insurance, please.
L'amende est de ___ euros, et vous pouvez me la régler directement. *lah-maw~d ay duh ___ oehr-oh ay voo poo-vay muh lah reh-glay dee-rehkt-maw~*	The fine is ___, and you can pay me directly.
Votre passeport, s'il vous plaît? *voh-truh pahs-pohr seel voo play*	Your passport please?
Où allez-vous? *oo ah-lay-voo*	Where are you going?
Pourquoi êtes-vous si pressé(e)? *poohr-kwah eht-voo see prehs-say*	Why are you in such a hurry?

The car is a rental.	**C'est une voiture de location.** *seh-toon vwah-tuehr duh loh-kah-see-yoh~*
Am I supposed to pay the fine to you?	**Dois-je vous régler directement l'amende?** *dwah-zhuh voo reh-glay dee-rehkt-maw~ lah-maw~d*
Do I have to go to court? When?	**Dois-je passer en justice? Quand?** *dwah-zhuh pah-say aw~ zhue-stees; kaw~*

I'm sorry, my French isn't very good.	**Je suis désolé(e), je ne parle pas bien le français.**
	zhuh swee day-zoh-lay zhuh nuh pahrl pah bee-yeh~ luh fraw~-say
I need an interpreter.	**J'ai besoin d'un interprète.**
	zhay buh-zweh~ duh~-neh~-tayhr-preht
I'm sorry, I don't understand the ticket.	**Désolé(e), je ne comprends pas pourquoi vous voulez me donner une amende.**
	day-zoh-lay zhuh nuh koh~-praw~pah poohr-kwah voo voo-lay muh duh-nay oon ah-maw~d
May we call the embassy?	**Pouvons-nous appeler l'ambassade de notre pays?**
	poo-voh~-noo-zah-play law~-bah-sahd duh noh-truh pay-ee
I was robbed.	**J'ai été victime d'un vol.**
	zhay ay-tay veek-teem duh~ vohl
I was mugged.	**J'ai été attaqué(e).**
	zhay ay-tay ah-tah-kay
I was raped.	**J'ai été violé(e).**
	zhay ay-tay vee-yoh-lay
May I make a report?	**Puis-je faire une déclaration?**
	pwee-zhuh fayhr oon day-klah-rah-see-yoh~
Somebody broke into my room.	**Quelqu'un s'est introduit dans ma chambre.**
	kehl-kuh~ say-teh~-tro-dwee daw~ mah shaw~-bruh
Someone stole my purse / wallet.	**Quelqu'un m'a volé mon sac à main / portefeuille.**
	kehl-kuh~ mah voh-lay moh~ sahk ah meh~ / pohrt-foeh-yuh

DICTIONARY KEY

n	noun	m	masculine
v	verb	f	feminine
adj	adjective	s	singular
prep	preposition	pl	plural
adv	adverb	interj	interjection

All verbs are listed in infinitive (to + verb) form, cross-referenced to the appropriate conjugations page. Adjectives are listed first in masculine form, followed by the feminine ending.

For food terms, see the Menu Reader (p98) and the Grocery section (p105) in Chapter 4, Dining.

ENGLISH—FRENCH

A

able, to be able to (can) *v pouvoir* **p34**

above *adv au-dessus de* p86

accept, to accept *v accepter* **p24**

Do you accept credit cards? *Acceptez-vous les cartes de crédit?*

accident *n l'accident m*

I've had an accident. *J'ai eu un accident.* **p64**

account *n le compte m* **p142**

I'd like to transfer to / from my checking / savings account. *Je désire transférer des fonds sur / de mon compte courant / épargne.*

acne *n l'acné f* **p193**

across *prep en face de / de l'autre côté de* **p5**

across the street *de l'autre côté de la rue* **p6**

actual *adj réel / réelle*

adapter plug *n l'adaptateur m* **p163**

address *n l'adresse f*

What's the address? *Quelle est l'adresse?*

admission fee *n le prix d'entrée*

in advance *adv à l'avance*

African American *n adj afro-américain(e)*

afternoon *n l'après-midi m*

in the afternoon *durant l'après-midi*

age *n l'âge m* **p124**

What's your age? *Quel âge avez-vous?*

agency *n l'agence f* **p58**

car rental agency *l'agence de location de voitures*

agnostic *n adj agnostique*

air conditioning *n la climatisation f* **p76**

Would you lower / raise the air conditioning? *Pouvez-vous baisser / monter la climatisation?*

airport n l'aéroport m p44
  I need a ride to the airport.
  Je désire aller à l'aéroport.
  **How much does the trip to
  the airport cost?** *Combien
  coûte le trajet jusqu'à
  l'aéroport?*
airsickness bag n le sac vomitoire m p56
aisle (in store) n le rayon m
  Which aisle is it in? *Dans
  quel rayon cela se trouve-
  t-il?* p106
alcohol n l'alcool m p96
  Do you serve alcohol?
  Vendez-vous de l'alcool?
  I'd like nonalcoholic beer. *Je
  voudrais une bière sans
  alcool.*
all n tout m
  all of the time tout le temps
all adj tout(e) / tous pl p11
allergic adj allergique p197
  I'm allergic to ____. *Je suis
  allergique à ____.* See p197
  for common allergens.
altitude n l'altitude f
aluminum n l'aluminium m
ambulance n l'ambulance f
American n adj américain(e)
amount n le montant m
angry adj fâché(e) p128
animal n l'animal m
another adj autre
answer n la réponse f
answer, to answer v répondre (à) p25

Answer me, please.
  *Répondez-moi, s'il vous
  plaît!*
antibiotic n l'antibiotique m
  I need an antibiotic. *J'ai
  besoin d'un antibiotique.*
antihistamine n l'antihistaminique m p192
anxious adj impatient(e)
any adj n'importe lequelle m
  / laquelle f
anything n n'importe quoi
anywhere adv n'importe où
April n l'avril m p14
appointment n le rendez-
  vous m p130
  Do I need an appointment?
  *Est-ce que j'ai besoin d'un
  rendez-vous?*
are v See être (to be) p27.
Argentinian n adj argentin(e)
arm n le bras m p196
arrive, to arrive v arriver p24
arrival(s) n l'arrivée f / les
  arrivées f pl p44
art n l'art m
  exhibit of art l'exposition
  d'art
  art museum le musée d'art
artist n l'artiste m f
Asian n adj asiatique
ask, to ask v demander p24
  (request) / poser **(ask)** p24
  to ask for a drink demander
  une boisson
  to ask a question poser une
  question

aspirin n l'aspirine f p193

assist, to assist v aider **p24**

assistance n l'assistance f

asthma n l'asthme m p197

I have asthma. Je fais de l'asthme.

atheist adj athée

ATM n le distributeur automatique de billets (DAB) m / la billetterie automatique f

I'm looking for an ATM. Je cherche un distributeur automatique de billets.

attend, to attend v participer (à) / assister (à) **p24**

audio adj audio p73

August n le août m p15

aunt n la tante f p123

Australia n l'Australie f

Australian n adj australien m / australienne f

autumn n l'automne m p15

available adj disponible

B

baby n le bébé m

baby adj pour bébés

Do you sell baby food? Vendez-vous des aliments pour bébés?

babysitter n le / la baby-sitter f

Do you have babysitters who speak English? Avez-vous des baby-sitters qui parlent anglais?

baby stroller n la poussette f

back n le dos m p196

My back hurts. J'ai mal au dos.

back rub n le massage dorsal m

backed up (toilet) adj bouchées f pl

The toilet is backed up. Les toilettes sont bouchées.

bag n le sac m

airsickness bag le sac vomitoire p56

My bag was stolen. On a volé mon sac.

I lost my bag. J'ai perdu mon sac.

bag, to bag v emballer **p24**

baggage n le bagage m

baggage adj des bagages m pl

baggage claim la récupération des bagages p56

bait n l'appât m p174

balance (bank account) n le solde m p142

balance, to balance v se balancer **p24, 38**

balcony n le balcon m p77

ball (sport) n le ballon m / la balle f

ballroom dancing n la danse de salon f

band (musical ensemble) n le groupe m

band-aid n le pansement (adhésif) m p193

bank *n* la banque *f* p140

Can you help me find a bank? *Pouvez-vous m'indiquer une banque?*

bar *n* le bar *m* p90

barber *n* le coiffeur *m* p164

bass (instrument) *n* la basse *f*

bath *n* le bain *m*

bathe, to bathe *v* (se) baigner p24, 38

bathroom (restroom) *n* les toilettes *f pl* / les WC *m pl*

Where is the nearest public bathroom? *Où sont les toilettes publiques les plus proches?*

bathtub *n* la baignoire *f*

battery *n* la pile (for flashlight) *f* / la batterie (for car) *f*

be, to be *v* être p27

beach *n* la plage *f* p177

beard *n* la barbe *m* p165

beautiful *adj* beau *m* / belle *f*

bed *n* le lit *m* p75

pull-out bed *le canapé-lit*

bed-and-breakfast (B & B) *la chambre d'hôte* / *le bed-and-breakfast* p74

bee *n* l'abeille *f*

I was stung by a bee. *J'ai été piqué(e) par une abeille.*

beer *n* la bière *f* p96

draft beer *la bière pression*

begin, to begin *v* commencer (à) p24

behave, to behave *v* se tenir p24, 38

behind *prep* derrière p5

beige *adj* beige

Belgian *n adj* belge

Belgium *n* la Belgique *f*

below *prep* en dessous de

belt *n* la ceinture (clothing) *f*

bet, to bet *v* miser / parier (sur) p24

best *adj* le / la meilleur(e)

best *adv* le mieux *pl*

better *adv* mieux

big *adj* grand(e) p12

bilingual *adj* bilingue

bill *n* le billet (currency) *m* / la note / la facture (tab) *f*

bill, to bill *v* facturer p24

biography *n* la biographie *f*

biracial *adj* biracial(e)

bird *n* l'oiseau *m*

birth control (pill) *n* la pillule *f*

I need more birth control pills. *J'ai besoin d'une ordonnance pour la pillule.* p197

bit (small amount) *n* un peu *m*

black *adj* noir(e)

blanket *n* la couverture *f* p55

bleach *n* l'eau de Javel *f*

blind (visually impaired) *adj* aveugle / malvoyant(e)

block, to block *v* bloquer p24

blond(e) *adj* blond(e)

blouse *n* le chemisier *m*

blue *adj* bleu(e)

blurred vision *n* la vision trouble *f*

board (transportation) n le bord m
on board à bord
board, to board v embarquer p24
boarding pass n la carte d'embarquement f p54
boat n le bateau m p70
bomb n la bombe f
book n le livre m p162
bookstore n la librairie f p162
boss n le / la patron(e) m f
bottle n la bouteille f / le biberon (baby) m

May I heat this bottle someplace? Puis-je réchauffer ce biberon quelque part?

box (seat) n la loge m
box office n le guichet m
boy n le garçon m
boyfriend n le petit ami m
braid n la tresse f p164
braille, American n le braille américain m
brake, to brake v freiner p24
brandy n l'eau-de-vie f / le cognac m p97
bread n le pain m
break n la cassure f
break, to break v (se) casser p24, 38
breakfast n le petit déjeuner m

What time is breakfast? À quelle heure est le petit déjeuner? p81

bridge n le pont (across a river) m / le bridge (dental structure) m
briefcase n la serviette f p57
bright adj lumineux m / lumineuse f
broadband n adj (à) large bande f
bronze (color) adj mordoré
brother n le frère m p120
brown adj marron
brunette n le / la brun(e) m f
Buddhist n adj bouddhiste
budget n le budget m
buffet n le buffet m p89
bug n l'insecte m p85
burn, to burn v brûler (fire) / graver (disk) p24

Can I burn a CD here? Puis-je graver un CD ici?

bus n le car (school bus, motorcoach) m / l'autobus (city bus) m / la navette (shuttle bus) f p68

Where is the bus stop? Où se trouve l'arrêt d'autobus? p68
Which bus goes to ____? Quel autobus va à ____?

business n l'entreprise (a business) f / les affaires (in general) f pl

Here's my business card. Voici ma carte de visite.

business center le centre d'affaires

busy adj plein (restaurant) m
/ occupée (phone line) f
but conjunction mais
butter n le beurre m
buy, to buy v acheter **p24**

C

café n le café m
  Internet café le cybercafé
call, to call v (s')appeler **p24, 39**
camp, to camp, to go camping v camper **p24**
  Do we need a camping permit? Avons-nous besoin d'une autorisation de camper? **p87**
camper (motor home) n le camping-car m
campsite n le terrain de camping m **p87**
can n la boîte de conserve f
can (to be able to) v pouvoir **p34**
Canada n le Canada m
Canadian n adj canadien / canadienne
cancel, to cancel v annuler **p24**
  My flight was canceled. Mon vol a été annulé.
canvas n la toile f **p57**
cappuccino n le cappucino m
car n la voiture f **p58**
  car rental agency l'agence de location de voitures
  I need to rent a car. Je voudrais louer une voiture.

card n la carte f **p140**
  Do you accept credit cards? Acceptez-vous les cartes de crédit?
  May I have your business card? Puis-je avoir votre carte de visite?
car seat (child's safety seat) n le siège auto m **p59**
  Do you rent car seats for children? Louez-vous des sièges auto pour enfants?
car sickness n le mal des transports m
cash n les espèces f **p140**
  cash only espèces uniquement
cash, to cash v encaisser **p24**
  to cash out (gambling) v toucher les gains **p24**
cashmere n le cachemire m
casino n le casino m **p190**
cat n le / la chat(e) m f
Catholic adj catholique
cavity (tooth) n la carie f
  I think I have a cavity. Je pense que j'ai une carie.
CD n le CD m
CD player n le lecteur de CD m
celebrate, to celebrate v fêter **p24**
cell phone n le téléphone portable m
centimeter n le centimètre m
chamber music n la musique de chambre f

change (money) n la mon-
naie f p139

I'd like change, please. Je
voudrais de la monnaie,
s'il vous plaît.

**This isn't the correct
change.** Ce n'est pas la
monnaie exacte. See p7
for numbers.

change, to change v changer
(de) / langer (a baby diaper) p24

changing room n la cabine
d'essayage f

charge, to charge v mettre
(money) p25 / recharger
(battery) p24

charmed adj enchanté(e)

charred (meat) adj très cuite
(viande) p93

charter, to charter (transportation) v affréter p24

cheap adj pas cher / pas
chère p59

check n le chèque (money) m
/ l'addition (tab) f

**Do you accept travelers'
checks?** Acceptez-vous les
chèques de voyage?

Check, please! L'addition,
s'il vous plaît! p98

check, to check v vérifier p24

checked (pattern) adj à car-
reaux m

check-in n l'enregistrement
m p44

What time is check-in? À
quelle heure est l'enreg-
istrement?

check-out n la libération de
la chambre f

What time is check-out? À
quelle heure doit-on
libérer la chambre?

check out, to check out (of
hotel) v libérer la chambre
p24

cheese n le fromage m p107

chicken n le poulet (meat) m

child n l'enfant m f

children n les enfants m f

Are children allowed? Les
enfants sont-ils acceptés?

**Do you have children's pro-
grams?** Avez-vous des
spectacles pour enfants?

**Do you have a children's
menu?** Avez-vous un menu
pour enfants? p93

China n la Chine f

Chinese n adj chinois(e)

chiropractor n le chiropracticien m / la chiropracticienne f p194

Christian adj chrétien m /
chrétienne f

church n l'église f p133

cigar n le cigare m

cigarette n la cigarette f

pack of cigarettes le paquet
de cigarettes

cinema n le cinéma m p151

city n la ville f

claim n la réclamation f

  I'd like to file a claim. Je voudrais faire une réclamation.

clarinet n la clarinette f

class n la classe f p49

  business class la classe affaires

  economy class la classe économique

  first class la première classe

classical (music) adj de musique classique f

clean adj propre

clean, to clean v nettoyer p24

  Please clean the room today. Veuillez nettoyer la chambre aujourd'hui.

clear, to clear v enlever p24

clear adj clair(e)

climbing n l'escalade f / la varappe (rock climbing) f

climb, to climb v escalader (mountain) p24 / monter (stairs) p24

close, to close v fermer p24

close (near) adj près de, proche de

closed adj fermé(e)

cloudy adj couvert(e) p131

clover n le trèfle m

go clubbing, to go clubbing v sortir en boîte p36

coat n le manteau m

coffee n le café (espresso) m

  iced coffee le café glacé

cognac n le cognac m p97

coin n la pièce f p139

cold n le rhume m p192

  I have a cold. J'ai un rhume.

cold adj froid(e)

  I'm cold. J'ai froid.

collect adj en PCV

  I'd like to place a collect call. Je voudrais faire un appel en PCV.

collect, to collect v ramasser / collectionner p24

college n l'université f

color n la couleur f

color, to color v colorer p24

come, to come v venir p36

computer n l'ordinateur m

concert n le concert m p137

condition n l'état m

  in good / bad condition en bon / mauvais état

condom n le préservatif m

  Do you have a condom? As-tu un préservatif sur toi?

  not without a condom pas sans préservatif

confirm, to confirm v confirmer p24

  I'd like to confirm my reservation. Je voudrais confirmer ma réservation. p50

confused adj confus(e) p128

congestion n la congestion (respiratory) f / l'embouteillage (traffic) m

connection speed n la vitesse de connexion f p147

constipated adj constipé(e)

I'm constipated. Je suis constipé(e). p193

contact lens n la lentille de contact f p197

continue, to continue v continuer p24

convertible (car) n la voiture décapotable f / le cabriolet m

cook, to cook v cuisiner p24

I'd like a room where I can cook. Je voudrais une chambre où il est possible de cuisiner.

cookie n le petit gâteau m

copper adj cuivre (color)

cork n le bouchon m

corkscrew n le tire-bouchon m

corner n le coin m

on the corner au coin p5

correct, to correct v corriger p24

correct adj bon m / bonne f

Am I on the correct train? Suis-je dans le bon train?

cost, to cost v coûter p24

How much does it cost? Combien est-ce que cela coûte?

costume n le déguisement m

cotton n le coton m

cough n la toux f p192

cough, to cough v tousser p24

counter (in bar) n le comptoir m

country-and-western n la country f

country-and-western adj country

court n la justice (legal) f / le court (sports) m

courteous adj courtois(e)

cousin n le / la cousin(e) m f

cover charge (in bar) n l'entrée f p184

cow n la vache f

crack (in glass object) n la fissure f

craftsperson n l'artisan(e) m f

cream n la crème f

credit card n la carte de crédit f p139

Do you accept credit cards? Acceptez-vous les cartes de crédit?

crib n le lit d'enfant m p77

crown (dental) n la couronne f

curb n la bordure de trottoir f

curl n la boucle f

curly adj bouclé(e)

currency exchange n le change m p140

Where is the nearest currency exchange? Où se trouve le bureau de change le plus proche?

current (water) n l'eau courante f

customs n la douane f p52

cut (wound) n la coupure f / l'entaille f

I have a bad cut. Je me suis fait une vilaine entaille.

cut, to cut v couper p24

cybercafé n le cybercafé m

Where can I find a cyber-café? Où puis-je trouver un cybercafé?

D

damaged adj abîmé(e)

Damn! expletive Mince!

dance, to dance v danser p24

danger n le danger m

dark n le noir m

dark adj sombre

daughter n la fille f p120

dawn n l'aube f p13

at dawn à l'aube

day n le jour m

the day before yesterday avant-hier

these last few days ces derniers jours

deaf adj sourd(e) / malenten-dant(e) (hearing-impaired)

deal (issue) n l'affaire f

deal, to deal (cards) v donner p24

Deal me in. Tu peux compter sur moi! p190

December n le décembre m

declined adj rejeté(e)

Was my credit card declined? Ma carte de crédit a-t-elle été rejetée?

declare, to declare v déclarer p24

I have nothing to declare. Je n'ai rien à déclarer. p52

deep adj profond(e)

delay n le retard m p51

How long is the delay? De combien est le retard?

delighted adj ravi(e) p107

democracy n la démocratie f

dent, to dent v cabosser p24

He / She dented the car. Il / Elle a cabossé la voiture.

dentist n le / la dentiste m f

denture n la prothèse den-taire f p198

denture plate la plaque de prothèse dentaire

departure(s) n les départs m pl

designer n le / la styliste m f

dessert n le dessert m p102

dessert menu la carte des desserts

destination n la destination f

diabetic adj diabétique

dial, to dial (phone number) v composer p24

to dial direct composer directement le numéro

diaper n la couche f

Where can I change a dia-per? Où puis-je langer mon enfant?

diarrhea n la diarrhée f p193

dictionary n le dictionnaire m

different (other) adj dif-férent(e)

difficult adj difficile

dinner n le dîner m

directory assistance (phone) n les renseignements m pl

disability n le handicap m

disappear, to disappear v *disparaître* **p25**

disco n *la disco* f

disconnected adj *discon coupé(e)*

Operator, I was disconnected. *Opératrice, j'ai été coupé(e).*

discount n *la réduction* **(store)** f / *le tarif reduit* **(ticket)** m

Do I qualify for a ___ discount? *Ai-je droit à une réduction pour ___?*

children's *enfants*

senior *personnes âgées*

student *étudiants*

dish (meal) n *le plat* m

dive, to dive v *plonger* **p24**

scuba diving *la plongée sous-marine* **p175**

divorced adj *divorcé(e)* **p123**

dizzy (to be) adj *avoir des vertiges* **p195**

do, to do v *faire* **p33**

doctor n *le médecin* m f **p194**

doctor's office n *le cabinet du médecin* m

dog n *le chien* m / *la chienne* f

guide dog *le chien guide* **p73**

door n *la porte* f

double adj *à deux / double*

double bed *lit à deux*

to have double vision *voir double*

down adj *déprimé(e)*

download, to download v *télécharger* **p24**

downtown n *le centre-ville* m

dozen n *la douzaine* f **p11**

drain n *le tuyau d'évacuation* m

drama n *le drame* m

drawing n *le dessin* m

dress (garment) n *la robe* f

dress code n *la tenue de rigueur* f / *le code vestimentaire* m

What's the dress code? *Quel est le code vestimentaire?*

dress, to dress v *s'habiller* **p24, 39**

dressing (salad) n *la sauce* f

dried adj *séché(e)*

drink n *la boisson* f **p96**

I'd like a drink. *Je voudrais quelque chose à boire.*

drink, to drink v *boire* **p31**

drip, to drip v *fuire* **p25**

drive, to drive v *conduire* **p25**

driver n *le conducteur* m / *la conductrice* f

driving range n *le terrain d'exercice* m

drum n *la batterie* f / *le tambour* m

dry adj *sec* m / *sèche* f

This towel isn't dry. *Cette serviette n'est pas sèche.*

dry, to dry v *sécher* **p24**

I need to dry my clothes. *J'ai besoin de sécher mes vêtements.*

dry cleaner n *le pressing* m

dry cleaning n *le nettoyage à sec* m **p82**

duck n le canard m
duty-free adj hors-taxe
duty-free shop n la boutique hors-taxe f p45
DVD n le DVD m p59
  Do the rooms have DVD players? Les chambres ont-elles des lecteurs de DVD?
  Where can I rent DVDs or videos? Où puis-je louer des DVD ou des cassettes vidéo?

E

early adv tôt p13
  It's early. Il est tôt.
eat, to eat v manger / déjeuner (lunch) / dîner p24
to eat out sortir dîner
economy n l'économie f p58
editor n le rédacteur m / la rédactrice f p129
educator n l'éducateur m / l'éducatrice f p129
eight adj huit p7
eighteen adj dix-huit p7
eighth adj huitième m p7
eighty adj quatre-vingt p7
election n l'élection f
electrical hookup n le raccordement m p87
elevator n l'ascenseur m p65
eleven adj onze p7
e-mail n le courriel m
  May I have your e-mail address? Puis-je avoir votre adresse courriel?

e-mail message le message courriel
e-mail, to send e-mail v envoyer un courriel p24
embarrassed adj embarrassé(e)
embassy n l'ambassade f
emergency n l'urgence f
  emergency brake n le frein à main m
  emergency exit n la sortie de secours f p49
employee n l'employé(e) m f
employer n l'employeur m / l'employeuse f
engine n le moteur m p62
engineer n l'ingénieur m f
England n l'Angleterre f
English n adj anglais(e)
  Do you speak English? Parlez-vous anglais?
enjoy, to enjoy v aimer p24
enter, to enter v entrer p24
enthusiastic adj enthousiaste
entrance, entry n l'entrée f
  Do not enter. Entrée interdite.
environment n l'environnement m
escalator n l'escalier roulant m
espresso n le café m
exchange rate n le taux de change m p140
  What is the exchange rate for U.S. / Canadian dollars? Quel est le taux de change du dollar américain / canadien?

excuse, to excuse (pardon) v excuser / pardonner **p24**

> **Excuse me.** Excusez-moi.

exhausted adj épuisé(e)

exhibit n l'exposition f

exit n la sortie f

exit, to exit v sortir **p36**

> **not an exit** ne pas sortir par cette issue

expensive adj cher m / chère f

explain, to explain v expliquer **p24**

express adj express

> **express check-in** l'enregistrement express **p48**

extra (additional) adj supplémentaire

extra-large adj très grand(e)

eye n l'œil m / les yeux m pl

eyebrow n le sourcil m **p126**

eyeglasses n les lunettes f pl

eyelash n le cil m **p126**

F

fabric n le tissu m / la matière f

face n le visage f **p126**

faint, to faint v perdre connaissance **p25**

fall (season) n l'automne m

fall, to fall v (se) tomber **p24, 38**

family n la famille f **p120**

fan n le ventilateur m **p85**

far adv loin **p5**

> **How far is it to _____?**
> Combien y a-t-il jusqu'à _____?

fare n le prix m

fast adj adv rapide / vite

fat adj gros m / grosse f **p12**

father n le père m **p120**

faucet n le lavabo m **(bathroom)** / l'évier m **(kitchen)**

fault n / **at fault** adj la faute f / fautif m / fautive f

> **I'm at fault.** C'est moi le fautif / la fautive. **p64**
> **It was his / her fault.** C'est sa faute.

fax n la télécopie m **p130**

February n le février m **p14**

fee n le prix m

female adj féminin(e)

fiancé(e) n le / la fiancé(e) m f

fifteen adj quinze **p7**

fifth adj cinquième **p7**

fifty adj cinquante **p7**

find, to find v trouver **p24**

fine (for traffic violation) n l'amende f **p64**

fine adv bien

> **I'm fine.** Je vais bien. **p1**

Fire! Au feu!

first adj premier m / première f

fishing pole n la canne à pêche f **p175**

fitness center n le club de remise en forme f **p167**

fit, to fit (clothes) v aller **p30**

> **This doesn't fit.** Cela ne va pas.
> **Does this look like it fits?** Est-ce que ça a l'air d'aller?

fitting room n la cabine d'essayage f

five *adj cinq* p7

flight *n le vol m* p46

Where do domestic flights arrive / depart? *Où se trouve la zone d'arrivée / de départ des lignes intérieures?*

Where do international flights arrive / depart? *Où se trouve la zone d'arrivée / de départ des vols internationaux?*

What time does this flight leave? *À quelle heure part ce vol?*

flight attendant *le steward m / l'hôtesse de l'air f*

floor (level) *n l'étage m*

ground floor *le rez-de-chaussée*

first floor *le premier étage*

flower *n la fleur f*

flush (gambling) *n le flush m*

flush, to flush *v tirer la chasse d'eau* p24

This toilet won't flush. *La chasse d'eau de ces toilettes ne marche pas.*

flute *n la flûte f*

food *n la nourriture f / les aliments m pl*

foot *n le pied m* p196

forehead *n le front m* p126

format *n le format m*

formula *n la préparation lactée (baby) f / la formule (math) f*

Do you sell infants' formula? *Est-ce que vous vendez des préparations lactées pour nourrisson?*

forty *adj quarante* p7

forward *adv en avant*

four *adj quatre* p7

fourteen *adj quatorze* p7

fourth *n le quart m / la quatrième f* p9

one-fourth *un quart*

fragile *adj fragile*

freckle *n la tache de rousseur f*

free *adj gratuit(e) (complimentary) / libre (having freedom) / disponible (available, open)*

French *n adj français(e)*

fresh *adj frais m / fraîche f*

Friday *n le vendredi m* p14

friend *n l'ami(e) m f* p120

front *adv de devant*

front desk *n la reception f*

front door *n la porte d'entrée f*

fruit *n le fruit m* p113

fruit juice *n le jus de fruit m*

full *adj / to be full (after a meal) v ne plus avoir faim*

Full house! *Complet!* p191

fuse *n la bougie (car) f / le fusible (home) m*

G

gallon *n le gallon m*

garlic *n l'ail m* p115

ENGLISH–FRENCH

gasoline n l'essence f p160

gas gauge la jauge d'essence p62

I'm out of gas. Je suis en panne d'essence.

gate (at airport) n la porte f

German n adj allemand(e)

gift n le cadeau m

gin n le gin m p97

girl n la fille f

girlfriend n la petite amie f

give, to give v donner p24

glass n le verre m

Do you have it by the glass? Est-ce qu'il est possible de le commander au verre?

I'd like a glass, please. Je voudrais un verre, s'il vous plaît.

glasses (spectacles) n les lunettes f pl p159

I need new glasses. J'ai besoin de nouvelles lunettes.

glove n le gant m

go, to go v aller p30

goal (sport) n le but m

goalie n le gardien de but m

goat n la chèvre f

gold n l'or (metal)

golden adj doré (color)

golf n le golf m p178

golf, to golf v jouer au golf p24

good adj bon m / bonne f

goodbye n au revoir

goose n l'oie m

grade school n l'école primaire f

gram n le gramme m

grandfather n le grand-père m

grandmother n la grand-mère f p123

grandparents n les grands-parents m pl p123

grape n le raisin m

gray adj gris(e)

Great! adj Super!

Greek n adj grec m / grecque f

green (golf) n le vert m

green (color) adj vert(e)

groceries n les provisions f pl

group n le groupe m

grow, to grow (get larger) v grandir p24

Where did you grow up? Où avez-vous grandi?

guard n le garde m / l'agent m

security guard l'agent de sécurité p44

guest n l'hôte m / l'hôtesse f

guide (tour) n le / la guide m f

guide (publication) n le guide m

guide, to guide v guider p24

guided tour n l'excursion guidée f p155

guitar n la guitare f

gym n la gymnastique f p167

gynecologist n le / la gynécologue m f p194

H

hair *n le cheveu m / les cheveux m pl*

haircut *n la coupe f* p164

  I need a haircut. *J'ai besoin d'une coupe.*

  How much is a haircut? *Combien coûte une coupe?*

hairdresser *n le coiffeur m / la coiffeuse f* p164

hair dryer *n le séchoir m* p87

half *n la moitié n*

half *adj demi(e)*

  one half *une moitié*

hallway *n le couloir* (**building**) *m / l'entrée* (**house**) */ le hall d'entrée m*

hand *n la main f*

handicapped-accessible *adj accessible aux personnes à mobilité réduite* p73

handle, to handle *v manipuler* p24

handsome *adj beau m / belle f*

hangout (hot spot) *n lieu de rencontre m*

hang out, to hang out (to relax) *v traîner / passer du temps* p24

hang up (end a phone call) *v raccrocher* p24

happy *adj heureux m / heureuse f* p128

hard *adj dur(e)*

hat *n le chapeau m* p159

have, to have *v avoir* p25

hazel *adj noisette*

headache *n le mal de tête m*

headlight *n le feu (avant) m*

headphones *n le casque m s*

hear, to hear *v entendre* p25

hearing-impaired *adj malentendant(e)* p73

heart *n le cœur m*

heart attack *n la crise cardiaque f*

hectare *n l'hectare m* p10

hello *n bonjour / salut* (**informal**) */ allô* (**telephone**)

Help! *Au secours!*

help, to help *v aider* p24

hen *n la poule f*

her *adj sa f / son m / ses m f pl*

herb *n l'herbe f* p109

here *adv ici* p5

high *adj haut(e)*

highlights (hair) *n les mèches f pl* p165

highway *n l'autoroute f*

hike, to hike *v faire de la marche* p33

him *pron lui*

Hindu *n adj hindou(e) adj*

hip-hop *n le hip-hop m*

his *adj son m / sa f / ses m f pl*

historical *adj historique*

history *n l'histoire f*

hobby *n le passe-temps m*

hold, to hold *v tenir* (**something**) p24 */ attendre* (**pause**) p25 */ rester en ligne* (**on telephone**) p24 */ conserver* (**gambling**) p24

to hold hands *se tenir par la main*

Would you hold this for me? *Pouvez-vous tenir cela pour moi?*

Hold on a minute! *Attendez une minute!*

I'll hold. *Je reste en ligne.*

holiday *n les vacances f pl*

home *n le domicile m*

homemaker *n l'homme m / la femme f au foyer* p129

horn (automobile) *n le klaxon m*

horse *n le cheval m*

hostel *n l'auberge f* p74

hot *adj chaud(e)*

hot chocolate *n le chocolat chaud m* p97

hotel *n l'hôtel m* p74

Do you have a list of local hotels? *Avez-vous une liste des hôtels de la région?*

hour *n l'heure f* p12

hours (at museum) *n les heures d'ouverture f pl*

how *adv comment (manner) / combien (amount)* p3

humid *adj humide* p132

hundred *n adj cent* p8

hurry, to hurry *v être pressé(e)* p27 / *se dépêcher* p24, 38

I'm in a hurry. *Je me suis pressé(e).* p65

Hurry, please! *Dépêchez-vous, s'il vous plaît!*

hurt, to hurt *v avoir mal* p25 / *faire mal* p33

Ouch! That hurts! *Aïe! Ça fait mal!*

My head hurts. *J'ai mal à la tête.*

husband *n le mari m* p122

I

I *pron je* p22

ice *n la glace f / le glaçon m (ice cube)*

with ice cubes *avec des glaçons*

identification *n la pièce d'identité f*

inch *n le pouce m*

include, to include *v comprendre* p25

Is breakfast included? *Le petit-déjeuner est-il compris?*

India *n l'Inde f*

Indian *n adj indien m / indienne f*

indigestion *n l'indigestion f*

inexpensive *adj pas cher m / pas chère f*

infant *n le petit enfant m*

Are infants allowed? *Les enfants en bas âge sont-ils acceptés?*

information *n l'information f / les renseignements m pl*

information booth *n le stand d'information*

injury *n la blessure f*

insect repellent *n* l'insectifuge *m*

inside *prep* dans *l* à l'intérieur de

insult, to insult *v* insulter **p24**

insurance *n* l'assurance *f*

intercourse (sexual) *n* les rapports sexuels *m pl*

interest rate *n* le taux d'intérêt *m* **p141**

intermission *n* l'entracte *m*

Internet *n* l'Internet *m* **p145**

high-speed Internet
l'Internet à haut débit
**Do you have Internet
access?** Offrez-vous un
accès à Internet?
**Where can I find an
Internet café?** Où puis-je
trouver un cybercafé?

interpreter *n* l'interprète *m f*
I need an interpreter. J'ai
besoin d'un interprète.

introduce, to introduce *v*
présenter **p24**
**I'd like to introduce you to
____.** Laissez-moi vous
présenter ____.

Ireland *n* l'Irlande *f*

Irish *n adj* irlandais(e)

is *v* est See être **(to be) p27**.

Italian *n adj* italien *m* / italienne *f*

jacket *n* le blouson *m* / la
veste *f*

January *n* le janvier *m* **p14**

Japanese *n adj* japonais(e)

jasmine *n* le jasmin *m*

jazz *n* le jazz *m*

Jewish *adj* juif *m* / juive *f*

jogging *n* le jogging *m*

jog, to go jogging *v* faire du
jogging **p33**

juice *n* le jus *m*

June *n* le juin *m* **p15**

July *n* le juillet *m* **p15**

keep, to keep *v* / **to mind
(children)** *v* garder **p24**

kilo *n* le kilo *m* **p10**

kilometer *n* le kilomètre *m*

kind (type) *n* la sorte *f*

kind (nice) *adj* gentil *m* / gentille *f*
What kind of car is it?
Quelle sorte de voiture
est-ce?
You're very kind! C'est très
gentil de votre part!

kiss *n* le baiser *m*

kiss, to kiss *v* donner un
baiser (à) **p24**

kitchen *n* la cuisine *f*

know, to know *v* savoir **(a
fact) p35** / connaître **(a
person or place) p31**

kosher *adj* kasher

ENGLISH—FRENCH

L

lactose-intolerant *adj allergique aux produits laitiers* p94

land, to land *v atterrir* **p24**

language *n la langue f*

laptop *n l'ordinateur portable m*

large *adj grand(e)*

last, to last *v durer* **p24**

last *adj dernier m / dernière f*

late *adj en retard* **p13**

Please don't be late. *Ne soyez pas en retard, s'il vous plaît.*

later *adv plus tard* **p4**

See you later. *À bientôt.*

laundry *n la lessive f*

lavender *adj bleu lavande*

law *n la loi f*

lawyer *n l'avocat(e) m f*

least *adv le moins*

leather *n le cuir m* **p57**

leave, to leave (depart) *v partir* **p34**

left *n la gauche f* **p5**

on the left *à gauche*

leg *n la jambe f* **p196**

less *adj moins*

license *n le permis m*

driver's license *le permis de conduire*

life preserver *n le gilet m / la bouée de sauvetage f*

light *n la lumière (lamp) f / le voyant (car) m / le feu (for cigarette) m*

May I offer you a light? *Puis-je vous offrir du feu?*

lighter (cigarette) *n le briquet m*

like, to like *v vouloir (want)* **p37** */ aimer (take pleasure in)* **p24**

I would like _____. *Je voudrais _____.*

limousine *n la limousine f*

liqueur *n la liqueur f* **p97**

liquor *n les boissons alcoolisées f*

liter *n le litre m* **p10**

little *adj petit(e)*

live, to live *v vivre* **p25** */ habiter (place)* **p24**

Where do you live? *Où habitez-vous?*

living *n la vie f*

What do you do for a living? *Que faites-vous dans la vie?*

local *adj local(e)*

lock *n le verrou (on door) m / le cadenas (on locker) m*

lock, to lock *v verrouiller* **p24**

I'm locked out. *Je me suis enfermé(e) dehors.* **p85**

locker (storage) *n le local de stockage m*

locker room *n le vestiaire m*

long *adv longtemps* **p10**

For how long? *Pendant combien de temps?*

long *adj long m / longue f*

look, to look v regarder
(observe) p24 / aller (clothing) p30
  I'm just looking. Je ne fais
  que regarder.
  Look here! Regarde ça!
  How does this look? Ça me
  va comment?
look for, to look for (search)
v chercher p24
  I'm looking for a porter. Je
  cherche un porteur.
loose adj flottant(e)
lose, to lose v perdre p25
  I lost my passport / wallet.
  J'ai perdu mon passeport /
  porte-monnaie.
  I'm lost. Je suis perdu(e).
lost adj perdu(e)
loud adj fort(e)
loudly adv fort
  Please speak more loudly.
  Parlez plus fort, s'il vous
  plaît.
lounge n le salon m / le bar m
lounge, to lounge v se
  prélasser p24, 38
love n l'amour m
love, to love v aimer p24
  to love (family) aimer
  to love (a friend) bien aimer
  to love (a lover) aimer
  to make love faire l'amour
low adj bas m / basse f
lunch n le déjeuner m

luggage n le bagage m
  **Where do I report lost lug-
  gage?** Où puis-je déclarer
  la perte d'un bagage?
  **Where is the lost luggage
  claim?** Où se trouve la
  zone de récupération des
  bagages?

M

machine n la machine f
made of adj en / fait à partir
  de
magazine n le magazine m
maid (hotel) n la femme de
  chambre f
maiden adj de jeune fille
  That's my maiden name.
  C'est mon nom de jeune
  fille.
mail n le courrier m p147
  registered mail courrier
  recommandé
make, to make v faire p33
makeup n le maquillage m
make up, to make up v se
  réconcilier (apologize)
  p24, 38 / se maquiller
  (apply cosmetics) p24, 38
male (man) n l'homme m
male adj masculin
mall n le centre commercial m
manager n le directeur m / la
  directrice f p80
manual (instruction booklet)
  n le guide d'utilisation m

many *adj beaucoup de* p11

map *n la carte f / le plan* (subway) *m* p71

March (month) *n le mars m*

market *n le marché m* p160

flea market *le marché aux puces*

open-air market *le marché en plein air*

married *adj marié(e)* p123

marry, to marry *v (s')épouser* p24, 39

massage, to massage *v masser* p24

match *n le match* (sport) *m / l'allumette* (fire) *f*

book of matches *la boîte d'allumettes*

match, to match *v aller avec* p30

May (month) *n le mai m* p15

may (permission) *v pouvoir* p34

May I ____? *Puis-je ____?*

meal *n le repas m*

meat *n la viande f* p100

medication *n le médicament m*

medium (size) *adj moyen(ne)*

medium rare (meat) *adj saignant(e)* p92

medium well (meat) *adj rouge* p92

member *n le / la membre mf*

menu *n le menu m* p92

May I see a menu? *Puis-je avoir un menu?* p92

metal detector *n le détecteur de métaux m*

meter *n le mètre m*

Mexican *n adj mexicain(e)*

middle *prep au milieu de*

midnight *n minuit* p13

mile *n le mile m* p10

military *n l'armée f / le militaire m*

milk *n le lait m* p97

milk shake *le milk-shake / le lait frappé*

milliliter *n le millilitre m* p10

millimeter *n le millimètre m*

minute *n la minute f* p12

in a minute *dans une minute*

miss, to miss *v manquer* (a flight) p24

missing *adj manquant(e)*

mistake *n l'erreur f*

moderately priced *adj pas trop cher m / chère f*

mole (facial feature) *n le grain de beauté m*

Monday *n le lundi m* p13

money *n l'argent m / les fonds m* p139

money transfer *le transfer de fonds* p139

month *n le mois m*

morning *n le matin m* p13

in the morning *le matin*

mosque *n la mosquée f* p133

mother *n la mère f* p120

motorcycle *n la moto f* p58*

mountain *n la montagne f*
mountain climbing
l'escalade f
mouse *n la souris f*
moustache *n la moustache*
mouth *n la bouche f* p126
move, to move (change homes) *v déménager* p24
movie *n le film m* p151
moving walkway *n le trottoir roulant m*
much *adv beaucoup*
mugged *adj agressé(e)* p196
museum *n le musée m* p155
music *n la musique*
live music *la musique live*
musician *n le musicien m / la musicienne f* p129
muslim *adj musulman(e)*
mystery (novel) *n le roman policier m*

N

name *n le nom m*
My name is ___. *Je m'appelle ___.* p1
What's your name?
Comment vous appelez-vous?
first name *le prénom*
last name *le nom de famille*
napkin *n la serviette f*
narrow *adj étroit(e)* p12
nationality *n la nationalité f*
nausea *n la nausée f* p193
near *adj proche* p5
nearby *adv près d'ici*

neat (tidy) *adj bien rangé(e)*
need, to need *v avoir besoin de* p25
neighbor *n le / la voisin(e) m f* p121
nephew *n le neveu m* p123
network *n le réseau m*
new *adj nouveau m / nouvelle f*
news (current events) *n les actualités f pl*
newspaper *n le journal m*
newsstand *n le kiosque à journaux m* p162
New Zealand *n la Nouvelle-Zélande f*
New Zealander *adj néo-zélandais(e)*
next *adj prochain(e)* p5
next *prep à côté de*
the next station *la prochaine station*
next *adv puis* **(then)** */ après* **(later)**
nice *adj gentil m / gentille f*
niece *n la nièce f* p123
night *n la nuit f* p13
at night *pendant la nuit*
per night *par nuit* p78
nine *adj neuf* p7
nineteen *adj dix-neuf*
ninety *adj quatre-vingt-dix*
ninety-one *adj quatre-vingt-onze* p8
ninth *adj neuvième* p9
No. *Non.* p1
no (not any) *adv pas de*

noisy adj bruyant(e)

none pron aucun(e) p11

nonsmoking adj non fumeur

noon n le midi m p13

nose n le nez m p126

novel n le roman m

November n le novembre m

now adv maintenant p4

number n le numéro m / le chiffre (digit, figure) p7

Which room number? Quel numéro de chambre?

May I have your phone number? Puis-je avoir votre numéro de téléphone?

nurse n l'infirmier m / l'infirmière f p129

nurse, to nurse (breastfeed) v allaiter p24

Do you have a place where I can nurse? Y a-t-il un endroit où je puisse allaiter?

nursery n la crèche f

Do you have a nursery or playground? Avez-vous une crèche ou une aire de jeu?

nut la noix f p95

O

o'clock adv heures p13

October n l'octobre m p15

offer, to offer v offrir p24

officer n l'officier m / l'agent m

oil n l'huile f

Ok. D'accord. p1

Are you okay? Ça va?

old adj vieux m / vieille f / âgé(e) (person)

I'm six years old. J'ai six ans. See p7 for numbers.

olive n l'olive f

one adj un(e)

one way (traffic sign) adj sens unique m

open (business) adj ouvert(e)

Are you open? Êtes-vous ouvert?

open v ouvrir p33

opera n l'opéra m p153

opera house n l'opéra m

operator (phone) n l'opérateur m / l'opératrice f

optometrist n l'optométriste f

orange adj orange (color)

orange juice n le jus d'orange m

order, to order v ordonner / demander / commander (a meal) p24

organic adj biologique

Ouch! Aïe!

outside adv dehors

overcooked adj trop cuit(e)

overheat, to overheat v (car)chauffer

The car is overheating. La voiture chauffe.

overflow, to overflow v déborder p24

oxygen tank n la bouteille d'oxygène f

P

package n le colis m p147

pacifier n la tétine f

page, to page (someone) v faire appeler **p33**

paint, to paint v peindre **p25**

painting n la peinture f

pale adj pâle

paper n le papier m

parade n le défilé m

parent n le parent m p123

park n le parc m

parking n le parking m / le stationnement m

no parking stationnement interdit p61

park, to park v se garer **p24, 38**

parking fee le prix du stationnement **p61**

parking garage le parking couvert **p61**

partner n le / la partenaire m f

party n la soirée (event) f / le parti (political) m

pass, to pass (gambling) v passer **p24**

I'll pass / double. Je passe.

passenger n le passager m / la passagère f

passport n le passeport m

I've lost my passport. J'ai perdu mon passeport. **p54**

password n le mot de passe m

pay, to pay v payer **p24**

peanut n la cacahuète f p95

pedestrian n le piéton m / la piétonne f

pediatrician n le / la pédiatre m f

Can you recommend a pediatrician? Pouvez-vous me recommander un(e) pédiatre?

permit n le permis f

Do we need a permit? Avons-nous besoin d'un permis?

permit, to permit v permettre **p25**

phone n le téléphone m

Do you have a phone directory? Avez-vous un annuaire (téléphonique)?

May I have your phone number? Puis-je avoir votre numéro de téléphone?

Where can I find a public phone? Où puis-je trouver un téléphone public?

phone operator l'opérateur / l'opératrice téléphonique

Do you sell prepaid phones? Vendez-vous des téléphones portables prépayées?

phone call n l'appel m p143

I need to make a collect phone call. Je dois faire un appel en PCV.

an international phone call un appel à l'étranger

photocopy, to photocopy v photocopier **p24**

piano n le piano m

pillow n l'oreiller m p82

down pillow l'oreiller en
duvet d'oie

pink adj rose

pint n la pinte f / la bière
(pint of beer) f p10

pizza n la pizza f

place, to place v mettre p25

plastic n le plastique m

play n la pièce de théâtre f

play, to play v jouer (à) (de)
(game, instrument) p24

playground n l'aire de jeu f

Do you have a playground
or nursery? Avez-vous une
aire de jeu ou une crèche?

please (polite entreaty) adv
s'il vous plaît p1

please, to be pleasing to v
plaire p25 / faire plaisir (à)
p33

pleasure n le plaisir m

It's a pleasure. C'est un
plaisir.

plug n la prise (electrical out-
let) f

plug in, to plug in v brancher
p24

point, to point v montrer p24

Would you point me in the
direction of ___? Pouvez-
vous me montrer dans
quelle direction se trouve
___?

police n la police f

police station n le bureau de
police m p198

pool n la piscine (swimming)
f / le billard (game) m

pop music n la musique pop f

popular adj populaire

port n le porto (beverage) m
/ le port (ship) m

porter n le porteur m p14

portrait n le portrait m

postcard n la carte postale f

post office n le bureau de
poste m p140

Where is the nearest post
office? Où se trouve le
bureau de poste le plus
proche?

poultry n la volaille f p101

pound n la livre f

prefer, to prefer v préférer
p24

pregnant adj enceinte p195

prescription n l'ordonnance f

price n le prix m

print, to print v imprimer p24

private berth / cabin n la
couchette particulière f / le
compartiment privé m

problem n le problème m

process, to process (transaction) v traiter p24

product n le produit m

professional adj professionnel m / professionnelle f

program n le programme m /
le spectacle m

May I have a program?
Puis-je avoir un pro-
gramme?

Protestant n adj le / la protestant(e)

publisher n l'éditeur m / l'éditrice **(person)** f / la maison d'édition **(publishing house)** f

pull, to pull v tirer p24

pump n la pompe f

purple adj violet

purse n le sac à main m p54

push, to push v pousser p24

put, to put v miser p24

Q

quarter adj le quart m

one-quarter un quart

Quebec n le Québec m

Quebecois n adj québécois(e)

quiet adj calme

R

rabbit n le lapin m p101

radio n la radio f p59

satellite radio la radio par satellite

rain, to rain v pleuvoir

Is it supposed to rain? Est-ce qu'il va pleuvoir?

It's rainy. Le temps est pluvieux. p131

ramp, wheelchair n la rampe d'accès f p65

rape n le viol m p196

I was raped. Je suis violé(e).

rare (meat) adj bleue p92

rate (car rental, hotel) n le tarif m p60

What's the rate per day? Quel est le tarif par jour?

What's the rate per week? Quel est le tarif hebdomadaire?

rate plan (cell phone) n le forfait m

Do you have a rate plan? Offrez-vous des forfaits?

rather adv mieux

read, to read v lire p25

really adv vraiment

receipt n le reçu m p140

receive, to receive v recevoir p37 (like VOIR)

recommend, to recommend v recommender p24

red adj rouge

redhead n le roux m / la rousse f

refill n la même boisson **(beverage)** f / le renouvellement d'une ordonnance **(prescription)** m

reggae n le reggae m

relative n le membre de la famille m

remove, to remove v ôter p24

rent, to rent v louer p24

I'd like to rent a car. Je voudrais louer une voiture.

repeat, to repeat v repeater p24

Would you please repeat that? Pourriez-vous répéter ce que vous venez de dire, s'il vous plaît?

reservation n la réservation f

I'd like to make a reservation for ___ people. Je voudrais faire une réservation pour ___ personnes. See p7 for numbers.

restaurant n le restaurant m

Where can I find a good restaurant? Où puis-je trouver un bon restaurant? p88

restroom n les toilettes f pl / les WC m pl p44

Do you have a public restroom? Avez-vous des toilettes publiques?

return, to return v retourner p24

ride, to ride v conduire p25

right adj droit(e) p5

It is on the right. C'est à droite.

Turn right at the corner. Tournez à droite au coin de la rue.

rights n les droits m pl

civil rights les droits civiques

river n la fleuve f / la rivière f

road n la route f / la rue (street) f

road closed (sign) n route fermée f p61

rob, to rob v voler p24

I've been robbed. J'ai été victime d'un vol. p200

rock and roll n le rock m

rock climbing n la varappe f

rocks (iced beverage) adj avec des glaçons p96

I'd like it on the rocks, please. Avec des glaçons, s'il vous plaît.

romantic adj romantique

room (hotel) n la chambre f

room service le service en chambre p81

rooster n le coq m

rope n la corde f

rose n la rose f

royal flush n la quinte royale f

rum n le rhum m p97

run, to run v courir p24

S

sad adj triste p128

safe (for valuables) n le coffre-fort m p83

Do the rooms have safes? Les chambres sont-elles équipées de coffres-forts?

safe (secure) adj sûr(e) / sans danger

Is this area safe? Ce quartier est-il sûr? p83

sail n la voile f / la navigation f

sail, to sail v appareiller p24

When do we sail? À quelle heure le navire appareille-t-il?

salad n la salade f

salesperson n le / la représentant(e) commercial(e)

salt *n le sel m* p93

Is that low-salt? *Est-ce à faible teneur en sel?* p93

satellite *n le satellite m* p59

satellite radio *la radio par satellite* p59

Saturday *n le samedi m* p14

sauce *n la sauce f* p103

say, to say *v dire* p32

scan, to scan (document) *v scanner* p24

schedule (of events) *n le programme m*

school *n l'école f*

high school *le lycée*
law school *l'université de droit*

scooter *n le scooter m* p58

score *n le score m*

Scottish *n adj écossais(e)*

scratched *adj rayé(e)*

scuba dive, to scuba dive *v faire de la plongée sous-marine* p33

sculpture *n la sculpture f*

seafood *n les poissons et fruits de mer* p99

search *n la fouille f* p53

search, to search *v chercher* p24

seasick (to be) *adj avoir le mal de mer* p25

I am seasick. *J'ai le mal de mer.* p70

seasickness pill *le cachet contre le mal de mer m*

seat *n la place f / le siège m*

child seat *le siège pour enfant* p59

second *adj second(e)*

security *n la sécurité f*

security guard *l'agent de sécurité* p45

sedan *n la berline f* p58

see, to see *v voir* p37

May I see it? *Puis-je le / la voir de plus près?* p37

self-serve *adj en libre-service m*

sell, to sell *v vendre* p25

seltzer *n l'eau de Seltz f*

send, to send *v envoyer* p24

separated (marital status) *adj séparé(e)* p123

September *n le septembre m*

serve, to serve *v server* p24

service *n le service m / l'office (religious) m*

out of service *hors service*
service charge *n frais de traitement m*

seven *adj sept*

seventy *adj soixante-dix*

seventeen *adj dix-sept*

seventh *adj septième*

sew, to sew *v coudre* p25

sex (gender) *n le sexe m*

sex, to have intercourse *v avoir des rapports sexuels* p25

sheet *n le drap (bed) m / la feuille (paper) f*

shellfish *n les fruits de mer m*

ship *n le navire m* p70
ship, to ship *v expediter* p24
   How much to ship this to ____? *Combien cela coûte-t-il pour expédier cela en ____?*
shipwreck *n le naufrage m*
shirt *n la chemise* **(man's)** *f / le blouson* **(woman's)** *m*
shoe *n la chaussure f*
shop *n la boutique f*
shop, to shop *v faire des achats / chercher* **(to look for)** */ faire des courses* p33
   I'm shopping for ____ clothes. *Je cherche des vêtements pour ____* **men's** *hommes.*

shorts *n les shorts m*
shot (liquor) *n le verre m*
shout, to shout *v crier* p24
show (performance) *n le spectacle m* p155
   What time is the show? *À quelle heure est le spectacle?*
show, to show *v montrer* p24
   Would you show me? *Pouvez-vous me montrer?*
shower *n la douche f* p76
   Does it have a shower? *Est-ce qu'il y a une douche?*
shower, to shower *v se doucher* p24, 38

shrimp *n la crevette f*
shuttle bus *n la navette f*
sick *adj malade*
   I feel sick. *Je ne me sens pas bien.*
side *adv à part*
sidewalk *n le trottoir m*
sightseeing *n l'excursion m*
   sightseeing bus *n le car d'excursion m*
sign, to sign *v signer* p24
   Where do I sign? *Où dois-je signer?*
silver *adj argent*
sing, to sing *v chanter* p24
single *n adj le / la célibataire* **(unmarried)** */ seul(e)* **(alone, only)** p123
   Are you single? *Êtes-vous célibataire?*
   single bed *le lit à une place*
sink *n le lavabo* **(bathroom)** *m / l'évier* **(kitchen)** *m*
sister *n la sœur f* p120
sit, to sit *v s'asseoir* p39
six *adj six* p7
sixteen *adj seize* p7
sixty *adj soixante* p7
size (clothing, shoes) *n la taille f* p158
skin *n la peau f*
sleeping berth *n la couchette f*
sleeping car *n le wagon-lits m*
slow *adj lent(e)*
slow, to slow *v ralentir* p24
   Slow down! *Ralentissez! / Veuillez ralentir!* p65

ENGLISH—FRENCH

slowly *adv lentement*
  Please speak more slowly.
  Parlez plus lentement, s'il vous plaît.
slum *n les bas quartiers m pl*
small *adj petit(e)* **p24**
smell, to smell *v sentir* **p24**
smoke, to smoke *v fumer* **p24**
smoking *adj (pour) fumeurs*
  smoking area *la zone fumeurs*
  no smoking *interdit de fumer*
snack *n le snack m*
Snake eyes! *Paire d'as!* **p190**
snorkel, to snorkel *v faire de la plongée avec un tuba* **p33**
soap *n le savon m*
sock *n la chaussette f* **p159**
soda *n la boisson gazeuse f / le coca (cola) m* **p96**
  diet soda *la boisson gazeuse allégée*
soft *adj doux m / douce f*
software *n le logiciel m*
sold out *adj complet m / complète f*
some *adj du m / de la f / des m f pl* **p21**
someone *n quelqu'un (definite) / on (indefinite)*
something *n quelque chose f*
son *n le fils m* **p120**
song *n la chanson f*
sorry *adj désolé(e)*
  I'm sorry. *Je suis désolé(e).*
soup *n la soupe f* **p98**
spa *n le spa m* **p75**

Spain *n l'Espagne f*
Spanish *n adj espagnol(e)*
spare tire *n la roue de secours f*
sparrow *n le moineau m*
speak, to speak *v parler* **p24**
  Do you speak English?
  Parlez-vous anglais? **p120**
  Please speak louder. *Parler plus fort, s'il vous plaît.*
  Please speak more slowly.
  Parler plus lentement, s'il vous plaît. **p120**
special (featured meal) *n le plat du jour m*
specify, to specify *v spécifier* **p24**
speed limit *n la limite de vitesse f* **p64**
  What's the speed limit in town? *Quelle est la limite de vitesse en ville?*
speedometer *n l'indicateur de vitesse m*
spell, to spell *v peeler* **p24**
  Would you spell that, please?
  Pourriez-vous épeler ce mot, s'il vous plaît?
spices *n les épices f pl* **p104**
spill, to spill *v renverser* **p24**
split (gambling) *v partager* **p24**
sports *n les sports m pl*
spring (season) *n le printemps m* **p15**
stadium *n le stade m* **p169**
staff (employees) *n le personnel m / les employés m pl*

stamp (postage) n le timbre m

stair n l'escalier m

 Where are the stairs? Où sont les escaliers?

stand, to stand v se tenir debout p24, 38

start, to start v commencer (begin) / démarrer (a car) p24

state n l'état m

station n la station f

 Where is the nearest gas station? Où se trouve la station essence la plus proche?

 Where is ___ Où se trouve ___

 the bus station? la station de bus?

 the subway station? la station de métro?

 the train station? la gare?

stay, to stay v rester p24

 We'll be staying for ___ nights. Nous resterons ___ nuits. See p7 for numbers.

steakhouse n le grill m p88

steal, to steal v voler p24

stolen adj volé(e)

stop n l'arrêt m p24, 71

 Is this my stop? Est-ce mon arrêt?

 I missed my stop. J'ai manqué mon arrêt.

stop, to stop v (s')arrêter p24, 39

 Please stop. Arrêtez-vous, s'il vous plaît.

STOP (traffic sign) STOP

Stop, thief! Au voleur! Arrêtez-le!

store n le magasin m p156

straight (gambling) n la quinte f p191

straight adj droit(e) / raide (hair) / sec (drink)

straight ahead adv tout droit

street n la rue f

 across the street de l'autre côté de la rue

 down the street en bas de la rue

 Which street? Quelle rue?

 How many more streets? Dans combien de rues?

stressed adj stressé(e)

striped adj à rayures f pl

stroller n la poussette f

 Do you rent baby strollers? Est-ce que vous louez des poussettes?

suburb n la banlieue f

subway n le métro m p71

 subway line la ligne de métro

 subway station la station de métro p71

 Which subway do I take for ___? Quelle ligne de métro dois-je prendre pour aller à ___?

subtitle n le sous-titre m

suitcase n la valise f p57

suite n la suite f p74

summer n l'été m p15

sun *n le soleil m*

sunburn *n le coup de soleil m*

  I have a bad sunburn. *J'ai un mauvais coup de soleil.*

Sunday *n le dimanche m* p14

sunglasses *n les lunettes de soleil f*

sunny *adj ensoleillé(e)* p131

  It's sunny out. *Il fait du soleil.*

sunroof *n le toit ouvrant m*

sunscreen *n la crème solaire f*

  Do you have sunscreen SPF _____? *Avez-vous une crème solaire indice _____?* See p7 for numbers.

supermarket *n le super-marché m* p105

surf, to surf *v surfer* p24

  surfboard *n la planche de surf f*

suspiciously *adv d'une manière étrange* p56

swallow, to swallow *v avaler* p24

sweater *n le pull m* p159

swim, to swim *v nager* p24

  Can one swim here? *Peut-on nager ici?*

  swimsuit *n le maillot de bain m*

  swim trunks *n le caleçon de bain m*

Swiss *n adj suisse*

Switzerland *n la Suisse f*

symphony *n l'orchestre sym-phonique m*

T

table *n la table f* p90

  table for two *la table pour deux* p90

tailor *n le tailleur m* p82

  Can you recommend a good tailor? *Pourriez-vous me recommander un bon tailleur?*

take, to take *v prendre* **p35** / *emmener* **p24**

  Take me to the station. *Emmenez-moi à la gare, s'il vous plaît.*

  How much to take me to _____? *Quel est le prix de la course d'ici à _____?*

  takeout menu *n le menu des plats à emporter m*

talk, to talk *v parler* **p24**

tall *adj grand(e)*

taste *n le goût m*

taste, to taste *v goûter / déguster* **p24**

tax *n la taxe f* p161

  value-added tax (VAT) *la taxe sur la valeur ajoutée (TVA)*

taxi *n le taxi m* p65

  Taxi! *Taxi!*

  Would you call me a taxi? *Pouvez-vous m'appeler un taxi?*

tea *n le thé m* p97

  herbal tea *la tisane*

team *n l'équipe f* p169

techno *n la musique techno f*

television n la télévision f p76

temple n le temple m p133

ten adj dix p7

tennis n le tennis m p168

tennis court le court de tennis

tent n la tente f p87

tenth adj dixième p9

terminal n le terminal m

Thank you. Merci. p1

that (nearby) pron celui-ci m / celle-ci f p21

that (far away) pron celui-là m / celle-là f p21

theater n le théâtre m p151

them pron pl eux m / elles f

then adv alors (so, in that case) / puis (next)

there adv là

Is / Are there ____? Est-ce qu'il y a ____?

over there là-bas

these adj ces p21

thick adj épais m / épaisse f

thin adj fin(e)

third adj troisième p9

thirteen adj treize p7

thirteenth adj treizième p7

thirty adj trente p7

this adj ce m / cette f p21

those adj ces p21

thousand adj mille p8

three adj trois p7

Thursday n le jeudi m p14

ticket n le billet m p67

ticket counter le guichet

one-way ticket un aller simple p67, 72

round-trip ticket un aller-retour p67, 72

tight adj serré(e)

time n l'heure f p12

Is it on time? Est-il / Est-elle à l'heure?

At what time? À quelle heure?

What time is it? Quelle heure est-il? p12

timetable n l'horaire m

tip (gratuity) le pourboire m

tip included service compris

tire n le pneu m p61

I have a flat tire. J'ai un pneu crevé.

tired adj fatigué(e)

today n adv aujourd'hui p14

toilet n les toilettes f pl / la cuvette des toilettes f

The toilet is overflowing. La cuvette des toilettes déborde. p84

The toilet is backed up. Les toilettes sont bouchées.

toilet paper n le papier de toilette m

You're out of toilet paper. Il n'y a plus de papier toilette.

toiletries n le nécessaire de toilette m

toll n le péage m

tomorrow n adv demain p14

ton n la tonne f

too adv trop (excessively) / aussi (also) p12

tooth n la dent f
I lost my tooth. J'ai perdu une dent.
toothache n le mal de dents m
I have a toothache. J'ai mal à une dent.
total adv en tout
What is the total? Ça fait combien en tout?
tour n l'excursion f p155
Are guided / audio tours available? Y a-t-il des excursions guidées / audio-guidées?
towel n la serviette f p82
May we have more towels? Pouvons-nous avoir plus de serviettes?
toy n le jouet m
toy store le magasin de jouets
Do you have any toys for the children? Avez-vous des jouets pour enfants?
traffic n la circulation f
How's traffic? Comment est la circulation?
traffic rules le code de la route
trail n le sentier m p171
Are there trails? Y a-t-il des sentiers?
train n le train m p66
express train le train express
local train la ligne régionale
Does the train go to ____? Le train va-t-il à ____?
Where is the train station? Où se trouve la gare?

train, to train v entraîner p24
transfer, to transfer v transférer p24
I need to transfer funds. J'ai besoin de transférer des fonds.
wire transfer le virement
transmission n la transmission f
automatic transmission la transmission automatique
standard transmission la transmission standard
travel, to travel v voyager p24
travelers' check n le chèque de voyage m
Do you cash travelers' checks? Encaissez-vous les chèques de voyage?
trim, to trim v couper (hair) p24
trip n le voyage m
triple adj triple p8
trumpet n la trompette f
trunk n le coffre m p57
try, to try v essayer p24
Tuesday n le mardi m p13
turkey n la dinde f
turn, to turn v tourner p24
to turn left / right tourner à gauche / à droite
to turn off / turn on éteindre / allumer
turn signal n le clignotant m
twelve adj douze p7
twelfth adj douzième p9
twenty adj vingt p7
twentieth adj vingtième
two adj deux p7

U

umbrella n le parapluie m

uncle n l'oncle m p123

undercooked adj pas assez cuit(e)

understand, to understand v comprendre **p25**

I don't understand. Je ne comprends pas.

Do you understand? Vous comprenez?

underwear n le sous-vêtement m

United States n les États-Unis m

university n l'université f

up adv vers le haut p5

update, to update v mettre à jour **p25**

upgrade n la mise à niveau f

upload, to upload v télécharger **p24**

upscale adj huppé(e)

us pron nous

USB port n le port USB m

use, to use v utiliser **p24**

V

vacation n les vacances f

on vacation en vacances

to go on vacation partir en vacances

vacancy n les chambres libres f pl p75

no vacancy complet

van n le fourgon m p58

VCR n le magnétoscope m

Do the rooms have VCRs? Les chambres sont-elles équipées de magnétoscope?

vegetable n le légume m p114

vegetarian n végétarien m / végétarienne f

vending machine n le distributeur m

version n la version f

very adj très

video n la vidéocassette f

Where can I rent videos or DVDs? Où puis-je louer des cassettes vidéo ou des DVD?

view n la vue f p76

beach view la vue sur mer

city view la vue sur ville

vineyard n le vignoble m

vinyl adj en vinyle m p57

violin n le violon m

visa n le visa m

Do I need a visa? Ai-je besoin d'un visa?

vision n la vision f

visit, to visit v visiter (a place) **p24** / rendre visite à (person) **p25**

visually-impaired adj malvoyant(e) p73

vodka n la vodka f p97

volume n le volume m

Please turn up / turn down the volume. Veuillez augmenter / baisser le volume.

vote, to vote v voter **p24**

voucher n le bon m / le coupon m p52

meal voucher le coupon-repas

room voucher le coupon d'hébergement

W

wait, to wait v attendre p25

Please wait. Attendez, s'il vous plaît!

waiter n le serveur m / la serveuse f p94

waiting area n la salle d'attente f p44

wake-up call n le réveil téléphonique m p83

wallet n le portefeuille m

I lost my wallet. J'ai perdu mon portefeuille. p54

Someone stole my wallet. On a volé mon portefeuille.

walk, to walk v marcher p24 / aller à pied p28, 30

walker (ambulatory device) n le déambulatoire m

walkway n le trottoir m

want, to want v vouloir p37

war n la guerre f

warm adj chaud(e) p132

watch, to watch v regarder p24

water n l'eau f

Is the water drinkable? L'eau est-elle potable? p87

Do you have sparkling water? Avez-vous de l'eau pétillante?

wave n la vague (water)

waxing n l'épilation à la cire f

weapon n l'arme f

wear, to wear v porter p24

weather forecast n les prévisions météorologiques f pl

Wednesday n le mercredi m

week n la semaine f p4

this week cette semaine

last week la semaine dernière

next week la semaine prochaine

weigh v peser p24

I weigh ____. Je pèse ____.

It weighs ____. Cela pèse ____. See p7 for numbers.

weights n les altères f pl

welcome adv bienvenu(e)

You're welcome. Vous êtes le bienvenu / la bienvenue.

well adv bien

well done (meat) bien cuite

well done (task) bon travail

I don't feel well. Je ne me sens pas bien.

western adj western (movie)

whale n la baleine f

what adv quel m / quelle f p3

What sort of ____? Quelle sorte de ____?

What time is it? Quelle heure est-il?

wheelchair n la chaise roulante f p65

wheelchair access l'accès aux handicapés p65

wheelchair ramp la rampe d'accès pour handicapés

power wheelchair le fauteuil roulant motorisé

wheeled (luggage) adj à roulettes p57

when adv quand p1

where *adv* où p1

Where is it? *Où est-ce?*

which *adj lequel m / laquelle f / lesquels m pl / lesquelles f pl*

Which one? *Lequel / Laquelle?*

Which is it? *Lequel / Laquelle est-ce?*

white *adj blanc m / blanche f*

who *pron qui* p3

whose *pron à qui*

wide *adj large* p12

widow / widower *n la veuve f / le veuf m* p123

wife *n la femme f* p112

Wi-Fi *n la Wi-Fi f*

window *n la fenêtre f*

drop-off window *le guichet de dépôt* p149

pickup window *le guichet de récupération* p149

windshield *n le pare-brise m*

windshield wiper *n l'essuie-glace m* p62

windsurf, to windsurf *v faire de la planche à voile* p33

windy *adj du vent* p132

wine *n le vin m* p96

winery *n le vignoble m*

winter *n l'hiver m* p15

wiper *n l'essuie-glace m*

with *prep avec*

withdraw *v retirer* p24

I need to withdraw money. *J'ai besoin de retirer de l'argent.*

withdrawal *n le retrait m*

without *prep sans*

woman *n la femme f*

work, to work *v travailler* (job) p24 / *marcher* (function) p24

This doesn't work. *Cela ne marche pas.*

workout *n l'entraînement m*

worse *adj pire*

worst *adj le pire*

write, to write *v écrire* p32

Would you write that down for me? *Pourriez-vous m'écrire cela?*

writer *n l'écrivain* p129

X

x-ray machine *n l'appareil de radiographie m*

Y

yellow *adj jaune*

yes *adv oui* p1

yesterday *n hier m* p4

the day before yesterday *avant-hier*

yield sign *n panneau de priorité m* p61

you *pron tu s / vous pl* p22

you (s. informal) *tu*

you (s. formal) *vous*

you (pl. informal) *vous*

you (pl. formal) *vous*

your, yours *adj ton m / ta f / tes pl*

young *adj jeune*

Z

zoo *n le zoo m* p137

A

l'abeille f bee n

abîmé(e) damaged adj p10

accepter to accept v **p24**

accessible aux personnes à mobilité réduite handi-capped-accessible adj p73

l'accident m accident n

D'accord. Okay. adv p1

acheter to buy v **p24**

l'acné f acne n

actuel actual adj

l'adaptateur m adapter plug n

l'addition f check (tab) n

l'adresse f address n

l'aéroport m airport n p44

l'affaire f s deal n

les affaires f pl business n

Voici ma carte de visite. Here's my business card.

affréter to charter v **p24**

afro afro n adj

afro-américain(e) m f African-American n adj

l'âge m age n p124

Quel âge avez-vous? What's your age?

l'agence f agency n p58

l'agence de location de voitures car rental agency

l'agent m guard n

agnostique agnostic adj

agressé(e) mugged adj p196

l'aide f help n

aider to help v **p24**

Aïe! Ouch! exclamation

l'ail m garlic n p115

aimer to like, to enjoy / to love v **p24**

faire l'amour to make love

l'aire de jeu f playground n

l'alcool m alcohol n p96

allaiter to nurse v **p24**

allemand(e) German n adj

aller to go / to look (appear) / to fit (clothes) / to go with (match) v **p30**

l'aller simple m one-way ticket n p67, 72

l'aller-retour m round-trip ticket n p67, 72

l'allergie f allergy n

allergique allergic adj See p197 for common allergens.

allumer to turn on v **p24**

l'allumette f match n

la boîte d'allumettes book of matches

alors then adv / yet adv / so

l'altitude f altitude n

l'ambassade f embassy n

l'ambulance f ambulance n

l'amende f fine (for traffic violation) n p64

américain(e) American n adj

l'ami(e) m f friend n p120

l'amour m love n

l'amphithéâtre m coliseum n

anglais(e) English n adj

l'Angleterre f England n

l'animal m animal n

annuler to cancel v **p24**

Le vol ＿＿＿ a été annulé.
Flight ＿＿＿ has been canceled.

l'antibiotique *m antibiotic n*

l'antihistaminique *m antihistamine n* p192

anxieux *m* / **anxieuse** *f anxious adj*

le août *m August n* p15

l'appareil de radiographie *m x-ray machine n*

appareiller *to sail away v* p24

l'appel *m phone call n* p143

un appel en PCV *collect phone call*

l'appel à l'étranger *international phone call*

appeler *to call (on the phone) / to call (shout) v* p24

l'après-midi *m afternoon n*

l'argent *m money n / silver n*

l'arme *f weapon n*

l'armée *f military, army n*

l'arrêt *m stop n* p71

l'arrêt de bus *bus stop*

arrêter *to stop v* p24, 39

Arrêtez-vous, s'il vous plaît.
Please stop.

Je veux que vous vous arrêtiez. *I need you to stop.*

STOP *STOP (traffic sign)*

l'arrivée *f* / **les arrivées** *f pl arrival(s) n* p44

arriver *to arrive v* p24

l'art *m art n*

exposition d'art *exhibit of art*

d'art *art adj*

le musée d'art *art museum*

l'artisan(e) *m f craftsperson n*

l'artiste *m f artist n* p129

l'ascenseur *m elevator n* p65

asiatique *Asian n adj*

l'aspirine *f aspirin n* p193

s'asseoir *to sit v* p39

l'assistance *assistance, help n*

assister *to assist, to help v* p24

l'assurance *f insurance n*

la tierce collision *collision insurance*

l'assurance responsabilité civile *liability insurance*

l'asthme *m asthma n* p197

athée *atheist adj*

attendre *to wait / to hold (telephone) v* p25

Attendez, s'il vous plaît!
Please wait.

Attendez une minute! *Hold on a minute!*

l'attente *f wait n*

atterrir *to land v* p24

l'aube *f dawn n* p13

l'auberge *f hostel n* p74

aucun(e) *none n* p11

au-dessus de *above prep* p86

audio *audio adj* p73

l'assistance audio *audio assistance*

aujourd'hui *today n*

aussi *too (also) adv* p12

l'Australie *f Australia n*

australien *m* / **australienne** *f Australian n adj*

l'autobiographie *f autobiography n*

l'autobus *m bus n*

l'automne m *autumn (fall)* n

l'autoroute f *highway* n

autre *another* adj

de l'autre côté de *across* adv

de l'autre côté de la rue / en face *across the street*

avaler *to swallow* v **p24**

l'avance f *advance (money)* n

à l'avance *in advance* adv

en avant *forward* adj

avec *with* prep

avec des glaçons *on the rocks (beverage)* **p96**

Avec des glaçons ou sec? *On the rocks or straight?*

aveugle *blind* adj

l'avocat(e) m f *lawyer* n

avoir *to have* v **p25**

avoir besoin de *to need* v **p25**

avoir des rapports sexuels *to have intercourse* v **p25**

avoir mal *to hurt* v **p25**

Aïe! Ça fait mal! *Ouch! That hurts!*

l'avril m *April* n **p14**

B

le / la baby-sitter m f *babysitter* n

Les baby-sitters parlent anglais. *The babysitters speak English.*

les bagage(s) m pl *baggage, luggage* n

bagages perdus *lost baggage*

récupération des bagages *baggage claim* **p56**

se baigner *to bathe* v **p24, 38**

la baignoire f *bathtub* n

le bain m *bath* n

le baiser m *kiss* n

baiser *vulgar to fuck* v **p24**

le balai d'essuie-glace m *wiper blade* n

le balcon m *balcony* n **p77**

le ballon m / **la balle** f *ball (sport)* n

la banlieue f *suburb* n

la banque f *bank* n **p140**

bancaire *bank, banking* adj

le compte bancaire *bank account*

la carte bancaire *bank card*

le bar m *bar, lounge* n **p90**

la barbe f *beard* n

bas m / **basse** f *low* adj

les bas quartiers m *slum(s)* n

le bateau m *boat* n **p70**

la batterie f *battery (car)* n

le tambour m *drum* n

beau m / **belle** f *handsome, beautiful* adj

beaucoup *much* n

beaucoup de *many* adj

le bébé m *baby* n

beige *beige* adj

belge *Belgian* n adj

la Belgique f *Belgium* n

le berceau m *crib* n

la berline f *sedan* n **p58**

le beurre m *butter* n

le biberon m *baby bottle* n

bien *fine / well* adv

Je vais bien. *I'm fine.* **p1**

Je ne me sens pas bien. *I don't feel well.*

bienvenu(e) *welcome adv*

Vous êtes le / la bienvenu(e). *You're welcome.*

la bière *f beer n p96*

la bière pression *draft beer*

bilingue *bilingual adj*

le billard *m pool (game) n*

le billet *m ticket n / bill (currency) n p6*

le distributeur automatique *f ATM / cash machine n*

DAB (distributeur automatique de billets) *ATM p142*

la biographie *f biography n*

biologique *organic adj*

biracial *biracial adj*

blanc *m* / **blanche** *f white adj*

la blessure *f injury n*

bleu(e) *blue adj*

bleue *rare (meat) adv p92*

bleu lavande *lavender adj*

blond(e) *blond(e) adj*

bloquer *to block v p24*

le blouson *m jacket n*

le bœuf *m beef (meat) n*

boire *to drink v p31*

la boisson *f drink n*

la boisson gratuite *complimentary drink*

Voulez-vous quelque chose à boire? *Would you like something to drink?*

les boissons alcoolisées *f liquor n*

la boisson gazeuse *f soda n*

la boisson gazeuse allégée *diet soda*

la boîte de nuit *f nightclub n*

la bombe *f bomb n*

le bon *m voucher n p52*

bon *m* / **bonne** *f good / correct adj*

Bonjour. *Good morning.*

Bon après-midi. *Good afternoon.*

Bonsoir. *Good evening.*

Bonne nuit. *Good night.*

Bonjour. *Hello. (morning and daytime)*

le bord *m board n*

à bord *on board*

la bosse *f dent n*

la bouche *f mouth n p126*

la boucle *f curl n*

bouclé(e) *curly adj*

bouddhiste *m f Buddhist adj*

bouger *to move v p24*

la bougie *f fuse (car) / candle n*

la bouteille *f bottle n*

la bouteille de vin *wine bottle*

la bouteille d'oxygène *oxygen tank*

la boutique *f shop n*

la boutique hors-taxe *duty-free shop p45*

le braille américain *m braille, American n*

brancher *to plug v p24*

le bras *m arm n*

le bridge *m bridge (dental) n*

le briquet *m lighter (cigarette) n*

bronzé(e) *tanned adj*

brûler *to burn* v **p24**

brûn *brown (hair) adj*

la brune *f brunette n*

bruyant(e) *noisy adj*

le budget *m budget n*

budgéter *to budget* v **p24**

le buffet *m buffet n* **p89**

le bureau de police *m police station n* **p198**

le bureau de poste *m post office n* **p140**

le but (sport) *m goal (sport) n*

C

la cabine d'essayage *f changing room, fitting room n*

le cabinet du médecin *m doctor's office n*

cabosser *to dent* v **p24**

Il / Elle a cabossé la voiture. *He / She dented the car.*

la cacahuète *f peanut n* **p95**

en cachemire *cashmere adj*

le cachet contre le mal de mer *m seasickness pill n*

le cadeau *m /* **les cadeaux** *m pl gift n* **p52**

le café *m coffee / café n*

le café glacé *iced coffee*
le café au lait *latte*

le caleçon de bain *m swim trunks n*

calme *quiet adj*

camper *to camp* v **p24**

de camper *camping adj*

le camping-car *m camper n*

le Canada *m Canada n*

canadien *m /* **canadienne** *f Canadian n adj*

le canard *m duck n*

la canne à pêche *f fishing pole n*

le cappucino *m cappuccino n*

le car *m bus (coach) n* **p68**

le car d'excursion *m sightseeing bus n*

la carie *f cavity (tooth) n*

la carte *f card n* **p140**

Voici ma carte de visite. *Here's my business card.*

la carte *f map n*

la carte de crédit *credit card* **p139**

la carte d'embarquement *boarding pass* **p54**

la carte postale *postcard*

le casier *m locker n*

le casino *m casino n* **p190**

(se) casser *to break* v **p24, 38**

la cassure *f break n*

le casque *m headphones n*

catholique *Catholic adj*

le CD *m CD n*

ce *m /* **cette** *f this adj*

la ceinture *f belt (clothing) n*

célébrer *to celebrate* v **p24**

célibataire *single (unmarried)*

Êtes-vous célibataire? *Are you single?*

celui-ci *m /* **celle-ci** *f that (nearby) adj* **p21**

celui-là *m /* **celle-là** *f that (far away) adj* **p21**

cent *hundred adj* **p7**

centaine *f hundred n* **p7**

le **centimètre** *m centimeter n*

le **centre commercial** *m mall n*

le **centre-ville** *m downtown n*

ces *these / those adj* p21

la **chaise roulante** *f wheelchair n* p65

l'**accès aux handicapés** *wheelchair access* p65

la **rampe d'accès pour handicapés** *wheelchair ramp*

le **fauteuil roulant motorisé** *power wheelchair*

la **chambre** *f room n*

le **service en chambre** *room service* p81

la **chambre d'hôte** *bed-and-breakfast (B & B)*

chambres libres *vacancy*

complet *no vacancy*

le **change** *m currency exchange n*

changer *to change v* p24

la **chanson** *f song n*

chanter *to sing v* p24

le **chapeau** *m hat n* p159

charter *charter adj*

le **chat** *m /* la **chatte** *f cat n*

chaud(e) *hot / warm adj* p132

chauffer *to overheat v* p24

la **chaussette** *f sock n* p159

la **chaussure** *f shoe n* p159

la **chemise** *f shirt n* p159

le **chemisier** *m blouse n* p159

le **chèque** *m check n*

le **chèque de voyage** *travelers' check*

cher *m /* **chère** *f expensive adj*

pas cher *m /* **pas chère** *f cheap*

chercher *to look for, to search v* p24

le **cheval** *m horse n*

le **cheveu** *m /* les **cheveux** *m pl hair n*

la **chèvre** *f goat n*

le **chien** *m /* la **chienne** *f dog n*

le **chien accompagnant** *service dog* p73

la **Chine** *f China n*

chinois(e) *Chinese n adj*

le **chiropracticien** *m /* la **chiropracticienne** *f chiropractor n* p194

le **chocolat chaud** *m hot chocolate n* p97

chrétien *m /* **chrétienne** *f Christian adj*

le **cigare** *m cigar n*

la **cigarette** *f cigarette n*

le **cil** *m eyelash n* p126

le **cinéma** *m cinema n* p151

cinq *five adj* p7

cinquante *fifty adj* p7

le **/** la **cinquième** *fifth adj* p9

la **circulation** *f traffic n*

la **citronnade** *f lemonade n*

clair(e) *clear adj*

la **clarinette** *f clarinet n*

la **classe** *f class n* p49

la **classe affaires** *business class*

la **classe économique** *economy class*

la **première classe** *first class*

la **climatisation** *f air conditioning n* p76

le **clos** *vineyard / orchard n*

le club de remise en forme *f fitness center n* p167

le cochon *m pig n*

le code vestimentaire *m dress (general attire) n*

le cœur *m heart n*

le coffre (à bagages) *m trunk (luggage, car) n* p57

coffre-fort *m safe (for storing valuables) n* p83

le cognac *m cognac n* p97

le coiffeur *m* / **la coiffeuse** *f hairdresser n* p164

le coin *m corner n*

le colis *m package n* p147

collectionner *to collect v* p24

colorer *to color v* p24

commander *to order (a meal) v* p24

commencer *to start, to commence v* p24

comment / **combien** *how adv*

Comment allez-vous? *How are you?*

Combien de temps cela va-t-il prendre? *How long will it take?*

Combien est-ce que cela coûte? *How much does this cost?*

commencer *to begin v* p24

compenser *to make up (compensate) v* p24

complet *full house n*

complet *m* / **complète** *f sold out adj*

composer *to dial (a phone number) v* p24

composer directement le numéro *to dial direct*

comprendre *to understand v* p25

Vous comprenez? *Do you understand?* p1

compris(e) *included*

le compte *m account n* p142

le comptoir *m counter (in bar) n*

le concert *m concert n* p137

le conducteur *m* / **la conductrice** *f driver n*

conduire *to drive* / *to ride v* p25

confirmer *to confirm v* p24

Vous n'avez pas confirmé votre réservation. *You didn't confirm your reservation.*

la confirmation *f confirmation n*

confus(e) *confused adj* p128

la congestion *f congestion (sinus) n*

connaître *to know (someone) v* p31

constipé(e) *constipated adj*

continuer *to continue v* p24

le coquillage *m shellfish n*

la corde *f rope, twine n*

corriger *to correct v* p24

à côté (de) *next (to) prep*

le coton *m cotton n*

la couche *f diaper n*

la couche jetable *disposable diaper*

la couchette particulière *f private berth* / *cabin n*

coudre *to sew v* **p25**

la **couleur** *f color n*

le **coup de soleil** *m sunburn n*

la **coupe (de cheveux)** *f hair-cut n*

coupé(e) *disconnected adj*

couper *to cut / to trim (hair) v* **p24**

le **coupon** *m voucher n* **p52**

le **coupon-repas** *meal voucher*

le **coupon d'hébergement** *room voucher*

courir *to run v* **p24**

la **couronne** *f crown (dental) n*

le **courriel** *m e-mail n* **p147**

Puis-je avoir votre adresse courriel? *May I have your e-mail address?*

le **courrier** *m mail n*

courrier par avion *air mail*

courrier en recommandé avec accusé de réception *certified mail*

courrier exprès *express mail*

courrier première classe *first class mail*

courrier recommandé *registered mail*

le **court** *m court (sport) n*

court(e) *short adj* **p10**

courtois(e) *courteous adj*

coûter *to cost v* **p24**

le / la **cousin(e)** *m f cousin n*

la **couverture** *f blanket n* **p55**

la **crèche** *f nursery n*

la **crème** *f cream n*

la **crème solaire** *f sunscreen n*

la **crème solaire indice _____** *sunscreen SPF _____*

la **crevette** *f shrimp n*

crier *to shout v* **p24**

la **crise cardiaque** *f heart attack n*

le **cuir** *m leather n* **p57**

la **cuisine** *f kitchen n*

cuisiner *to cook v* **p24**

très cuite *charred (meat) adj*

trop cuit(e) *overcooked adj*

cuivre *copper (color) adj*

le **culte** *m service (religious) n*

le **cybercafé** *Internet café, cybercafé n*

D

le **danger** *m danger n*

la **danse** *f dance n*

danser *to dance v* **p24**

dans *in, inside prep*

le **déambulatoire** *m walker (ambulatory device) n*

déborder *to overflow v* **p24**

décapotable *convertible (car) adj*

le **décembre** *m December n*

déclarer *to declare v* **p24**

Vous n'avez rien à déclarer? *You don't have anything to declare?*

le **déguisement** *m costume n*

la **dégustation** *f tasting, sampling n*

déguster *to taste v* **p24**

dehors *outside n*

le **déjeuner** *m lunch n*

déjeuner to eat (lunch) v **p24**

demain tomorrow adv **p14**

demander / poser to ask v **p24**

démarrer to start (car) v **p24**

déménager to move (household) v **p24**

se dépêcher to hurry v **p24, 38**

déprimé(e) down, depressed adj

dernier m / **dernière** f last adv

derrière behind prep **p5**

désolé(e) sorry adj

Je suis désolé(e), je ne comprends pas. I'm sorry, I don't understand.

le dessert m dessert n **p102**

la carte des desserts dessert menu

le dessin m drawing n

en dessous de below prep

la destination f destination n

le détecteur de métaux m metal detector n

deux two adj

à deux / double double adj

à deux lits double room

devant front prep

diabétique diabetic adj

la diarrhée f diarrhea n **p193**

le dictionnaire m dictionary n

différent(e) different (other) adj

difficile difficult adj

le dimanche m Sunday n **p14**

la dinde f turkey n

le dîner m dinner n

dîner to eat v **p24**

sortir dîner to eat out

dire to say v **p32**

le directeur m / **la directrice** f manager n **p80**

la disco, la discothèque f disco / nightclub n

disparaître disappear v **p25**

disponible available adj

le distributeur m vending machine n

divorcé(e) divorced adj **p193**

dix ten adj **p7**

dix-huit eighteen adj **p7**

dix-neuf nineteen adj **p7**

dix-sept seventeen adj **p7**

dixième tenth adj **p9**

le docteur m / **la docteresse** f doctor n **p80**

le dollar m dollar n

le domicile m home n

donner to give / to deal (cards) v **p24**

doré(e) golden adj

le dos m back (body) n

la douane f customs n **p52**

la douche f shower n **p76**

se doucher to shower v **p24, 38**

doux m / **douce** f soft adj

la douzaine f dozen n **p11**

douze twelve adj **p7**

douzième twelfth adj **p9**

le drame m drama n

le drap *m* sheet (bed linen) *n*
la droite *f* right *n* p5
  les droits civiques civil rights
  droit(e) / raide straight adj /
    right adj
  tout droit straight ahead
  C'est à droite. It is on the right.
  **Tournez à droite au coin de
    la rue.** Turn right at the
    corner.
dur(e) hard adj
durer to last *v* **p24**
le DVD *m* DVD *n* p59

E

l'eau *f* water *n*
  l'eau chaude hot water
  l'eau froide cold water
l'eau courante *f* current
  (water) *n*
l'eau de Javel *f* bleach *n*
l'eau de Seltz *f* seltzer *n*
l'eau-de-vie de pommes *f*
  brandy *n*
échouer to beach *v* **p24**
l'école *f* school *n*
l'économie *f* economy *n* p58
l'Écosse *f* Scotland *n*
écossais(e) Scottish *n* adj
écrire to write *v* **p32**
  Pourriez-vous m'écrire cela?
    Would you write that
    down for me?
l'écrivain *m* *f* writer *n* p129
l'éditeur *m* / **l'éditrice** *f* editor *n* p129
l'éducateur *m* / **l'éducatrice** *f*
  educator *n* p129

l'église *f* church *n* p133
l'égratignure *f* scratch *n*
l'élection *f* election *n*
emballer to bag *v* **p24**
embarquer to board *v* **p24**
embarrassé(e) embarrassed adj
l'embouteillage *m* congestion (traffic) *n*
l'employé(e) *m* *f* employee *n*
l'employeur *m* / **l'employeuse**
  f employer *n*
encaisser to cash *v* **p24**
en-cas *m* snack *n*
enceinte pregnant adj p195
enchanté(e) charmed adj
l'enfant *m* infant / child *n*
enlever to clear, delete,
  remove *v* **p24**
l'enregistrement *m* check-in *n*
  **l'enregistrement électron-
    ique** electronic check-in
ensoleillé(e) sunny adj p131
l'entaille *f* cut (wound) *n*
entendre to hear *v* **p25**
enthousiaste enthusiastic adj
l'entracte *m* intermission *n*
l'entraînement *m* workout *n*
entraîner to train *v* **p24**
l'entrée *f* entrance / cover
  charge (in bar) *n* p184
  entrée interdite do not enter
l'entreprise *f* business *n*
entrer to enter *v* **p24**
l'enveloppe *f* envelope *n*
l'environnement *m* environment *n*
envoyer to send *v* **p24**

épais *m* / **épaisse** *f* thick adj

épeler to spell v **p24**

> **Pourriez-vous épeler ce mot,
> s'il vous plaît?** Can you
> spell this word, please?

les épices *f* spice n **p104**

l'épilation à la cire *f* waxing n

> **l'épilation ____ à la cire**
> **____** waxing
> **du maillot** bikini
> **des sourcils** eyebrow
> **des jambes** leg

(s')épouser to marry, to get
married v **p24, 39**

épuisé(e) exhausted adj

l'équipe *f* team n **p169**

l'erreur *f* mistake n

l'escalade *f* climbing n

escalader to climb v **p24**

l'escalier *m* stair n

l'escalier roulant *m* escalator n

l'Espagne *f* Spain n

espagnol(e) Spanish n adj

les espèces *f* cash n **p140**

> **espèces uniquement** cash only

essayer to try v **p24**

l'essence *f* gas n **p60**

l'essuie-glace *m* windshield
wiper n **p67**

est is v See **être** (to be) **p27**.

l'étage *m* floor n

> **le premier étage** first floor

l'état *m* condition / state n

l'été *m* summer n **p15**

éteindre to turn off v **p25**

êtes are v See **être** (to be) **p27**.

être to be v **p27**

étroit(e) narrow adj **p12**

eux *m pl* / **elles** *f pl* them pron

s'évanouir to faint v **p24, 39**

l'évier *m* sink (kitchen) n

l'excursion *m* sightseeing /
tour n **p155**

> **les excursions guidées**
> guided tours
> **les excursions audio**
> **guidées** audio tours

excuser to excuse (pardon) v
p24

> **Excusez-moi.** Excuse me.

expédier to ship v **p24**

expliquer to explain v **p24**

l'exposition *f* exhibit n

F

fâché(e) angry adj **p128**

facturer to bill v **p24**

faire to do, to make v **p33**

fait à partir de made of adj

la famille *f* family n **p120**

fatigué(e) tired adj

la faute *f* fault n

le fautif *m* / **la fautive** *f* at
fault adj

> **C'est moi le fautif / la fau-
> tive.** I'm at fault. **p64**
> **C'est sa faute.** It is his / her
> fault.

féminin(e) female adj

la femme *f* woman / wife n

la femme au foyer *f* homemaker n **p129**

la femme de chambre *f* maid
(hotel) n

la fenêtre *f* window n

fermé(e) *closed adj*

fermer *to close v* **p24**

le festival *m festival n*

le festival de rue *street festival*

Au feu! *m Fire! n*

le feu *m light n*

Puis-je vous offrir du feu?
May I offer you a light?

février *m February n* p14

le fiancé *m /* **la fiancée** *f*
fiancé(e) n p123

la fille *f girl, daughter n* p120

le film *m movie n* p151

le fils *m son n* p120

fin(e) *thin adj*

finir *to finish v* **p24**

la fissure *f crack (in glass*
object) n

la fleur *f flower n*

flottant(e) *loose adj*

le flush *m flush (gambling) n*

la flûte *f flute / small baguette n*

les fonds *m pl money (in an*
account) / stocks, securities n

le forfait *m rate plan n*

le format *m format n*

fort(e) *loud adj*

fort *loudly adv*

Parlez plus fort, s'il vous plaît.
Please speak more loudly.

la fouille *f search n* p53

le fourgon *m van n* p58

fragile *fragile adj*

frais *m /* **fraîche** *f fresh adj*

frais de traitement *m service*
charge n

la France *f France n*

français(e) *French n adj*

le frein *m brake n*

le frein à main *emergency*
brake

freiner *to brake v* **p24**

le frère *m brother n* p120

froid(e) *cold adj*

le fromage *m cheese n* p107

le front *m forehead n* p126

le fruit *m fruit n* p113

les fruits de mer *seafood n*

fumer *to smoke v* **p24**

les fumeurs *m pl smokers n*

la zone fumeurs *smoking area*

interdit de fumer *no smoking*

fuire *to drip v* **p25**

le fusible *m fuse (home) n*

G

le gallon *m gallon n*

le gant *m glove n*

le garçon *m boy n*

le garde *m guard n*

garder *to keep v* **p24**

se garer *to park v* **p24, 38**

la gauche *f left n* p5

à gauche *on the left*

gentil *m /* **gentille** *f kind*
(nice) adj

le gilet *m /* **la bouée** *f de*
sauvetage life preserver n

le gin *m gin n* p97

la glace *f ice / ice cream n*

avec des glaçons *with ice*
cubes / on the rocks

la machine à glaçons *ice*
machine

le golf *m golf n* p178

le terrain de golf *golf course*
le club de golf *golf club*
le goût *m taste n*
goûter *to taste v* **p24**
le grain de beauté *m mole (facial feature) n*
le gramme *m gram n*
grand(e) *big / tall adj* **p12**
très grand(e) *extra-large adj*
la grand-mère *f grandmother n*
le grand-père *m grandfather n*
les grands-parents *m f pl grandparents n* **p123**
grandir *to grow (get larger) v* **p24**

Où avez-vous grandi?
Where did you grow up?

gratter *to scratch v* **p24**
gratuit(e) *complimentary, free adj*
graver *to burn (CD) v* **p24**
grec *m /* **grecque** *f Greek adj*
le grill *m steakhouse n* **p88**
gris(e) *gray adj*
gros *m /* **grosse** *f fat adj* **p12**
le groupe *m band (musical ensemble) / group n*
la guerre *f war n*
le guichet *m ticket counter, box office n*
le / la guide *m f guide (of tours) n*
le guide *m guide (publication) n*
le guide d'utilisation *m manual (instruction booklet) n*
guider *to guide v* **p24**

la guitare *f guitar n*
la gymnastique *f gym n* **p167**
le / la gynécologue *m f gynecologist n* **p194**

H

s'habiller *to dress v* **p24, 39**

Vous devriez vous habiller pour cet événement. *You should dress up for that affair.*

habiter *to live v* **p24**
le hall d'entrée *m hallway n*
le handicap *m handicap, disability n*
haut(e) *high adj* **p5**
l'hectare *m hectare n*
l'herbe *f herb n* **p104**
l'heure *f hour / time n* **p12**
les heures d'ouverture *f pl hours (of operation) n*
heureux *m /* **heureuse** *f happy adj* **p128**
hier *yesterday adv* **p4**

avant-hier *the day before yesterday*

hindou(e) *Hindu adj*
hip-hop *hip-hop n*
l'histoire *f history n*
historique *historical adj*
l'hiver *m winter n* **p15**
l'homme *m /* **la femme** *f au foyer homemaker n*
l'homme *m /* **la personne de sexe masculin** *f man n / male n*
l'horaire *m timetable n*
hors-taxe *duty-free adj*

l'hôte *m* / l'hôtesse *f guest n*

l'hôtel *m hotel n* p74

l'huile *f oil n*

huit *eight adj*

huitième *eighth adj*

humide *humid adj* p132

huppé(e) *upscale adj*

I

ici *here n* p5

n'importe lequel *m* / laquelle *f any adj*

n'importe quoi *m f anything n*

n'importe où *anywhere adv*

imprimer *to print v* p24

l'Inde *f India*

indien *m* / indienne *f Indian n adj*

l'indicateur de vitesse *m speedometer n*

l'indigestion *f indigestion n*

l'infirmier *m* / l'infirmière *f nurse n* p129

l'information *f information n*

l'ingénieur *mf engineer n*

l'inscription *f membership n*

l'insecte *m bug n85*

l'insectifuge *m insect repellent n*

l'institution de crédit *f credit bureau n*

insulter *to insult v* p24

à l'intérieur de *inside prep*

l'Internet *m Internet n* p145

l'Internet à haut débit *high-speed Internet*

l'interprète *m f interpreter n*

l'Irlande *f Ireland n*

irlandais(e) *Irish n adj*

l'Italie *f Italy n*

italien *m* / italienne *f Italian n adj*

J

la jambe *f leg n*

le janvier *m January n14*

le Japon *m Japan n*

japonais(e) *Japanese n adj*

jaune *yellow adj*

le jazz *m jazz n*

je *I pron* p22

le jeudi *m Thursday n* p14

jeune *young adj*

de jeune fille *maiden adj*

J'ai gardé mon nom de jeune fille. *I kept my maiden name.*

le jogging *m jogging n*

jouer *to play v* p24

le jouet *m toy n*

le magasin de jouets *toy store*

le jour *m day n*

le journal *m* / les journaux *m pl newspaper n*

juif *m* / juive *f Jewish adj*

le juillet *m July n* p15

le juin *m June n* p15

le jus *m juice n*

le jus de fruit *fruit juice*

la justice *f* / le tribunal *m court (legal) n*

K

kasher *kosher adj*

le kilo *m kilo n* p10

le kilomètre *m kilometer n*

le kiosque à journaux *m*
    newsstand *n* p162
la kitchenette *f* kitchenette *n*
le klaxon *m* horn *n*

L

là *there adv* p5
    là-bas *over there*
le lait *m* milk *n* p97
    le milk-shake / le lait frappé
    milkshake
la langue *f* language *n*
le lapin *m* rabbit *n* p101
large *wide adj* p12
(à) large bande *f* broadband *n*
le lavabo *m* sink (bathroom) *n*
la leçon *f* lesson *n*
le lecteur de CD *m* CD player *n*
le légume *m* vegetable *n*
lent(e) *slow adj*
lentement *slow(ly) adv*
    Parlez plus lentement, s'il
    vous plaît. *Please speak*
    more slowly. p120
les lentilles de contact *f* con-
    tact lens *n* p197
lequel *m* / laquelle *f* /
    lesquels *m pl* / lesquelles *f*
    pl which adj p3
    Lequel? *m* / Laquelle? *f*
    Which one?
    Lequel *m* / Laquelle *f* est-
    ce? *Which is it?*
la lessive *f* laundry *n*
la libération de la chambre *f*
    check-out *n* p24
    l'heure de libération de la
    chambre *check-out time*

la librairie *f* bookstore *n*
en libre-service *self-serve adj*
le lieu de rencontre *m* hang-
    out (hot spot) *n*
la limite de vitesse *f* speed
    limit *n* p64
la limousine *f* limo *n*
la liqueur *f* liqueur *n*97
lire *to read v* p25
le lit *m* bed *n*75
    le très grand lit *king-sized bed*
    le canapé-lit *pull-out bed*
    le grand lit *queen-sized bed*
    le lit à une place *single bed*
le litre *m* liter *n* p10
le livre *m* book *n* p162
la livre *f* pound *n*
local(e) / locaux *pl local adj*
la loge *f* box (seat) *n*
le logiciel *m* software *n*
la loi *f* law *n*
loin *far adj* p5
long *m* / longue *f* long adj*
longtemps *long adv* p10
louer *to rent v* p24
lui *him pron*
la lumière *f* light (lamp) *n*
lumineux *m* / lumineuse *f*
    bright adj
le lundi *m* Monday *n* p13
les lunettes *f pl* glasses (spec-
    tacles) *n*
    les lunettes protectrices
    safety glasses
    les lunettes de soleil
    sunglasses

M

la machine f machine n

le magasin m store n p156

le magazine m magazine n

le magnétoscope m VCR n

le mai m May (month) n p15

le maillot de bain m swimsuit n

la main f hand n

mais but conjunction

maintenant now adv p4

malade sick adj

le mal de tête m headache n

le mal des transports m car sickness n

malentendant(e) hearing-impaired adj73

malvoyant(e) visually-impaired adj p73

manger to eat v p24

d'une manière étrange suspiciously adv

manipuler to handle v p24

manquant(e) missing adj

manquer to miss / to lack v p24

le manteau m coat n

le maquillage m makeup n

se maquiller to make up (apply cosmetics) v p24, 38

le / la marchand(e) ambulant(e) m f street vendor n

la marche f walk n

le marché m market n

  le marché aux puces flea market

  le marché en plein air open-air market

marcher to walk v p24

le mardi m Tuesday n p13

le mari m husband n p122

marié(e) married adj p123

marron brown adj

le mars m March (month) n

masculin male adj

le massage dorsal m back rub n

masser to massage v p24

le match (sport) m match (sport) n

la matière f subject matter, content / fabric n

le matin m morning n p13

les mèches f highlights (hair) n

le / la médecin m f doctor n

le médicament m medication n

meilleur(e) best adj

le / la membre m f member n

même same adj

le menu m menu n p92

  le menu des plats à emporter m takeout menu

Merci. Thank you. p1

le mercredi m Wednesday n

la mère f mother n p120

le mètre m meter n

le métro m subway n p71

  la ligne de métro subway line

mettre to place / to charge (money) v p25

mettre à jour to update v p25

le Mexique m Mexico n

mexicain(e) Mexican n adj

le midi m noon n adv p13

mieux best / better / rather adj

le mile m mile n p10

au milieu de in the middle prep

le / la militaire *m f* military *n*

mille *thousand adj* p8

le millilitre *m* milliliter *n* p10

le millimètre *m* millimeter *n*

mince *damn expletive / slender adj*

le minuit *m* midnight *n* p13

la minute *f* minute *n* p12

la mise *f* / le pari *m* bet *n*

Je veux connaître votre mise. *I'll see your bet.*

la mise à niveau *f* upgrade *n*

miser *to put / to bet v* **p24**

moins *less adv / least adv*

le mois *m* month *n*

la moitié *f* half *n*

une moitié *one half*

la monnaie *f* change (money) *n*

Vous voudrais de la monnaie? *Would you like change back?*

la montagne *f* mountain *n*

le montant *m* amount *n*

monter *to climb / to get in (a vehicle) v* **p24**

montrer *to show / to point v* **p24**

mordoré(e) *bronze adj*

la mosquée *f* mosque *n* p133

le mot de passe *m* password *n*

le moteur *m* engine *n*

la moto *f* motorcycle *n* p58

le mousqueton *m* carabiner *n*

la moustache *f* moustache *n*

moyen(ne) *medium (size) adj*

le musée *m* museum *n* p155

le musicien *m* / la musicienne *f* musician *n* p129

la musique *music n*

musulman(e) *Muslim adj*

N

nager *to swim v* **p24**

défense de nager *no swimming*

la nationalité *f* nationality *n*

le naufrage *m* shipwreck *n*

la nausée *f* nausea *n* p193

la navette *f* shuttle bus *n* p68

le navire *m* ship, boat *n* p70

le nécessaire de toilette *m* toiletries *n*

le nettoyage à sec *m* dry cleaning *n* p82

nettoyer *to clean v* **p24**

neuf *nine adj* p7

neuvième *ninth adj* p9

le neveu *m* / les neveux *m pl* nephew *n* p123

le nez *m* nose *n* p126

la nièce *f* niece *n* p123

le noir *m* dark *n*

noir(e) *black adj*

noisette *hazel adj*

la noix *f* nut *n* p95

le nom *m* name *n*

Quel est ton nom? *What's your (sur)name?*

le nom de famille *last name*

non fumeur *nonsmoking adj*

zone non fumeurs *nonsmoking area*

voiture non fumeurs *nonsmoking car*

chambre non fumeurs *non-smoking room*

la nourriture *f food n*

nous *us pron*

nouveau *m* / **nouvelle** *f new adj*

la Nouvelle-Zélande *f New Zealand n*

le novembre *m November n*

nuageux *cloudy adj*

la nuit *f night n* p13

par nuit *per night* p78

le numéro *m number n* p7

Puis-j'avoir votre numéro de téléphone? *May I have your phone number?*

O

occupé(e) *busy, occupied adj*

l'octobre *m October* p15

l'œil *m* / **les yeux** *m pl eye(s) n*

l'officier *m officer n*

offrir *to offer v* p24

l'oie *f goose n*

l'oiseau *m bird n*

l'olive *f olive n*

l'once *f ounce n*

l'oncle *m uncle n* p123

onze *eleven adj* p7

l'opéra *m opera / opera house n*

l'opérateur *m* / **l'opératrice** *f operator (phone) n*

l'optométriste *m f optometrist n*

l'or *m gold n adj*

l'orange *f orange n adj*

l'orchestre symphonique *m symphony n*

l'ordinateur *m computer n*

l'ordinateur portable *m laptop n*

l'ordonnance *f prescription n*

l'oreiller *m pillow n* p82

l'orgue *m organ n*

orthodoxe *orthodox adj*

ôter *to remove v* p24

où *where adv*

oui *yes adv*

ouvert(e) *open adj*

Nous ne sommes plus ouvert. *We're not open anymore.*

P

le pain *m bread n*

pâle *pale adj*

panneau de priorité *m yield sign n* p61

le pansement (adhésif) *m band-aid n* p193

le papier *m paper n*

le papier de toilette *m toilet paper n*

le parapluie *m umbrella n*

le parc *m park n*

le pare-brise *m windshield n*

le parent *m parent n* p123

parier (sur) *to bet (on), to gamble (on) v* p24

le parking *m parking n*

parler *to speak, talk v* p24

Parlez-vous français? *Do you speak French?* p120

Pourriez-vous parler plus fort, s'il vous plaît? *Would you speak louder, please?*

partager *to divide / to split (gambling) v* p24

le / la partenaire *m f partner n*

le parti *m party n*

participer (à) *to attend v* **p24**

partir *to leave, depart v* **p25**

pas de *no adv*

le passager *m* **/ la passagère**
f passenger n

le passe-temps *m hobby n*

le passeport *m passport n*

le pâté de maisons *m block
(residential) n*

le patron *m* **/ la patronne** *f
boss n* **p12**

payer *to pay v* **p24**

en PCV *collect adv*

Veuillez faire votre appel en
PCV. *Please make your call
collect.*

le péage *m toll n*

la peau *f skin n*

le / la pédiatre *mf pediatrician n*

peindre *to paint v* **p25**

la peinture *f painting n*

perdre *to lose v* **p25**

perdu(e) *lost adj*

le père *m father n* **p120**

permettre *to permit v* **p25**

le permis *m license, permit n*

le permis de conduire *driver's license*

le personnel *m staff, employees n*

peser *to weigh* **p24**

Combien de kilos pèsez-
vous? *How much do you
weigh (in kilos)?*

petit(e) *little, small adj* **p11**

le petit ami *m* **/ la petite amie**
f boyfriend / girlfriend n

le petit déjeuner *m breakfast n*

On ne sert plus le petit
déjeuner. *Breakfast is no
longer being served.*

le petit gâteau *m cookie n*

un peu *m bit (small amount) n*

un peu de *some adj*

le phare *m headlight n*

le piano *m piano n*

la pièce *f coin / room (of
house) / play (theater) n*

la pièce d'identité *f identification n* **p54**

le pied *m foot n*

à pied *walking, on foot adj*

le piéton *m* **/ la piétonne** *f
pedestrian n*

la pile *f battery (for flashlight) n*

la pillule contraceptive *f
birth control pill n*

la pinte *f pint n* **p10**

pire *worse / worst adj adv*

la piscine *f swimming pool n*

la piste de décollage *f runway n*

la pizza *f pizza n*

la place *f seat n / plaza, square n*

la plage *f beach n*

le plaisir *m pleasure n*

le plastique *m plastic n*

le plat *m dish n*

le plat du jour *special
(featured meal)*

plein *adj busy (restaurant) adj*

pleuvoir *to rain v* **p24**

plonger *to dive v* **p24**

pluvieux m / **pluvieuse** f
    rainy adj p131
le pneu *tire* n
la poignée f *handle* n
la police f *police* n
le pont m *bridge (across a
    river)* n
populaire *popular* adj
le port m *port (for ship
    mooring)* n
le port USB m *USB port* n
la porte f *door* / *gate (air-
    port)* n
le portefeuille m *wallet* n
porter *to wear* v p24
le porteur m *porter* n p44
le porto m *port (beverage)* n
poser une question *to ask a
    question* v p24
le pouce m *inch* n
le poulet m *chicken* n
le pourboire m *tip (gratuity)* n
pousser *to push* v p24
la poussette f *stroller* n
pouvoir *can (able to)* v / *may* v
    p34

Puis-je _____? *May I _____?*

préférer *to prefer* v p24
se prélasser *to lounge* v p24,
    38
premier m / **première** f *first* adj
prendre *to take* v p35

Cette place est-elle prise? *Is
    this seat taken?*

la préparation lactée f *for-
    mula* n
préparé(e) adj *prepared* adj
près de *close (near)* prep

présenter *to introduce* v p24

Laissez-moi vous présenter
    à _____. *I'd like to introduce
    you to _____.*

le préservatif m *condom* n

pas sans préservatif *not
    without a condom*

le pressing m *dry cleaner* n
**les prévisions météorolo-
    giques** f pl *weather fore-
    cast* n
le printemps m *spring (sea-
    son)* n p15
la prise f *plug* n
privé(e) *private* adj
le prix m *fee* n / *price* n
le prix d'entrée m *admission
    fee* n
le prix du traject m *fare* n
le problème m *problem* n
prochain(e) *next* adj p5
proche *near* adj p5
le produit m *product* n
professionnel m / **profession-
    nelle** f *professional* adj
profond(e) *deep* adj
le programme m *schedule* n /
    program n
propre *clean* adj
protestant(e) *Protestant* adj
la prothèse dentaire f *den-
    ture* n p198
les provisions f pl *groceries* n
puis *next, then* adv
le pull m *sweater* n p159

Q

Quand *when* adv
quarante *forty* n adj p7

le quart m quart n / fourth n / quarter n adj

quatorze fourteen adj p7

quatre four adj p7

quatre-vingt eighty adj7

quatre-vingt-dix ninety adj

quatre-vingt-onze ninety-one adj p8

quatrième fourth adj p9

le Québec m Quebec n

québécois(e) Quebecois n adj

quel m / **quelle** f what adv

quelque chose f something

quelqu'un m someone pron

qui who adv p3

à qui whose adj

la quinte f straight (gambling) n

la quinte royale f royal flush n

quinze fifteen adj7

Quoi de neuf? What's up?

R

le raccordement m electrical hookup n p87

raccrocher hang up (end a phone call) v p24

la radio f radio n p59

le raisin m grape n

ralentir to slow v p24

Ralentissez! Slow down!

ramasser to collect v p24

la rampe d'accès f ramp (wheelchair) n p65

rapide fast adj

les rapports sexuels m pl intercourse (sexual) n

ravi(e) delighted adj p107

rayé(e) scratched adj

le rayon m aisle (in store) n

à rayures striped adj

recevoir to receive v p24

recharger to charge (a battery) v p24

le récif m reef (coral) n

la réclamation f claim n

Voulez-vous faire une réclamation? Do you want to file a claim?

recommander to recommend v p24

se réconcilier to make up (apologize) v p24, 38

le reçu m receipt n p140

le rédacteur m / **la rédactrice** f editor n p129

la réduction f discount n

la réduction pour enfants children's discount

la réduction pour personnes âgées senior discount

la réduction étudiante student discount

regarder to look (observe) / to watch v p24

le reggae m reggae n

régler la note to check out (of hotel) v p24

rejeté(e) declined adj

Votre carte de crédit a été rejetée. Your credit card was declined.

le rendez-vous m appointment n p130

rendre visite à to pay a visit to v p25

renoncer à to wave v **p24**

le renouvellement m refill (prescription) n

les renseignements m pl information / directory assistance (phone) n

rentrer to return (to a place, usually home) v **p24**

renverser to spill v **p24**

le repas m meal n

répéter to repeat v **p24**

> **Pourriez-vous répéter ce que vous venez de dire, s'il vous plaît?** Would you please repeat that?

répondre to answer v **p25**

la réponse f answer n

le / la représentant(e) commercial(e) m f salesperson n

le réseau m / **les réseaux** m pl network n

la réservation f reservation n

le restaurant m restaurant n

rester to stay v **p24**

> **Combien de nuits est-ce que vous resterez?** For how many nights will you be staying?

rester en ligne to hold (telephone) v **p24**

en retard late adj **p13**

le retard m delay n **p51**

retirer withdraw v **p24**

retourner to return v **p24**

le retrait m withdrawal n

le réveil m alarm clock n

le réveil téléphonique m wake-up call n **p83**

Au revoir! Goodbye!

le rhum m rum n **p97**

le rhume m cold (illness) n

la rivière f river n

le robinet m faucet n

le rock m rock and roll n

la roue de secours f spare tire n

le roman m novel n

romantique romantic adj

la rose f rose n

rose pink adj

rouge red / medium well (meat) adv **p92**

à roulettes wheeled adj **p57**

la route f road n

route fermée f road closed (sign) n **p61**

le roux m / **la rousse** f redhead n

la rue f street n

> **de l'autre côté de la rue** across the street
>
> **en bas de la rue** down the street

S

sa f his, her adj

le sac bag n

le sac à main m purse n **p54**

le sac de vol m carry-on bag n

le sac vomitoire m airsickness bag n **p56**

saignant(e) medium rare (meat) / bloody adj **p92**

la salade f salad n

la salle d'attente f waiting area n **p44**

la salle de dégustation f tasting room n

le salon m lounge, bar n

le samedi m Saturday n p14

sans without prep

la sauce f dressing (salad) n / sauce n p103

savoir to know (something) v p35

le savon m soap n

scanner to scan (document) v p24

le scooter m scooter n p58

le score m score n

la sculpture f sculpture n

se oneself, himself, herself pron

sec m / **sèche** f dry adj

séché(e) dried adj

sécher to dry v p24

le séchoir m hair dryer n p83

second(e) second n adj

Au secours! Help!

la sécurité f security n

  le contrôle de sécurité security checkpoint

  l'agent de sécurité security guard p45

seize sixteen adj p7

le sel m salt n p93

  Ce plat est à faible teneur en sel. This is a low-salt dish.

la semaine f week n p4

  cette semaine this week

  la semaine dernière last week

  la semaine prochaine next week

sens unique m one way adj

le sentier m trail n p171

sentir to smell v p24

séparé(e) separated (marital status) adj p123

sept seven adj p7

le septembre m September n

septième seventh adj p9

serré(e) tight adj

le serveur m / **la serveuse** f waiter n p94

le service m service n

  hors service out of service

la serviette f napkin / towel / briefcase n p57, 82

servir to serve v p24

ses mf pl his, her adj

seul(e) single (one) adj

le sexe m sex (gender) n

les shorts m shorts n

le siège auto m car seat (child's safety seat) n p59

signer to sign v p24

  Signez ici, s'il vous plaît. Sign here, please.

s'il te plaît s please (informal)

s'il vous plaît please (formal)

six six adj p7

la sœur f sister n p120

la soie f silk n

soixante sixty adj p7

soixante-dix seventy adj p7

le solde m balance (bank account) / sale (discount) n

le soleil m sun n

sombre dark adj

sommes are v See être (to be) p27

son m / **sa** f / **ses** m f his, her adj

sont are v See être (to be) p27

la sorte *f* kind (type) *n*

la sortie *f* exit *n*

la sortie de secours *f* emergency exit *n* p49

sortir to exit / to go out *v* **p36**

ne pas sortir par cette issue not an exit

sortir en boîte to go clubbing *v* **p36**

la soupe *f* soup *n* p98

le sourcil *m* eyebrow *n* p126

sourd(e) deaf *adj*

le sous-titre *m* subtitle *n*

le sous-vêtement *m* underwear *n*

le spa *m* spa *n* p75

spécifier to specify *v* **p24**

le spectacle *m* show (performance) *n* p155

les sports *m* sports *n*

le stade *m* stadium *n* p169

le stand d'information *m* information booth *n* p45

la station *f* station *n*

la station essence gas station

la station de bus bus station

la station de métro subway station p71

stationner to park (a vehicle) *v* **p24**

stationnement interdit no parking p61

stressé(e) stressed *adj*

le / la styliste *m f* designer *n*

la substitution *f* substitution *n*

la Suisse *f* Switzerland *n*

suisse Swiss *n adj*

la suite *f* suite *n* p74

la suite avec terrasse *f* penthouse *n*

super great *adj*

superficiel shallow *adj*

le supermarché *m* supermarket *n* 105

supplémentaire extra (additional) *adj*

sur on, over *prep*

sûr(e) safe (secure) *adj*

Ce quartier n'est pas sûr. This area isn't safe.

surfer to surf *v* **p24**

T

ta *f* / **ton** *m* / **tes** *m f pl* your, yours *pron*

la table *f* table *n* p90

la taille *f* size (clothing, shoes) *n*

le tailleur *m* tailor *n* p158

la tante *f* aunt *n* p123

plus tard *adv* later *adv* p7

le tarif *m* rate (car rental, hotel) *n*

le tarif par jour daily rate

le tarif hebdomadaire weekly rate

le taux de change *m* exchange rate *n* p140

le taux d'intérêt *m* interest rate *n* p141

la taxe *f* tax *n* p161

la taxe sur la valeur ajoutée (TVA) value-added tax (VAT)

le taxi *m* taxi *n* p65

télécharger to download / to upload *v* **p24**

la télécopie *f* fax *n* p130

le téléphone *m* phone *n*

Nous n'avons pas de téléphone public. *We don't have a public phone.*

le téléphone portable *m cell phone n*

téléphonique *phone adj*

la carte téléphonique *phone card*

l'annuaire téléphonique *phone directory*

la télévision *f television n*

la télévision par câble *cable television*

la télévision par satellite *satellite television*

le temple *m temple n* p139

tenir *to hold v* **p24**

se tenir *to behave v* **p24, 38**

se tenir debout *to stand v* **p24, 38**

le tennis *m tennis n* p168

la tente *f tent n* p87

la tenue de rigueur *f* / **le code vestimentaire** *m dress (general attire) n*

le terminal *m terminal (airport) n*

le terrain de camping *m campsite n* p87

le terrain d'exercice *m driving range n*

la terrasse *f terrace* / *sidewalk seating n*

Voulez-vous dîner sur terrasse? *Would you like to be seated outdoors?*

tes *m f pl* / **ton** *m* / **ta** *f your, yours pron*

la tétine *f pacifier n*

le thé *m tea n* p97

le théâtre *m theater n* p151

le timbre *m stamp (postage) n*

le tire-bouchon *m corkscrew, bottle opener n*

tirer *to pull v* p24

tirer la chasse d'eau *to flush v* p24

le tissu *m fabric n*

la toile *f canvas n57*

la toilette *f s toilet (fixture) n*

les toilettes *f pl bathroom n*

les toilettes pour hommes *men's restroom*

les toilettes pour femmes *women's restroom*

les toilettes publiques *public restroom*

le toit ouvrant *m sunroof n*

tomber *to fall v* p24

ton *m* / **ta** *f* / **tes** *mf pl your, yours adj*

la tonne *f ton n*

tôt *early adj* p13

tourner *to turn v* p24

tourner à gauche / **à droite** *to turn left / right*

tousser *to cough v* p24

tout *all n* p11

en tout *total adv*

Ça fait ___ euros en tout. *It comes to ___ euros.*

tout *m* / **toute** *f* / **tous** *m pl* / **toutes** *f pl all adj*

la toux *f cough n* p192

le train *m train n*

un horaire des trains *train schedule*

traîner *(passer du temps) to hang out (to relax)* v **p24**

traiter *to process (a transaction)* v **p24**

la transaction *f transaction n*

transférer *to transfer* v **p24**

le transfert *m transfer n*

la transmission *f transmission n*

la transmission automatique *automatic transmission*

la transmission standard *standard transmission*

travailler *to work* v **p24**

en travers de *across prep*

treize *thirteen adj* p7

treizième *thirteenth adj* p7

trente *thirty adj* p7

très *very adj*

la tresse *f braid n*

le tribunal *m court (legal) n*

le tribunal des infractions à la circulation *traffic court*

triple *triple adj* p8

triste *sad adj* p128

trois *three adj* p7

troisième *third adj* p9

la trompette *f trumpet n*

trop *too (excessively) adv* p12

le trottoir *m sidewalk n / walkway n*

trouble *blurry adj*

trouver *to find* v **p24**

tu *you (singular, informal) pron*

le tuyau d'évacuation *m drain n*

U

un(e) *one adj* p1

l'université *f university / college n*

l'urgence *f emergency n*

utiliser *to use* v **p24**

V

les vacances *f pl holidays n / vacation n*

la vache *f cow n*

la valise *f suitcase n* p57

la varappe *f rock climbing n*

végétarien *m /* **végétarienne** *f vegetarian adj*

vendre *to sell* v **p25**

le vendredi *m Friday n* p14

le ventilateur *m fan n* p85

du vent *windy adj* p132

vérifier *to check* v **p24**

le verre *m glass n / shot (liquor) n*

Ce vin se sert au verre ou à la carafe. *This wine is served by the glass or by the carafe.*

le verrou *m lock (on door) n*

verrouiller *to lock* v **p24**

vers le haut *up adv*

la version *f version n*

le vert *m green (golf) n*

vert(e) *green adj*

des vertiges (avoir) *dizzy (to be) adj* p194

la veste *f jacket n*

la veuve *f /* **le veuf** *m widow, widower n* p123

viande f *meat n* p100

la vidéocassette f *video n*

la vie f *living n* / *life n*

Que faites-vous dans la vie?
What do you do for a living?

vieux m / **vieille** f *old adj*

la vigne f *vine n*

le vignoble m *vinyard,*
winery n

la ville f *city n*

le vin m *wine n* p96

la carte des vins *wine list*
le vin sec *dry wine*
le vin doux *sweet wine*
le vin rosé *blush wine*
le vin mousseux *sparkling*
wine

vingt *twenty adj* p7

vingtième *twentieth adj* p9

le vinyle m *vinyl n* p57

violer *to rape v* p24, 199

violet *purple adj*

le violon m *violin n*

le visa m *visa n*

le visage f *face n* p126

la vision f *vision n*

visiter *to visit v* p24

vite *fast adv*

vivre *to live v* p25

la vodka f *vodka n*97

la voile f *sail n*

voir *to see v* p37

le voisin m / **la voisine** f
neighbor n p121

la voiture f *car n* p58

agence de location de
voitures *car rental agency*

le vol m *flight n* p46

Vous allez changer de vol.
You have a connecting
flight.

la zone d'arrivée des vols
internationaux *interna-*
tional arrivals

la zone de départ des vols
internationaux *interna-*
tional departures

la volaille f *poultry n* p101

volé(e) *stolen adj*

voler *to rob, to steal v* p24

le volume m *volume n*

voter *to vote v* p24

vouloir *to want, to desire v* p37

le voyage m *trip n*

voyager *to travel v* p24

le voyant m *light (car) n*

le voyant de contrôle *check*
engine light
le voyant du niveau d'huile
oil light

vraiment *really adj*

la vue f *view n* p76

W

le wagon-lits f *sleeping car n*

les WC f pl *restrooms n*

la Wi-Fi f *Wi-Fi n*

Z

le zoo m *zoo n* p137